RETURNING TO REALITY

KALOS

The word *kalos* (καλός) means beautiful. It is the call of the good; that which arouses interest, desire: "I am here." Beauty brings the appetite to rest at the same time as it wakens the mind from its daily slumber, calling us to look afresh at that which is before our very eyes. It makes virgins of us all, and of everything—there, before us, lies something that we never noticed before. Beauty consists in *integritas sive perfectio* [integrity and perfection] and *claritas* [brightness/clarity]. It is the reason why we rise and why we sleep— that great night of dependence, one that reveals the borrowed existence of all things, if, that is, there is to be a thing at all, or if there is to be a person at all. Here lies the ground of all science, of philosophy, and of all theology, indeed of our each and every day.

This series will seek to provide intelligent-yet-accessible volumes that have the innocence of beauty and of true adventure, and in so doing remind us all again of that which we took for granted, most of all thought itself.

SERIES EDITORS:
Conor Cunningham, Eric Austin Lee, and Christopher Ben Simpson

Returning to Reality

CHRISTIAN PLATONISM FOR OUR TIMES

. . .

Paul Tyson

CASCADE *Books* · Eugene, Oregon

RETURNING TO REALITY
Christian Platonism for Our Times

Kalos Series 2

Cascade Books
A Division of Wipf and Stock Publishers
199 W. 8th Ave., Suite 3
Eugene, OR 97401

www.wipfandstock.com

ISBN 13: 978-1-61097-924-5

Cataloging-in-Publication data:

Tyson, Paul G.

Returning to reality : Christian Platonism for our times / Paul Tyson.

Kalos 2

x + 218 p. ; 23 cm. Includes bibliographical references.

ISBN 13: 978-1-61097-924-5

1. Plato. 2. Platonists. 3. Christianity—Philosophy. 4. Religion and culture. 5. Secularism. I. Title.

BV800 T97 2014

Manufactured in the U.S.A.

This book is dedicated to my father, Graham Roland Tyson, and to three of my children, Daniel Dubrelle Tyson, Lucy Anastasia Tyson, and Francis Tyson. Great souls all.

I do not say dedicated to their memory, for though they have all died, the vision of reality which the church upholds finds them living amongst that great crowd of witnesses who surround us, in the Church Triumphant. In that vision there is only one church, there is not the church of the living and the church of the dead; for all within her have died in the death of Christ and all have been made forever alive in his resurrection. This unity means that the fellowship of love is ever there between us fumbling travellers in the Church Militant and those who have arrived via the eternal shalom of God at the city of joy called the Church Triumphant. Here there is indeed only one fellowship of love, and that fellowship is not divided up by the spatio-temporal boundaries we normally experience between those gone, those to come, and those here for a few fleeting moments in what we call, in such a small manner, the present. In God's love we are all in the eternal Being and Now of God, always and together.

I find it most appropriate to dedicate a book on the Christian understanding of reality to four people who the knowledge of faith tells me—beyond tangible evidence, beyond conceptual mastery—are alive in the life of Christ. And yet, to the reality vision common to our times, these saints are considered to have left the sphere of the real, to no longer exist, and to live only as memory traces found in others now present.

Saint Paul teaches that we must be transformed by the renewing of our mind. Perhaps he means that we are transformed when we come to see Reality as it has been revealed to us, and live in the truths of the kingdom of heaven here and now, however unrealistic and fantastic those truths must seem to the wisdom and workings of this present age. These four saints in my family have greatly enabled me to see that kingdom in the witness of their lives, and so they inspire me to darkly see, and to attempt falteringly to live, in the Real, even here, even now. To them I dedicate this book.

Contents

Acknowledgements

There are many people I wish to acknowledge and thank. Some of them are international intellectual superstars, some are non-academic friends, some former students, some are very fine scholars, some are the most generous and gracious opponents, and some have given astonishing practical and spiritual aid even though they will never read this book.

My wife and four daughters have endured years of relative poverty and insecurity so that I can think and write on these big picture matters. To them in particular I owe more than I can ever repay. Thank you Annette, Hannah, Claire, Aurora, and Emma. This book could not have been written without your grace and patience towards me or without your astonishing confidence in me. To Karl and Ursula Wiethoff, many thanks for your material support over many years. To John and Donna Obezuk, thanks for the protracted loan of your car. To Anthony and Alison Bartolo, thank you for facilitating many happy hours of writing whilst soaking up the wonderful hospitality of your coffee shop. To Ben Tarren, Stuart Weierter, David Reynolds, and Matthew Tan, thank you for your fellowship of mind and heart and your clear understanding of the concerns I have tried to address in this book.

Some very fine scholars have read the text for this book and given me detailed and insightful feedback. My very appreciative thanks go to Andrew Davison, Spike Bucklow, Charles Ringma, Michael Hanby, David C. Schindler, Tracey Rowland, Johannes Hoff, and Richard Colledge. John and Alison Milbank have been strongly supportive of this project from its beginning and the encouragement and feedback of William Desmond has been invaluable. All of these learned and beautiful people have shown astonishing generosity towards me in the gifts of their time and their deep and constructive insights.

Special thanks to Andrew Stumer, Katherine Gainey, Luke Costa, Sue Garlick, Andrew Tyson, and Celia Duffy for crunching through (or at least attempting) the text and giving me intelligent feedback from outside the world of professional philosophy and theology. Your gifts of time and feedback are greatly appreciated.

Of all the people who have enabled this project to come to completion as an actual book, my first thanks go to Robin Parry, editor at Wipf and Stock. Thanks Robin for taking this project on in the first place and then doing a great deal of fine work in bringing it to the press.

With so many gifted and brilliant people aiding the writing of this book you must suspect that this is a masterpiece to read that contains no error. Yet, I cannot assure you of that, for even though the above have saved me from many a mistake, false inference, impossibly un-nuanced generalization, and so on, the book remains my own work and I am responsible for it. It has been a burden and a delight to write and I have been very encouraged to discover just how many people I know who are also thinking over the same sort of issues and concerns that are raised in this book.

Introduction

Everyone does metaphysics. Whenever we endeavor to understand the nature of reality we are doing metaphysics. Such an enterprise is not an abstract mind game—to the contrary, nothing could be more mundane, more practical than our operational understanding of reality. Even so, no operational understanding of reality is simply pragmatic; every time we plan or perform any activity in what we take to be a realistic manner, we do so by putting our confidence in a set of deeply held beliefs about the nature of reality itself.

As integral with realistic action as our metaphysical beliefs are, most of the time we do not explicitly think about metaphysics but simply accept the reality outlook that is assumed by our way of life. This is because—as sociologists ably point out—our deepest belief assumptions about reality are more like organic operational reflexes arising from the actual human communities in which we live than they are like clear and timeless conceptual propositions. Bearing this in mind, it is not surprising that if we try to think clearly about what we really believe to be real, what often comes to the surface is how contextually plastic and defiantly impervious to first order explanation our metaphysical convictions actually are. Metaphysics is a notorious intellectual minefield.

As organically resistant to mechanical analysis as lived metaphysics no doubt is, even so, there are problems with simply accepting the validity of the reality assumptions that we have grown up with. The first problem concerns power. Because we are social beings, we inherit our operational assumptions about reality from the common practices, ideas, and values assumed by those around us. That is, the norms governing our interpersonal and cultural environment, and the political, legal, and economic norms that shape our public environment, define and limit our assumed field of realistic action. These operational norms and the assumptions about the nature of reality that go with them are at least partly shaped by the vested power interests of those who govern us. Thus shared reality

1

beliefs are intimately enmeshed in the necessary power structures, with all their vested interests, in which we live. This is by no means an inherently bad thing, yet even so it may well be that those power structures are as interested in promoting zones of illusion that hide oppression within our assumed understanding of reality as they are in facilitating the true flourishing, freedom, and dignity of our lives. Those who never question the realities with which they are presented are easily controlled by those who set up the power structures and wield influence in any given society. But secondly, if one believes that reality itself is meaningful and reasonable in a way that is "bigger" than the humanly constructed and often incoherent layers of our socio-cultural evolution, then incoherence and illusion are real problems. Now I know that many highly educated people today no longer believe that reality itself is meaningful or that some divine Reason above human minds upholds reality and makes it intelligible. To these people, metaphysical incoherence is not, in itself, a problem. This stance does not think that Meaning and Reason are there *in Reality*; rather it holds that all meaning and reasoning and all reality beliefs are human constructions and functions of use and power, rather than defensible claims concerning how things ultimately really are. However, if one is philosophical in the mainstream classical sense of that word, then philosophy is about the ardent pursuit of wisdom, and wisdom is a type of intellectual and practical harmony with the divine order, moral goodness, and innate purpose that generates and upholds the cosmos. So a philosopher, in this old and original sense of the word, cannot simply live with metaphysical incoherence as if there is no real meaning about reality to be known. Likewise, a religious person—certainly within the mainstream Christian traditions of the West—equally believes that reality is the creation of divine Reason (Christ the *Logos*), such that wrong metaphysical beliefs entail error, and life grounded in error falls short of truth in serious ways. The Christian maintains that the passive acceptance of culturally constructed errors regarding reality will result in false valuations, false loyalties, and futile and destructive lifestyles. Such error results in idolatrous impiety in the living of one's life. So to philosophical and religious people, metaphysical incoherence, and treating metaphysics simply as an entirely natural function of the vested power structures and operational norms of any society, cannot be mildly accepted.

Taking the traditional understanding of philosophy and religion seriously, this book is an essay on Christian metaphysics. That is, this book is concerned with the Christian understanding of reality and with the type of lived action compatible with the Christian vision of reality. Specifically, the central idea put forward in this book is that Christian Platonism is right about the nature of reality. This, I fully appreciate, is a very big claim. Not only is it big (who is entitled to say what reality is really like?) it is also, to put it politely, amazingly audacious. For by various scholarly estimates, Christian Platonism has been deemed redundant in mainstream Western intellectual circles for between eight hundred and two hundred years. However, in this book I shall argue that the Christian Platonist outlook on the nature of reality is simply the Christian outlook, so whether or not such an outlook is considered obsolete, Christians who want their thinking about reality to be integral with their beliefs and their actions should take it seriously.

Christian Platonism holds that the unseen God really is the present source and ongoing ground of all created reality. Further, Christian Platonism holds that the qualities of beauty, goodness, and truth, wherever they are in some measure discovered, are divine revelations of *real* meanings that give the world in which we live its value and purpose. That is, by modern functionally materialist and methodologically atheist standards, such a Christian view of reality is entirely laughable (magical, unrealistic). Yet such an outlook cannot be disentangled from mainstream Christian faith, and such an outlook is not obsolete because there are still many Western Christians who believe in the truth of the claims about God and reality that I have described above, whether or not they have even heard of Christian Platonism.

Yet—and this is the interesting thing—we modern Western people typically "believe in" discretely "religious" understandings of reality in a very strange way. For even if a doctrine is not obsolete as an article of faith, it can be functionally obsolete in terms of how we see and function within "the real world" of secular modernity. We have an astonishing capacity to happily believe Christian doctrines that are strikingly incompatible with the very materialistic, value neutral, and pragmatic realism that we largely accept as valid in our work-a-day lives. The conventions of the secular world have isolated our specifically religious beliefs such that they are now largely understood to be private convictions, held discrete from "the real world" of factual and public affairs. To amplify this, in ordinary speech "the real world" refers to quantifiable facts, amoral financial and political necessities, and the sheer instrumental power of spiritually indifferent techniques of mastery over nature. So the vision of reality that is presupposed in mainstream Christian doctrine is, for all practical purposes, held discretely outside of "the real world" of today's techno-consumer reality. But . . . what if it is really the *real* world that Christian doctrine is concerned with, and what if the value-neutral mechanical determinism of secular reality is in fact something of a bizarre fantasy that is not, after all, faithful to reality?

Before seeking to go further we must note that, in practice, posing a simple binary question such as, "either materialistic consumerism is real or Christian Platonism is real" does not help us much. For experience tells us that our usual readings of reality can contain different levels of meaning, and there is a complex relationship between what we collectively believe about the nature of reality and the human environments civilizations construct. So the "real world" of secular modernity is governed by the shared beliefs and practices of our day, and this is the actual world in which we live, whether we have reason to believe it fully accounts for the *real* world or not. Yet, if we happen to inherit a defective cultural vision of reality then three things follow. Firstly, there will be something hollow, something wrong about the world we inhabit. Perhaps the relentless rat race of working and spending, tied to merely tangible or financial "reality" is not a true reflection of reality. Perhaps the callous "realism" of how power often works in the workplace is not quite right, even if we think it is inevitable. Perhaps pop materialism has a hollowness to it that is exposed and challenged by something as simple as the smile of a child. Secondly, even if there really is "something wrong" with our human world, reality is still there, and still upholds us, even when we are deluded in our beliefs about reality, and even when many of the seemingly necessary activities we spend our lives doing are, in reality, exercises in futility. For however functionally materialist our actions and beliefs are and however spiritually futile our ambitions and aspirations in the world may be, the child still smiles, the beauty of nature still amazes us, and a deep qualitative vitality still reaches us. In such experiences of intrinsically meaningful reality a window in our soul opens up onto a larger world than mere facts and manipulative power and a breeze from the True Outside stirs our hair and enlivens our being with joy, however unable we might be to give that divine breath in real life a name. Thirdly, reality has its way of emerging even if we would rather it did not. A bit like a collective Freudian suppression, when the conscious social reality we live in is actually delusional, reality still pops up in odd, often distorted, sometimes profoundly challenging ways. If real reality is locked out from our understanding of "the real world," reality then bites us from behind in our daydreams and nightmares, in our fantasies and bored despair, in moments of extremity and disorientation, in experiences of startling delight, or in revelations of beauty, goodness, and truth, which the so called "real world" has no words for.

If thinkers like G. K. Chesterton and C. S. Lewis are right, Reality has never left us. Reality is still there even when our day-to-day "real world" minds have largely turned from the divinely situated fount of meaning and purpose in the world. Our work-a-day gaze has shifted from the heavens to the earth, and from divine meaning to human power. We are like Nebuchadnezzar who lives like an ox and will not turn his eyes to heaven. This is the modern world. Yet the heavens and Reality are still there. All we need do is return to that which has never left us. But *can* the ox of modernity now turn its eyes to that which stands above human knowledge and power, and in so doing have its civilizational sanity restored?

Could it really happen? Could we imagine and enact another world from within the iron cage of modern bureaucratic efficiency? Could we now live without the celebration of enticing superficiality and the continuous priming of our acquisitive desires that is consumerism? Could we now reign in the blindly pragmatic realism of global financial and military power? To seek to imagine reality otherwise than how it is presently governed is to seek to exercise what the Old Testament scholar Walter Brueggemann calls the prophetic imagination. And, of course, it is definitionally *un*realistic to dream of another human world from *within* any powerful and pervasive system of constructed human reality. So could it be done? Could we indeed imagine and enact a world more faithful to the true world to come than the world governed by "oh so fallen" normalities? But this, surely, is what it means for the church to seek to live in the kingdom of heaven now, to live before the eschaton as a sign of the eschaton. If we are too comfortable in "the real world," too defined by and relevant to the realism of our age, have we lost our eschatological vision?

But here another objection springs to mind. For while there may well be good gospel reasons for Christians to imagine and enact a counter reality to the "real world" of modern secular consumerism, is it yet simply wrong headed to dream of the kingdom of heaven in Christian Platonist terms? For surely such terms are defined by a philosophical and theological outlook that has long been obsolete and that only really had world forming power in a very different time and context to our own.

Given this concern, I should say a word about the notion of *return-ing* to reality. In this book I seek to re-habilitate a way of thinking about reality that was powerfully advocated by some of the best and wisest minds in classical, patristic, and medieval times, but which has largely fallen out of favor with the fashions of intellectual credibility in modern times. So I will indeed be advocating that we recover significant features of a pre-modern understanding of reality. Immediately I hear someone cry "ah, nostalgia!," as if it is my intention (*per impossibile*) to take us back to the life-world of the Middle Ages. This is *not* my intention. Fundamen-tal to the Christian Platonist understanding of reality is that God, the transcendent source of the qualitative richness of the reality we inhabit, is beyond our rational capture. This means that all human attempts to understand God and to build a human world that has some analogical relation to reality, are situated in their own particular contexts, can never attain perfection, are always richly laced with historically specific and explicitly human creative motifs, and cannot be the same. To seek to live faithfully to reality now will not be a copy of previous attempts to do that by patristic and medieval thinkers and communities. There is something fundamentally new about each generation's attempt to live in reality and for this reason the human worlds constructed within history are always moving feasts. But while no human world is the kingdom of heaven real-ized on earth, each attempt to build a world can be a partnership between perennial truths—if meaning is not merely a socio-biological efferves-cence—and the distinctive interpretations of that meaning by the great thinkers, artists, activists, power holders, and prophetic outsiders of any given place and time. If we are to be Christian Platonists *today*, and if we are to imagine and seek to enact the human world that best reflects the truths we hold to, then it will be a world that has things in common with all good worlds, but it will be distinctively *our* world and not the world of another time or place.

Another matter that must be brought up at the outset concerns the belief that it is terribly hubristic to make any strong claim about the true nature and meaning of what reality really is. If this book is claiming that Christian Platonism is, simply, right about reality, this must sound as a proclamation of preposterous hubris that way oversteps the bounds of what it is possible for any serious philosophical outlook to demonstrate.

This is a very interesting sort of objection for a number of reasons. Firstly, the modern understanding of small "r" realism (deeply tied to modern Liberalism) does not claim to be an understanding of the true meaning of reality, it only claims to be an understanding of how one can use the tangible and immediately apparent world for whatever meaning or purpose each individual so chooses. But this is not as humble a claim as it might at first appear to be. In fact, there are two great prides bubbling away under such a claim. Firstly, this supposedly small "r" realism is often functionally a big "R" Realism because a pragmatic understanding of reality tends easily to presuppose that all meanings are merely subjective human projections onto a meaningless reality. That is, modern "Realism" really holds that reality (really) has *no* meaning. This is actually a very big, and very hard to defend "ultimate meaning" claim, yet this nihilistic orthodoxy is terribly offended by the idea that people might be so backward and unrealistic as to believe that reality has a meaning that transcends any human evaluation. Secondly, this metaphysical nihilism (often cloaked as pragmatic realism) is grounded in a very strong commitment to a particular outlook on the nature of human knowledge that is entirely anthropocentric. Modern philosophers will only believe something to be true if it is "smaller" than our minds, if it fits within what we can, at least in principle, master with our knowledge. Valid knowledge is only that which can be demonstrated in purely rational and empirical terms. This outlook assumes that when it comes to knowledge and meaning, we are at the top of the tree, and whatever we cannot see when we look down does not exist (like the ox Nebuchadnezzar, we never look above ourselves for knowledge and meaning).

Both of these proud stances are impossible for the Christian to believe, for it is basic to our faith that we are not the self-generating pinnacle of knowledge and meaning, but that only Meaning (Christ, the *Logos* of God) is primarily real, albeit beyond our capacity to master. So this means that Christian Platonism can be entirely frank about not being able to bottle meaning and reality in the terms to which contained human knowledge is adequate (so this position *cannot* be proud). Yet the Christian Platonist can still discover some analogical[1] understanding of

---

1. Very briefly, analogical knowledge is not the knowledge of direct correspondence, and yet it is real knowledge all the same. This idea comes from Thomas Aquinas who makes a distinction between using a word like "father" in a direct manner (referring to a male biological progenitor) and speaking of God as "our Father." As with all analogies, the analogy of God as our Father is not *literally* valid—God is Spirit, neither male nor female, and God is not our biological progenitor—and yet as a divinely revealed truth, this analogy gives us a knowledge of realities that are *more* primary than the knowledge of immediate tangible perception. Thus God is our Father more perfectly than any tangible biological father, for biological fathers derive the essence of

the real meaning that is beyond merely human origin, something that no metaphysical nihilist committed to only believing what can be decisively demonstrated within the terms of human knowledge (precious little, by the way) would ever countenance. So it cannot be helped; Christian Platonism will claim *in some manner* to know truths about real meaning and this will offend the qualitatively nihilistic Realism of our day; but who is being proud and who is being deluded is a matter for serious debate.

One final comment: this book is firstly written with a Christian readership in mind. This is because Christians—so I believe—are already committed to the kind of metaphysics I am advocating. Indeed, I hope that Christians will find this book exciting to access, even though we live in an intellectual milieu that is remarkably averse to the type of metaphysical perspective I am advocating. Yet even though it has a predominantly Christian readership in mind, this book is making claims about reality. Thus, because I am making metaphysical claims that I believe to be true, this book does not have a restrictedly Christian or even religious audience in mind. So there is a complex texture involved in writing about the truth of reality in a manner that is firmly situated within one specific religio-philosophical tradition (and how else can any ultimate claim to metaphysical truth be made?), which claims to be valid and defensible to all comers, but which also expressly appreciates that no propositional formulation does the most ordinary experience of reality full justice. To write clearly while carefully respecting this complexity of texture is not easy to do; and if at times the road is difficult, this may well be because things that are genuinely complex can only be simplified so far.

A Brief Summary of the Argument

Part One aims to be as accessible and clear as possible. Here the basic ideas of Christian Platonism are introduced without any reference to the likes of Augustine or Aquinas, and with little reference to the period of Western

---

their father nature from the creative and providing nature of God. In Thomas' Christian vision of reality God is the grounds of all that is, so the spiritual is more basic than the material, though this in no manner demotes the material but rather exalts it. Plato too shares this outlook of the priority of the spiritual over the material. To Plato eternal intelligible realities inform all material bodies and so all material bodies gesture beyond their temporality and contingency to the unchanging essences that define their distinctive natures within their concrete, changing, and particular existence. In this sense, one could say that the material is an analogy of the spiritual and that the knowledge of divine things is more primary than the knowledge of immediate sensations.

history (some centuries ago) when the metaphysics of Christian Platonism was more or less assumed to be valid. Part One mainly draws on my daughter Emma and on C. S. Lewis and Tolkien to unpack what it is I mean when I talk about the vision of reality that arises from Christian Platonism.

Chapter 1 points out that the long traditions of Western metaphysics are divided into basically two camps. On the one hand, there are metaphysical traditions that assume that the only reality we can reasonably speak of is apparent reality. One might call this outlook the metaphysics of "what you see is what you get." This is really the only form of the long tradition of Western metaphysics to survive in modern philosophy. The other type of metaphysics maintains that there is a strongly derivative relationship between the world that appears to us in our perceptions and the transcendent reality that goes beyond what we are able to directly perceive. Here the real is always seen in some measure *through* the apparent, but the apparent is never adequate to the task of fully containing and defining the real. To this outlook intangible qualities are more primary than tangible quantities, timeless truths are more basic than any temporal expression of truth, and true meaning, which is always of divine origin, is reflected partially in the human mind rather than generated there. To this outlook there is more to reality than simply what meets the eye. Here reality exceeds that which can be discretely quantified, mathematically modeled, or logically demonstrated.

Chapter 1 also notes that this second outlook on metaphysics is the most natural and obvious outlook of these two stances, even though the educated realism of our modern times tends to assume that the real is exclusively a function of the quantifiably apparent and the mechanistically necessary. Thus we live in times where a great deal that *is* immediately obvious (such as the radiance of a child's smile) is often strangely held to be separate from the realm of factual and pragmatic reality. We often live in a context where there is a powerful disjunction between our ordinary experience of reality and the outlook of what might be called "scientific realism." For example, when a person is standing in front of us we do not actually treat them as if they are just a gene machine constructed out of so many grams of carbon-based organic matter. In real life it is *obvious* to us that there is more to being a person than simply what is quantifiably apparent and mechanistically determinate. Further, as any child knows, the world itself is apprehended as full of meaning and value. Yet meaning and value are not considered to be real features of nature by the quasi-scientific realism of our day. Could it be, this chapter wonders, that modern pragmatic realism is an abstract and unrealistic outlook on reality and that the outlook of a child is both more natural and more realistic?

Chapter 2 shows that Christian Platonism is not a distant academic curiosity unknown to ordinary modern people. In fact, via the rich fantasy stories of C. S. Lewis and J. R. R. Tolkien, twentieth-century Westerners have a very good idea of what the basic metaphysical shape of Christian Platonism is. So this chapter seeks to make explicit what most readers of Lewis and Tolkien already know about Christian Platonism.

The bridge from Part One to Part Two notes that contrary to the imaginative visions of Lewis and Tolkien, modern philosophy and theology almost invariably maintains that Christian Platonism is obsolete, impossible, and corrupting. Part Two, then, looks to address these concerns in order to see if they are well founded or not. Part Two contains most of the argument and intellectual history of this book.

Chapter 3 looks more closely at why a distinctly modern outlook finds Christian Platonism incredible. The case is made that it is the very mythos of modernity that is the real grounds of objection against a contemporary understanding of reality being framed in Christian Platonist terms.[2] For it is indeed correct that the mythos of modernity is in most regards incompatible with the mythos of Christian Platonism. But this modern mythos is itself problematized in this chapter, and this makes it possible to consider Christian Platonism as a serious alternative to modern approaches (and modern anti-approaches) to metaphysics.

Chapter 4 briefly identifies where we can see some clearly Platonic ideas expressed in the New Testament. Chapter 5 then looks at the usual range of modern *theological* objections to Christian Platonism. The case is made that because modern theology operates within the mythos of modernity it is committed to willful mis-readings of Christian Platonism; these mis-readings are unjustified in the light of the actual history of what Christian Platonism stands for and how it evolved within early, patristic, and medieval Christianity.

Chapter 6 considers more closely what Christian Platonism entails intellectually, and at how the downfall of Christian Platonism actually happened in Western intellectual history. Five stages of the demise of Christian Platonism are outlined: Abelard's attack on naïve medieval realism; the trajectory towards the parting of faith and reason dating from 1277; the innovations of Duns Scotus and William of Ockham; the

2. "Mythos" refers to the collectively imagined stories that orientate meaning within any given cultural life form.

invention of "pure nature" in the sixteenth century; and—finally—the scientific revolution of the seventeenth century. The long passage away from the Christian Platonist vision of reality needs to be well understood, for this is the genealogy of the rise of the modern vision of reality; and modernity—so I argue—starts rising from Abelard on and is in profound continuity with a particular stream of medieval metaphysical and epistemological innovation. If these cumulative innovations are to be challenged they must be well understood.

Bearing the expansive history of the medieval genealogy of modernity in mind, chapter 7 focused down on the last stage of the fall of Christian Platonism—the scientific revolution of the seventeenth century. I draw on Thomas Kuhn, Michel Henry, and Lloyd Gerson to analyze and critique what really happened in the scientific revolution, and my findings are that this revolution was never philosophically justifiable in the terms of the distinctly modern outlook on reality it assumes, but is rather "justified" because of the pragmatic manipulative power scientific reductionism unleashed. Further, I argue that the modern understanding of scientific truth, and science's key role in the very structure of modernity as the life-world in which we actually live, is not at all believable as the total vision of reality that it has functionally become. Indeed, Plato's appreciation of the problems of epistemological foundationalism have proved to be entirely correct. Hence, there is no powerful philosophical reason why the reality vision of modernity need be taken seriously, or why the alternative understanding of reality that Christian Platonism adheres to should not be taken seriously.

Part Three is the last chapter of this book, chapter 8. Here I endeavor to imagine the impossible; what would our world look like if we tried to return to a Christian Platonist view of reality today? How would things look to us and how would we act in the world if we thought that reality itself was intrinsically meaningful, if we really believed that wisdom was more primary than manipulative knowledge? How differently would Christians live if our piety was not neatly contained in the sphere of personal belief and private morality as the supposedly value neutral sphere of the public and political realm in modern liberal secularism requires of us? I maintain that the metaphysics embedded in some key New Testament ideas—out of which Christian Platonism has arisen—is radical and revolutionary. I argue that if the church better understood the manner in which the New Testament vision of reality challenged the realism of its day, and equally challenges the realism of our day, then some radical and revolutionary implications would follow. The church would be far more clearly differentiated from the world in its very mode of operation, and this differentiation would enable the church to better pursue its mission to be salt and light *for* the world. In this concluding chapter I hope to show how practically important the metaphysical vision of Christian Platonism could yet be for us in the Western church.

The Nature of this Book

This book is enormously ambitious in its scope and argumentative intentions, and it is a work of overview and synthesis.

On the ambition front, I do not flinch from arguing that the much-maligned metaphysical lens of Christian Platonism gives us a far clearer picture of reality than the lenses we are now accustomed to wearing. Against the prevailing intellectual fashions, I also argue for the practical and theological significance of metaphysics itself. I think it compellingly clear that metaphysics is inescapably tied to the operational structures of every actual life-world in which people really live. Whatever the seductions and derangements that metaphysical thought may be prone to, we avoid thinking about metaphysics at our very great practical peril. And where theology is concerned with reality, and with primary reality, it is *inescapably metaphysical*. Further, if the metaphysical implications of Christian theology are not deeply embedded in the corporate practice of the Christian life, then, I argue, the church is profoundly theologically ill, with dire practical consequences.

Concerning overview and synthesis; this book is an introduction to the metaphysics and practice of Christian Platonism for our times, and this book is a critical re-telling of the genealogy of modern realism grounded in an interdisciplinary synthesis of our philosophical, theological, and sociological cultural history. The integrative and panoramic nature of this book does not allow for much detail on any given matter and must brush over many complex matters lightly. That is, this book is written as a broadly educative aid designed to prime and provoke your own further exploration.

PART I

RE-DISCOVERING A CHRISTIAN
UNDERSTANDING OF REALITY

1

Two Views of Reality

Emma, my two-year-old daughter, has quite an astonishing understanding of reality. She is now adept at talking, but she does not just talk to her family and friends, she also talks to the cat, she talks to her breakfast, she talks to the flowers. And as far as she is concerned, her breakfast and the flowers talk back to her. It seems that she inhabits a cosmos that is intelligibly animate in its own right and where she is in rich communicative fellowship with, well, everything. And it is not just people, animals, and things she talks to. When we say grace to our unseen Father in heaven whose provision upholds us at every turn, she displays no incredulity. In fact, should someone other than her attempt to say grace she expresses her displeasure in no uncertain terms.

If you take the effort to get beside her and try to see the world from her perspective, if you really look into her eyes in order to look into her world, what we might call adult notions of objective reality start tumbling into disorder. For more than her paranormal communicative proclivities, it is who she herself *is* that most troubles any merely "factual" or scientifically "realistic" view of reality. As a normal two-year-old Emma is no angel (ask her sisters), and yet, perhaps, in some astonishing way all two year olds are beings of dazzling spiritual radiance. Her vibrant laughing eyes and her unreservedly open face can simply blow you away. Her eye contact reaches deeply into your being and her smile can cause even the parched spiritual desert of a tired and troubled soul to burst into bloom.

What are we to make of this? Is Emma simply a sweet and imaginative child who will grow up and lay aside her childish ways? Will the maturing of her outlook be demonstrated when she comes to understand the difference between scientific reality and imaginative fiction? Will her spirit of play, her delight in the joy and mystery of ordinary immediacy, her imaginative vitality, and her quickness to touch others in love, simply fade as she "grows up"? Or does she illustrate what Christ spoke of when he said that unless you become as a little child you cannot enter the kingdom of heaven?

The above questions expose the simple fact that the nature of reality can be understood in different ways. Metaphysics is the endeavor to understand what reality really is, and in the West there is a rather basic divide separating out two approaches to metaphysics. Let us call these two approaches the one-dimensional metaphysical outlook (1DM) and the three-dimensional metaphysical outlook (3DM). The 3DM outlook sees the moral dimension, the physical dimension, and the spiritual dimension of our experience as all equally integral to reality as a whole. The 3DM outlook maintains that in a human being, for example, you cannot try to unravel or functionally obliterate any of these dimensions without damaging or destroying a real understanding of what it means to be human. The particular type of 3DM this book will advocate is Christian Platonism. Here moral and spiritual realities you cannot immediately see or scientifically quantify nevertheless saturate the physical and tangible world. In contrast, the 1DM outlook maintains that reality is comprised of only one sort of stuff. Thus, what seem to be irreducibly different dimensions of reality to the 3DM outlook—quality, quantity, and the touch of divinity—are all seen as functions of a seamlessly undifferentiated reality by the 1DM outlook.

The type of 1DM outlook common in our day functionally reduces all of reality to its physical dimension. Even so, this 1DM outlook happily recognizes that we have what we experience as moral and spiritual states of awareness, but these states are seen as functions of our awareness, not functions of real (that is physical) reality itself. Further, to this type of realism our awareness itself must *really* be a physical thing in the final analysis. Thus 1DM physical realism employs a sophisticated interpretive apparatus that enables it to "understand" the qualitative and spiritual aspects of our experience of Emma—her beauty, value, moral capacities, and apparent intimacy with divinity—by reducing what these dimensions *really* signify to physical terms. For, as noted, to 1DM advocates the physical dimension of reality is the only dimension that is really real. The other "dimensions" are seen as subjective interpretations, psychological epiphenomena, and cultural glosses painted over the physical laws and material necessities of Emma's life.

The 3DM understanding of Emma does not reduce the moral and the spiritual to the physical. And note, here the qualitative dimension of reality includes not only moral categories concerning good and evil, but also aesthetic categories concerning beauty and ugliness; here the spiritual dimension of reality includes not only God and the mystery of personhood (the soul), but also meaning and intelligibility itself, which can be seen as given to all created things as their defining essence from the Creator. To the 3DM outlook that I will be advocating in this book, meaning is understood as a spiritual gift integral to all reality, not as a shimmering subjective by-product of brute physicality merely projected onto meaningless objective reality by our brains. To the 3DM outlook you can simply take your experience of Emma's beauty, her moral value, her personal dignity, her intimate relation to God, and her spiritual essence, as being experiences of moral and spiritual reality; you do not need to re-interpret your experience so that it conforms to the categories of reality defined only by materially demonstrable knowledge.

The point to notice is that both ways of understanding reality can look at the same "thing"—say Emma—but they interpret what they are seeing differently. Indeed, as already noted, the 1DM outlook uses an as-tonishingly sophisticated interpretive apparatus that applies highly com-plex forms of abstraction and reduction in formulating its understanding of *real* reality. In contrast the 3DM outlook is much more directly related to what we actually see and experience. The 1DM outlook really is more interpretively complex than a 3DM outlook, but whether this interpre-tive sophistication gives you greater contact with what reality really is or propels you into a region of fantastic disconnection with the moral and spiritual fabric of reality is a matter that is worth considering.

Could it be that our sophisticated 1DM outlook on reality has shaped our culture and the practices of modern power in such a way that we have lost contact with some very basic moral and spiritual realities? The global financial crisis of 2008 displayed an astonishing disconnection between high finance and ordinary reality, and yet only an entirely amoral and irreligious approach to financial and legal power could have allowed the abstract mathematical ingenuity of derivative trading to bring the USA and the global economic order it has built to its knees. And then again, if you happen to be a factory worker in Indonesia, a cotton picker in Uzbekistan, or a cocoa plantation worker in Africa, the way in which you are exploited by this global economic system may also strike you as re-markably blind to human and spiritual realities. Are we not, perhaps, just a little bit too good at abstracting and reducing the real world to merely mathematical relations and to calculations of practical manipulation for merely quantifiable outcomes? Have we become blind to the moral and spiritual dimensions of reality? Have we turned from reality as it really is?

Backing up a bit, it must be recognized that the relationship between the moral, the material, and the spiritual as seen from within a 1MD outlook is more complex than I have so far outlined. Significantly, the interpretive apparatus of the 1DM outlook usually only *functionally* ignores moral and spiritual reality. This is because the modern 1DM stance is grounded in a very deep commitment to the truth of scientific knowledge. Within this commitment the knowledge of objective material reality is real knowledge, but moral and spiritual truth claims, which cannot be scientifically tested, do not count as knowledge claims about reality. Thus our 1MD outlook typically only maintains that there are no scientifically *knowable* moral and spiritual realities, not that such realities positively do not exist. Hence, *beliefs* about moral truth and God are seen as optional subjective convictions that people can adhere to if they like, but which should always be held discretely separate from any verifiable knowledge claim about objective reality. Knowledge here pertains to what is physically real, and belief here pertains to that which is not physically real. Hence Goodness and God—as distinct from people's stated moral and religious beliefs and their observable moral and religious behaviors—are outside of our knowledge of reality. In this way the modern world isolates objective knowledge from subjective belief and this is seen as upholding the very essence of personal freedom in regard to belief commitments about morality and religion. This arrangement— so modern liberalism claims—liberates objective scientific truth from any sort of tyrannically mandated limitation from non-factual moral and religious convictions. This arrangement also liberates the individual conscience from the coercive use of civic power in all matters of moral and religious belief. Hence, one can functionally operate in a legal and pragmatic way within merely physical and social constructed reality at the same time as being passionately committed to deeply personal moral and religious convictions, provided one keeps one's religion and morality within the realm of private belief and out of the realm of knowledge and public power. Thus a strict demarcation between objective knowledge and subjective belief, grounded in a functionally 1DM understanding of reality, is the lynch pin of liberal secular society. (Notice how politically significant culturally assumed metaphysical understandings are.) Here, legality governs the operational rules of the public realm and this realm is not concerned with morality as such, and here good citizens who are members of religious societies are expected to respect the moral neutrality and spiritual pluralism upheld by the coercive powers of the secular state within the prevailing good order of society and commerce. So moral and spiritual dimensions reside in the personal and subjective arena of belief, and this arena has no direct bearing on public and objective matters concerning power and legality in the real world.

The collective dis-integration of knowledge from belief adhered to by liberal secular modernity did not come from nowhere. After the peace of Westphalia,[1] the modern uncoupling of religion from civic power started a revolution within Western culture that would effectively isolate matters of religion and morality to the discretely subjective and personal sphere of belief, and this would increasingly lean what was understood as the public and objective sphere of knowledge and power towards being functionally amoral and irreligious. By now—after the long cultural evolution of Western modernity—the separation of subjective belief from objective knowledge is in our mother's milk. Because the scientific knowledge and the secular power environment in which we live are basic to the objective realities of our very way of life, we readily perform the sophisticated interpretive isolations and reductions of the 1DM perspective effortlessly and without even being aware of it. Even so, this *is* an astonishing interpretive achievement that we—for the most part—willingly perform when we are dealing with objective knowledge claims and the accepted norms of public propriety. If you look at Emma, it is remarkably counter-intuitive to think that the moral and spiritual realities one sees and touches there are merely personal belief glosses that have no factual or publically significant connection to reality. Indeed, I cannot see that it would actually be possible to relate to real people and be an actor in the real world without assuming that reality had qualitative and meaningful dimensions.

So far we have outlined two approaches to metaphysics and noticed how a 1DM outlook is embedded in the objective and secular features

1. The peace of Westphalia was a series of peace treaties signed between rival European powers in 1648 that signaled the end of the Thirty Years' War and the end of the Eighty Years' War. The rivals were Catholic and Protestant powers, some of an imperial nature, some of a nascent nation state nature. This signaled the beginning of the modern era of international diplomacy in Europe and was a crucial development in political configuration, one that would eventually give birth to the modern secular nation state.

of our modern way of life. We will not here explore the history of the deep and intimate relationship between a distinctive type of Christian theology and the rise of modern secular liberalism,[2] but it is important to note that there is a naturally corrosive relationship between a way of life functionally embedded in a 1DM outlook and the unavoidably 3DM aspects of Christian doctrine. For clearly, Christian doctrine maintains that there really are moral and spiritual *realities* integral with (and prior to) the real material world of our everyday experience. To approach God and goodness as functions of our own personal belief freedoms, which we choose in our own identity construction, or to demarcate God to some discrete supernatural realm that is entirely discontinuous with material reality and to think of morality as inherently a personal matter, is to abandon a Christian understanding of reality itself. Yet Christianity within secular modernity often does just that. On the other side of this equation, given the functional dominance of a 1DM understanding of reality, Western culture is now in something of a serious metaphysical, spiritual, and moral bog. Increasingly our high culture is silent regarding what enduringly valid values, intrinsically worthwhile human goals, and the very point and meaning of our place in the cosmos might be. In short, wisdom is vanishing. Increasingly a deep cultural unknowing regarding what the point and meaning of our wondrous objective knowledge and

2. There are indeed some entirely Christian reasons why coercive civic power and religious authority are now separated in the secular West. Unlike, say, Judaism or Islam, Christianity was in its origin on the outside of civic/tribal power and there it functioned within a radically non-realist logic of power, as exemplified by the crucified Christ, by the Sermon on the Mount, and by the upside-down political nature of the kingdom of heaven expressed on earth by the church. In the fourth century, Saint Martin of Tours well understood the terrible consequences of entangling Christian authority in coercive civic power, as illustrated in his struggle with Emperor Maximus and Bishop Ithacus concerning executing heretics in the Priscillian Affair. To use civic power or state armies to wage violent war against those deemed heretics is to renounce the violence-receiving way of Christ on the cross. The blood bath of Catholics and Protestants killing each other from the time of the Reformation to the Peace of Westphalia was indeed a complete affront to the gospel, and the determination to keep matters of religious affiliation out of a Christian approach to state craft was entirely in keeping with the DNA of Christianity. Even so, the logic of the Lordship of Christ (which we shall examine in chapter 8) does mean that civic authorities are never treated as legitimate by the church if they deny moral truth in the pursuit of power, or if they promulgate idolatrous civic religion—be it flag worship of the worship of money and power. The idea of separate spheres—the non-political sphere of the sacred and the political sphere of the secular—where secular power is free from religious and moral restraint, has never been a legitimately Christian outlook on politics.

manipulative power might be is now a pervasive background feature of our cultural life form. This leaves us at the mercy of the brazen manipulative irrealism and the morally unconstrained instrumentalism of consumer culture. The vested power interests native to pragmatic consumerism delight in playing with our subjective beliefs and molding our objective behaviors to suit its merely instrumental ends. Market realism and the mass media age thrives on generating seductive ready-made consumer identities saturated in powerful illusions that prime our fantasies of desire and manipulate our inchoate fears, and all for the meaningless "point" of getting us to spend money. Once we are out of touch with thinking about moral and spiritual reality it does not take long for us to get out of touch with material reality as well (think of speculative trading and the non-material bubble worlds possible within cyberspace). The escapism, narcissism, and virtual brilliance of our powerful entertainment industry, and a flagrant disregard for the physical environment on which our very lives depend, is also characteristic of our times. Given these dynamics it seems that the entire edifice of the Western life form could be cooking up its own spiritual implosion.

In this context, perhaps Christians would do well to consider reclaiming an explicitly three-dimensional metaphysical outlook. Perhaps, Western culture can only find life-giving spiritual, moral, and political bearings if it can back out of the crass and finally pointless consumerism that our 1DM view of reality locks us into. For now we have power without wisdom or piety, existence without nobility, lives without any transcendently referenced point, birth and death without intrinsic meaning, time and seasons without liturgical reference, holidays without the holy. (Though, of course, we do have very fancy and cheap flat screen TVs.) Now the West has unleashed enormous instrumental and military forces on the globe and has built a set of global structures that facilitate unprecedented economic and material exploitation; but all this power is directed to no common good, to no intrinsically valuable end. Under this situation, if we have no sense of accountability to any moral truth or any sacred meaning in how we govern the world, then we may drag the whole world down into the West's spiritual bog and visit unprecedented destruction on the entire globe in the process. So in what seems to me to be an increasingly spiritually lost Western culture, "objective reality" is meaningless or merely manipulative and provides us with no collective anchor points for value and intrinsic meaning.

Today, ironically, it is only in fantasy that high moral and metaphysical truths can gain any purchase on the Western mind. But here, perhaps, in the waking visions of children and in the daydreams and fantasies of the Western mind, some sort of memory of the West's spiritual vitality lives on. Perhaps it is in the fantasy stories of Christian Platonists such as C. S. Lewis and J. R. R. Tolkien that real reality still speaks to us; reality undergirded by intrinsic moral meaning and (for want of a better term) "public" spiritual purpose, and overshadowed by divine goodness and love. Maybe it is via such fantasies that we can start to return to a richer understanding of reality, even in our times.

Indeed, I think the fantasy of Lewis and Tolkien is our most promising pathway back to reality now. Let us now turn to these two twentieth-century giants of letters and look for the vibrant three-dimensional metaphysical pathway their stories open up to us.

2

The Christian Platonism
of Lewis and Tolkien

If you go to Oxford today you can pop into a little pub and sit down in the room where Lewis and Tolkien and a few other likeminded friends used to have a pint and chat late into the night about what they were most seriously concerned with: imaginative stories. In our very down-to-earth times it may seem strange, even eccentric, for this bunch of English academics to take imagination so seriously, but, as we shall later unpack, imagination is indeed a very serious matter. What they were doing was seeking to clothe the Christian vision of reality, which they shared, in stories that engaged the hearts and imaginations of ordinary people. Given that Western culture is historically embedded in a Christian vision of reality, Lewis and Tolkien saw themselves as plugging into convictions and attitudes still dormant in the collective reality assumptions of modern Western consciousness. Once these near-forgotten visions had imaginative life, Lewis and his friends hoped that a quiet revolution would take root in people's minds. For this fellowship of storytellers believed that the loss of vitality in a distinctly Christian imaginative vision of reality was at the heart of the dying of the light that was so pervasive in the cultural trends of their times.

The metaphysical vision that Lewis and Tolkien were imaginatively clothing was, in fact, Christian Platonism. This means that if you have read and enjoyed the stories of Narnia and Middle Earth you already know a lot about Christian Platonism. So, let us start unpacking what Christian Platonism is by spelling out what we already know.

C. S. Lewis' Christian Platonism: His Metaphysical Vision

In *The Chronicles of Narnia* Lewis uses the mytho-poetic medium of the Narnia stories to carry a profoundly Christian message in a fresh, creative, and philosophically powerful way. This is not, of course, what Plato was doing, for Plato lived some four centuries before Christ, but the manner in which *The Chronicles of Narnia* can carry both a Christian message and an exposition of recognizably Platonist insights is what makes Lewis' works such a good illustration of Christian Platonism.

Let us note also that Lewis' choice of the children's story as a means of communicating both the Christian message and his Platonist metaphysical convictions is no accident. As already alluded to, something about the outlook of the child is crucially important both to the Christian understanding of faith and to the metaphysical outlook that believes in things it cannot directly see. Lewis grasped this "child-like" dynamic deeply. From within this stance, when it comes to the really profound truths of reality, we are all as children before them. So it is only in the openness, trust, wonder, and plasticity of the child's mind that any illumination of primary things comes to us at all. Here humility before a reality that always stands over us (that is, we *under*-stand and live *within* reality, we do not have a God's eye overview of reality) is a necessary requirement for any true illumination of reality. While Lewis was no stranger to complex and highly demanding intellectual endeavors, he clearly held that due to the intrinsic profundity and transcendent heights of reality, myth, imaginative analogy, and fairy tale can often go further than science and logic in disclosing truths regarding really primary things.

The entire *Chronicles of Narnia* are embedded in a three-dimensional metaphysical outlook. Lewis' books soak the imagination in an alternative reality perspective to the functionally 1DM outlook of what I will simply call modern Realism. So the best way to understand the reality outlook of Lewis' Christian Platonism is to sit down with a child and read them any of the Narnia books. But I am here going to focus on two specific passages to draw out how Lewis combines Christian doctrine with Platonist metaphysics.

"It's all in Plato . . ."

Towards the end of *The Last Battle* all the heroes of the story have died and find themselves in Aslan's country. But it is not a world where they are disembodied spirits and it is a world that they strangely recognize. Professor Kirke—Digory from *The Magician's Nephew*—explains that the true reality of all good things does not pass away. The mortal world that we call "real"— the realm of birth and death, change and struggle, chance and entropy—is really a realm of shadows, yet these shadows somehow participate in the reality to which they point. So when we die and our soul leaves the realm of shadows, we enter reality (still as embodied souls, but with a very different, yet strangely the same, body) properly for the first time. Aslan's country— the origin and destiny of all that is truly Real—is the home of all that we taste as true, beautiful, and good in the shadow lands. Aslan's country is the home of what reality we do know here in the realm of shadows, and it is the country to which we are travelling through our mortal lives.

After this explanation Digory Kirke observes that "It's all in Plato, all in Plato: bless me, what *do* they teach them at these schools!"[1] Here you can clearly see Lewis connect the belief frame of Christianity with the metaphysical outlook of Plato. Lewis' imagination discloses to us a reality outlook where there are transcendent dimensions to the world of immanent materiality and these dimensions are sourced in God. So the primary measure of reality is not tangible, perceivable, immediate materiality; not the stuff we can pick up, see, hear, smell, and taste. Rather, the ultimately real is unseen, inherently and eternally meaningful, transcending flux and contingency. Here immediately perceived reality is never simply what one's perceptions contact; here an enchanted cosmos undergirded by divine meaning is not simply an object of scientific knowledge, but the reality we experience is in some way alive and speaking and full of meanings beyond the small frame of human knowledge. The poet Gerard Manly Hopkins put it like this:

> The world is charged with the grandeur of God
> It will flame out, like shining from shook foil.[2]

It is important to note that for both Lewis and Hopkins, the world of immediate experience is not "seen through" and then discarded, but rather that world as we experience it is the necessary medium through which we hear the music of heaven.

1. Lewis, *The Last Battle*, 154.
2. Hopkins, *Poems and Prose*, 27.

Let us now skip across from Professor Kirke in *The Last Battle* to Puddleglum in *The Silver Chair*, via Plato's *Republic*.

The Analogy of the Cave in Plato's Republic

The dramatic center of *The Silver Chair* is a confrontation between evil enchantment and the liberating power of truth. This confrontation occurs in a cave. Lewis' cave scene has strong parallels to probably the most famous analogy in Plato's dialogues, which is also a struggle between enchantment and truth set in a cave. So let me quickly describe Plato's analogy of the cave to you so that you will be able to see how deeply Lewis draws on Plato in *The Silver Chair*.

In *The Republic* Plato asks us to imagine a cave.[3] The main chamber of this cave is a long way underground so that no natural light reaches it. This chamber is inhabited by people who are all chained so that they must look at the back wall of the cave and cannot easily turn their heads and look at what is behind them. On that back wall they see their own shadows and an entertaining show made up of other shadows. All the shadows are generated by a fire that is behind and above them, which is used by a small group of people who manipulate shadow puppets and cast their voices so that it echoes off the cave wall and seems to come from the wall. Because the chained up people have been in this cave for a long time, they no longer remember that the shadow show is an artifice, but think that the shadows of trees, animals, and themselves that they can see on the cave wall are real trees, animals, and people.

Now imagine that one of these cave dwellers is freed from their chains. Such a person—Plato discloses—is a philosopher, a lover of wisdom. What the philosopher sees when he is free and can turn around is the fire and the puppets and the controllers of this strange theatre. But the philosopher also sees a long narrow passage behind the fire that has just the hint of real daylight coming from it. So, when the philosopher's eyes are adjusted to the brightness of the fire and can clearly make out the nature of the illusions he has been living under, he then manages to creep past the fire and its sinister dramatic artists and struggle up the long passage towards the outside world. With much effort he makes it to the top. When he gets outside the cave his eyes are so unaccustomed to normal luminosity that it takes him a long time until he can bear to look at things clearly, even by starlight. But finally, he gets so familiar with the

3. Plato, *The Republic*, 514–17. This is found at the opening of book 7.

astonishing realm of the outside world that he can look on the sun itself, the source of all illumination and the true fount of life and beauty. At this point the philosopher remembers his former fellow prisoners down in the cave and decides he must return to them and try to liberate them. So back he goes, down the long tunnel into the darkness. His eyes are now very unaccustomed to the dark, and when he finally gets to the bottom, he can hardly make out the supposed meaning of the shadow drama on the cave wall. Not surprisingly, his inability to discern the meaning of what the cave dwellers take to be reality leads them to think that the philosopher has become blind to the real world because of his supposed journey. Further, should anyone try and unchain the non-philosophers, they will most likely turn on him and kill him, for cave dwellers of the shadow lands think themselves comfortable and secure in their little world of illusions and greatly fear any attempts to "free them" from the world they know and love.

We will unpack the meaning of this analogy further as we go, but at this point all that is needed is familiarity with this remarkable analogy. Let us return, now, to C. S. Lewis.

The Cave of Dark Enchantment

In *The Silver Chair* two children, Eustace and Jill, are sent on a mission by Aslan to find and free Rilian, a Prince of Narnia who has been missing for many years. They are assisted on their quest by Puddleglum, a Marsh-wiggle. Marsh-wiggles are a curious race of creatures that seem to have many of the dispositional characteristics often attributed to dower Scottish Calvinists. Their quest leads them to an underground realm ruled by a charming yet evil enchantress.

In chapter 12 of *The Silver Chair* the Prince, freed from his dark enchantment, and the two children and Puddleglum are locked in a cave in a life and death encounter with the enchantress. She tries to re-enchant the Prince and to entrance the other three and turns all her powers to that end.

The enchantress seeks to convince them that the world from which they come—reality outside the underground cave—is not real; instead, only that which they can directly see in the cave is real. In Plato's analogy of the cave there are keepers of the cave who are the manipulators of its shadowy show, and the enchantress in Lewis' story is such a keeper. She tries to get her four assailants to accept that the inner world of the cave is the only world, that anything they say of the supposed world outside of the cave is an imagined fiction composed out of things they see in the cave, and she tries to stop them from thinking clearly, to relax into her comforting enchantment and to go to sleep. She is determined to convince them that reality is only what she presents to them, reality is only what she manipulates and crafts for her own political ends.

The main obstacles of metaphysical resistance to the enchantress' purposes are their beliefs in the sun and in Aslan. The enchantress seeks to break their belief in this truth beyond her artifice by simple yet, under the conditions of enchantment, powerful means. She asks:

> "What is this *sun* that you speak of? Do you mean anything by the word?"
>
> "Yes we jolly well do," said [Eustace].
>
> "Can you tell me what it is like?" asked the Witch . . .
>
> "Please it your Grace," said the Prince, very coldly and politely. "You see that lamp. It is round and yellow and gives light to the whole room; and hangeth moreover from the roof. Now the thing which we call the sun is like the lamp, only far greater and brighter. It giveth light to the whole Overworld and hangeth in the sky."
>
> "Hangeth from what, my lord?" asked the Witch; and then, while they were all still thinking how to answer her, she added, with another of her soft silver laughs, "You see? When you try to think out clearly what this *sun* must be, you cannot tell me. You can only tell me it is like the lamp. Your *sun* is a dream; and there is nothing in that dream that was not copied from the lamp. The lamp is the real thing; the *sun* is but a tale, a children's story."[4]

The same strategy is employed on their belief in Aslan. They can only explain what a lion is to the Witch, who professes no knowledge of it, by using a cat as an analogy. Then the cat is taken for the real thing and the lion a fancy. So the Witch implores them, "Put away these childish tricks. I have work for you all in the real world. There is no Narnia, no Overworld, no sky, no sun, no Aslan. And now to bed all. And let us begin a wiser life tomorrow."[5]

It is Puddleglum who saves the day. He finds it simply impossible to believe that the world of impoverished darkness under the control of sinister manipulative power is able to generate such wonderful imaginative

4. Lewis, *The Silver Chair*, 141–42.

5. Ibid., 143–44.

fictions as the sun and Aslan. But, reasons Puddleglum, even if his beliefs are fictions they are so much better than the shallow and oppressive
"realities" of the Underworld (the real world, according to the Witch)
that he will be happier believing in fantasy than in reality and will by no
means accept such a dark reality. Puddleglum is prepared to be insane in
relation to the reality beliefs projected by the Witch, and there is nothing
she can do to change his mind. When Puddleglum defies the spell of the
Witch by acting on his crazy metaphysical stance he becomes impervious
to the technologies of enchantment the Witch has set in place and he
threatens the entire realm of illusion she has spun in order to entrap their
minds. She is forced out of her sweet and patronizing disguise then and
reverts to open violence as her true nature is unmasked.

   Lewis is here pointing out—as does Plato—that there are powerful,
vested interests at work that make the matter of the outlook of reality one
believes probably the most significant issue in relation to how the norms
and laws of the political context in which we live work. Metaphysics is
never simply metaphysics; metaphysics is always also politics, commerce,
technology, morality, religion, art, and knowledge. So what we assume
to be the nature of reality—what metaphysical beliefs we are committed
to—is a matter of the utmost practical and political significance.

Lewis, Reality, and Analogy

As with Jesus' use of parables, and as with Plato's use of dialogues, in the
Narnia stories Lewis speaks in imaginative, narrative, and analogous ways
about what reality is really like. Indeed, this very poetic mode of speaking
cannot be dispensed with when seeking to communicate truths about reality that cannot be contained within the quantifiable and logically necessary
order of human knowledge. We will look more closely at this later, but here
it is important to note that the one-dimensional "scientific" view of reality
seeks to describe and then control reality in explicitly non-poetic modes.
Modern notions of truth—be they probabilistic, correspondence, pragmatic, or coherence notions—all assume that only some direct and non-
analogous relation between reality and human knowledge is valid when one
is trying to think about what is real. This explains why Lewis is not often
studied in twentieth-century courses on philosophy in our universities, for
he is seen as a writer of fantasy, not as a serious philosopher at all. And this
has a lot to do with why Christian Platonism—strongly represented in the
cultural imaginary of the twentieth century by Lewis and Tolkien—remains

largely undetected in the modern academy. For who now seriously believes that multi-layered, meta-scientifically framed, deeply theistically located, and poetically expressed stories could have any valid relation to reality? Yet it is not simply Christian Platonist metaphysics that strikes our modern sensibilities as fantastic, it is the morality of Christian Platonism that is also radically out of place in our very pragmatic and one-dimensional understanding of reality. Here we can turn to Tolkien to get a feel for what the moral vision of a Christian Platonism outlook entails.

J. R. R. Tolkien's Christian Platonism: His Moral Vision

The most obvious points of contact between *The Lord of the Rings* and Plato is the myth of Gyges in the second book of Plato's masterpiece, *The Republic*. In Plato's myth a shepherd robs a grave and finds a plain gold ring that confers invisibility. This ring empowers its wearer with the ability to disregard all the usual constraints of piety and morality, without detection. The shepherd quickly learns how to use the ring in order to greatly advance his own situation, at the expense of all the people he kills, seduces, and manipulates along the way. With this myth Plato is setting up an argument against treating morality as simply humanly constructed by pointing to the notion that justice is not merely instrumental and conventional and that the corruption of good character by the lure of power is a spiritual disaster, even if it does confer material advantages. So while Tolkien shamelessly borrows Plato's imaginative idea of a ring of power as the key narrative device for his epic fantasy, more centrally, deep psychological and spiritual explorations of the relationship between power and morality are as basic to Tolkien's text as they are to *The Republic*. In this light it is not unreasonable to read *The Lord of the Rings* as something of an extended imaginative meditation on book two of *The Republic*.

Viewed thus—though without viewing Tolkien reductively so—it is easy to see that Hobbit morality has within it the promise of true moral greatness in Tolkien's eyes. Tolkien is, of course, well aware of the pettiness and pragmatic mean spiritedness that small people are prone to. The Sackville Baggins' long-standing interest in acquiring the real estate of Bag End makes it clear that Tolkien is no blind romantic regarding the explicitly small moral context of his hero. Yet, via Frodo, Sam, Merry, and Pippin, Tolkien presents us with the notion that what happy small people see as good—simple contentments, simple fairnesses, simple embodied and shared pleasures, guileless loyalty—has a profound moral beauty to it. Hobbit goodness is for small people who love and serve, for people who do not want to dominate and who refuse forceful ambition as a mode of operation. Hobbit morality is the opposite of Nietzschean greatness, the opposite of Wagnerian poetics, the opposite of the quest for self-defined personal glory that characterizes inherently agonistic and constructivist understandings of virtue. All too often grand enterprises in human greatness, like the grave-robbing shepherd in the myth of Gyges, explicitly defy the sanctities and mutual commitments of the common folk. Thus Plato and Tolkien set the wisdom of the little people against the power of the great. But—Nietzsche and Glaucon both wonder—are the good little people only "just" *because* they are not powerful?

In book two of *The Republic* Glaucon (Plato's brother) puts forward the argument that if there were two magic rings of invisibility and one was given to a just man and one to an unjust man, the difference between the just and the unjust would quickly disappear. For

> no man would keep his hands off what was not his when he could safely take what he liked out of the market, or go into houses and lie with anyone at his pleasure, or kill or release from prison whom he would, and in all respects be like a god among men. . . . [For] a man is just not willingly or because he thinks justice is any good to him individually, but of necessity, for wherever anyone thinks that he can safely be unjust, there he is unjust.[6]

Via Frodo, Tolkien examines the inner psychology of the type of just man who would not be corrupted by the ring of power. In doing so Tolkien, like Plato, means to show us that the difference between good and evil is not merely conventional and that justice is not merely an instrumental social construct. In this manner it is clear that Tolkien's understanding of morality and power has profound continuities with Plato. Further, in both Plato and Tolkien, the apprehension of true moral significance is tied to metaphysical vision: what one sees and does not see, what one takes as real and illusory, these matters are intimately tied up with the moral challenges of life for both Plato and Tolkien. Here again, this is an idea that is of profound significance for our day.

---

6. Plato, *The Republic*, 360b-c.

Plato and Tolkien on the Politics of Visibility
and Invisibility

Tolkien and Plato share the same type of outlook on the political significance of the relation between the visible and the invisible.

In Plato's cave analogy illusions are thrown onto the screen of the
cave wall by those who control the lives of the enslaved occupants of
the cave (such as the enchantress in Lewis' *Silver Chair*). This analogy
roughly means that the artifice of human culture, and the structures of
power linked to the control of human production—both material and
cultural—generates a life-world that only looks real to those who unphilosophically accept what they immediately see. The real controllers of
culture and power know it is an artifice, and the philosophers know it is
an artifice. But the controllers of culture and power have a vested interest in maintaining that the illusions they generate are real, whereas the
philosophers are seeking to liberate ordinary people from the shadows of
unreality so that they might know the truly real and value what is truly
important. Thus, philosophers and the powerful are typically locked in
combat for the hearts and minds of the people. And what the philosopher (prophet?) sees and says is real is what the controllers of culture and
power often say is delusional fantasy designed merely to trick and control
ordinary people. Likewise, what the controllers of culture and power say
is real and inevitable is what the philosophers often say is delusional fantasy designed to trick and enslave ordinary people.

Explicitly, Plato maintains that the Good is analogous to the sun
in the physical realm, and that the Good gives being itself[7] its life and
reality, and all real things are only seen aright in the light of the Good. So
that which gives moral value to the world transcends the world and is the
ground of reality in Plato, and thus power that moves one out of harmony
with the transcendent source of reality is actually power that makes one
less real, whatever temporal and material advantage it delivers. Thus
Plato has a means of understanding why power is not simply a matter of
instrumental use, but is always cutting either with the grain of deep and

---

7. In classical Greek thinking, existing in the world—being—is an astonishing action performed by every thing that in some manner *is*. Things within space and time
perform the action of being, but only partially, for they come into being, they change,
and they go out of being. So to Plato "being itself" is partially expressed in all physical
beings when they exist, perfectly expressed by the eternal intelligible realities Plato
calls "ideas" or "forms," and Goodness is an order of reality more primary even than
being itself. To Plato, being arises out of Goodness.

high reality or against that grain and "into" nothing. So Frodo, in refusing power that cuts against the moral grain of reality, is fighting evil without becoming evil, and this spiritual perspective regarding the intrinsically moral nature of the real is necessary for any genuine struggle against evil. So the central battle for goodness is not fought with arms and by soldiers in *The Lord of the Rings*, but the central struggle is spiritual and concerns how one sees what is real and free and what is false and necessary.

Plato, the New Testament, and Tolkien all maintain that the narrative trope of visibility and invisibility opens up an indispensable way of approaching the connections between knowledge, imagination, belief, and power.[8] This trope is of necessity imaginatively rich and both Christianity and Platonism understand this dynamic within a metaphysically three-dimensional outlook on reality. And perhaps, if Western culture can re-learn how important matters of visibility and invisibility are in the context of collective imagination, we may yet be able to integrate desire and imagination with reason again (not that these can really be dis-integrated) and this might be critical for philosophy's usefulness in relation to the central concerns of power in our times. For what different discourses of power consider as real and knowable, and what they do not perceive and thus label as unreal and unknowable, has enormous importance on how we actually live. Disciplines of desire and character formation are naturally aligned with the tacit collective goals of any given life form,[9] and these goals are only visible within shared frames of belief, and those shared frames of belief have deep leverage on our way of life because they are richly, imaginatively, and allegorically constructed.

Yet ironically—as Nietzsche himself understood—any view of reality that is only defined within the order of the tangibly apparent, the empirical realm, is just as much imaginatively constructed and a shared

8. This stance is also apparent in George MacDonald, C. S. Lewis, and G. K. Chesterton. See, for example, MacDonald's comment that "Seeing is not believing, it is only seeing" (*The Princess and the Goblins*, 177).

9. In this book I use the term "life form" in the manner that German sociologists and philosophers like Wittgenstein use it, to indicate the dynamic matrix of physical, cultural, political, religious, and linguistic conditions in which we actually live. Thus the broadly common life form experienced by people who live in New York is in many regards strikingly different to the broadly common life form experienced by people who lived in ancient Athens. For this reason there is no simple translation of meaning from one life form context to another, even if we know what the words might mean. Even so, that translations can, to some extent, be done, does indicate that all life forms have some areas of sociological function in common, and possibly, the basic meaning syntax out of which human culture as such is produced is not that extensive.

frame of *belief* as are outlooks situated within a metaphysically three-dimensional frame of belief. Formation in any collective belief alignment is deeply mytho-poetic and happens below the conscious and adult radar of our stated metaphysical convictions. The metaphysical formation that we absorb from the stories and ideas of our culture's collective imagination become the background cultural wallpaper of any given way of life. Thus, typically unknown to us, it is the distinctive narratives and particular imaginative landscapes of our culture that shape our sympathies, our apathies, and our social norms. These deep narratives discipline our desires and motivate our actions. Thus, the visibilities and invisibilities thrown up by a culture's mytho-poetic outlook shape its most basic moral and political framework.

Take buying a shirt. Here—from a first world consumer perspective—is what is functionally invisible: the inhuman exploitation of laborers (including children) in the manufacture of cotton in Uzbekistan and Bangladesh and in the sewing factories of Indonesia and China, and the disappearance of local and fairly paid clothing producers in the first world.[10] This is all out of sight in contrast to the highly visible and carefully crafted shopping mall experience of buying clothes. What we see when we shop are the illusions of "value for money," and we see our freedom to browse across a vast array of desirable personal identity images, which different labels and outlets suggest their product will secure for us. We see an attractive dynamic of illusion, identity construction, and consumer freedom, and this dynamic is the fuel of desire in the engine of consumption, which drives economic growth in the first world. And, as we all know, The Economy (an invisible aggregate whose health we can apparently measure by monitoring various crude quantities of financial exchange) must have ever more fuel or growth will collapse, the economy will go into recession, and our standard of living will drop. So those wealthy corporations, clever marketers, and financial institutions who drive the economy are essentially the rulers of our way of life. In light of this fact, our realistic politicians well understand that what the instrumental logic of market place success needs must be granted to those who rule our society, or else we will all fail to realize the happiness and fulfillment that a prosperous consumer society—so we believe—delivers.

Yet this dynamic of the normalization of exploitation via the techniques of skillfully-crafted marketing illusions and production

---

10. Siegle, *To Die For: Is Fashion Wearing Out the World?*

invisibilities—and instead of clothing we could have talked about coffee, chocolate, oil, minerals, flat screen TVs, high tech gizmos . . . almost any tradeable commodity—is tied to a deep cultural belief that makes the modern Western consumer way of life work. The belief that makes it all work is that *public facts and material things are objective and have no inherent value or meaning, for values and meanings are matters of personal preference and are thus up to individuals to select for themselves.* And that belief is a function of a one-dimensional metaphysical outlook where only objects that you can see and touch are really real.

However, the situation is subtle because it is not as if a 1DM outlook has no interest in values and meanings. Though we are deeply embedded in a way of life that could not function as it does without staggering levels of natural degradation and human exploitation, we still think of ourselves as good people and we still believe that our personal lives of remorseless activity and ever-increasing consumption are intrinsically meaningful. However, it is the functional assumption that meanings and values are not part of objective reality but are rather essentially personal and cultural constructions that means that financial and objective "realism" trumps personal and cultural values and meanings, without us even noticing that there is a contest.

When our way of life operates within a functionally materialistic consumer life form, an entirely instrumental outlook towards reality makes perfect sense. Yet, Plato and Tolkien, who hold to an objective understanding of the true source of value, maintain that a value-free understanding of objectivity—along with its way of seeing and not seeing and its vision of objective power and subjective value—is incurably morally inadequate. For this way of seeing and acting easily makes abstract fantasies (such as money) into real objects, and embodied normative realities (such as human dignity) into abstract fantasies. But if there is only one dimension to reality then both money and human dignity are equally artifices of manipulation, and there is no meaningful way of saying why one of them is more intrinsically important than the other. But what *is* clear to the practical metaphysical one-dimensionalist, is that money is more measurably useful than human dignity. So when it comes to making a rational and efficient decision regarding the management of "human resources," money will trump human dignity every time. Thus hardheaded market realists are typically brutally pragmatic in their treatment of the people and natural resources that are at the bottom of the global economic food chain. For, whatever one's personal values, the objective economic reality is that low cost production and high margin sales are the iron law of financial survival in the global economy. If a market place competitor is outperforming you then, if you want to survive in the "real" world, you also must employ whatever "immoral" means they are using to undercut your price and exceed your profit margin.

In old-fashioned terms, only *moral* realists can see that people are intrinsically more important than money.[11] Where reality only has the single dimension of immediate appearance, there is, in functional realistic terms, *no intrinsic meaning* and *no inherent moral value* to anything. Thus a culture's metaphysical perspective radically shapes the norms of its moral vision and practical action. Indeed, the very idea of moral realism presupposes a Platonist metaphysical vision, and if one gets rid of such a vision then Plato thought one also gets rid of the very comprehensibility of the idea of morality. If morality is simply conventional, simply a subjective and cultural construct, then it is, in reality, only concerned with the manipulation of people for non-moral purposes and loses what is distinctive about moral reasoning itself.

What makes *The Lord of the Rings* a work of Christian Platonism is its realist moral vision and its equation of evil with brute amoral and instrumental power. In the moral vision of both Plato and Tolkien connections between one's metaphysical outlook on reality, one's moral vision, and one's framework of political operation, are seen as both intimate and of vital human importance.

The Discarded Vision

So far we have noted that a 3DM approach to reality is very much embedded in the fantasy stories of Lewis and Tolkien. Further, the particular nature of the metaphysical outlook assumed by Lewis and Tolkien is not simply made up by them, but is, in fact, a contemporary imaginative expression of Christian Platonism. And yet, the manner in which Lewis and Tolkien are overwhelmingly *not* studied as two of the most important metaphysical minds of twentieth-century British thought—despite their astonishing cultural reach—tells us something very pointed about how Christian Platonism is seen by contemporary academia. That is, Lewis and Tolkien are seen as great scholars of the humanities in their fields and as great writers of wonderful stories, but they are not seen as serious philosophers, or even as seriously

---

11. Moral Realism is the philosophical stance that maintains that moral value is a real (and in modern terms, objective) feature of the world.

philosophical. Further Christian Platonism is not seen as a live option in contemporary philosophical circles. Indeed, every flavor of Platonist metaphysics is now almost entirely marginal in mainstream academic circles. Further, many modern Christian theologians think the historical partnership between Christian faith and Platonist philosophy seen in patristic and medieval times was a great disaster, and its residual ghost still needs exorcising. So it cannot be avoided: the fact is, Christian Platonism has long been a discarded vision of reality in Western high culture. But we need to ask, was this rich Christian vision of an inherently meaningful and God-upheld reality discarded for *good* reasons? And, is the reality this vision perceived still there and waiting to be recovered, even if our modern world does not see it? It is to these questions that we will now turn.

Bridge

In Part Two I will defend the metaphysical vitality of Christian Platonism from the strident antagonism this reality vision receives from the conceptual reflexes of modern philosophy and theology. The outlooks on truth, meaning, and power that are native to the modern world find it compellingly obvious that Christian Platonism is—thankfully—long obsolete, was always intellectually impossible, and remains theologically corrupting.

In order to clear the ground for Christian Platonism to engage fairly with the deep disdain it receives from the dominant reality outlook of modernity, we will have to get right down into the "subconscious" of the mindset of our times. So this defense is going to require some extended conceptual setting up and some involved historical argument.

Even so, it is worth remembering that the Western mindset and Christian Platonism were not always antagonistic. In ancient times Christian faith often found Platonist reason rather attractive. For Plato's philosophy has an ultimately spiritual view of the world where divine and unseen realities are the source of all meaning and value. Key Christian doctrines—such as the dependence of the visible creation on the invisible Creator—were seen to align nicely with much of what Plato taught. Indeed, Plato's philosophy *is* remarkably religious, and some of Plato's most profound insights and moral sympathies can quite easily be merged with Christian doctrine and practice.

But things have changed in the West. Today, as mentioned above, many learned people think that Christian Platonism is long gone, and gone for good. It is now broadly assumed that Christian Platonism was a bad idea in the first place. Claims in support of extinction appeal to historians who point out that Christian Platonism has not been a living force shaping the West's high intellectual culture for hundreds of years. Claims that Christian Platonism was a bad idea tend to be of two kinds. Firstly, philosophers committed to what could be called the Enlightenment Project seek to only believe things they know are not made up, and are very determined to ensure that philosophy (reason) is fully independent of theology (faith). To these philosophers, Christian Platonism was obviously a bad idea because such an outlook was full of grand sounding speculations about intangible "realities" that could never be rationally or scientifically proven, and any synthesis of theological and philosophical categories horribly mingles objective reason with subjective piety and superstitious fabrication. But secondly, many recent Christian theologians read Plato as advocating that the mind is good and the body is bad. So Christian thought influenced by Plato is seen as a body-denying and prudish corruption of a richly embodied and distinctly Jewish primitive Christianity.

Very briefly put, the anti-Platonist story often found in modern theology goes like this. With the fall of Jerusalem in 70 AD, the mindset of the Jesus movement became increasingly Greco-Roman. Over time Christian theologians of high to late Antiquity formed deep ties with the Hellenistic (that is, culturally Greek) philosophy that dominated that era (notably Middle Platonism and Neoplatonism) and so rationally framed doctrines, sexual repressions, and abstract notions of a disembodied world of pure spirit infiltrated and corrupted Christianity. Hellenistic ideas and attitudes are, so it is claimed, inherently foreign to Jesus and the apostles, possibly excepting the somewhat Stoic and already Hellenized Paul. So theologians who think Christian Platonism is a bad idea tend to find that the very down-to-earth and body-embracing outlook of modernity has finally purged classical and medieval theology of its anti-matter bias and its highly conceptualized Hellenistic corruption. We will explore this modern theological stance against Christian Platonism in considerable detail in chapter 5.

Yet, modern theology is not simply a return to some supposedly non-philosophical Hebraic purity characteristic of primitive Christianity. In reality the perspective of modern theologians is often profoundly shaped by the broader interpretive outlook of the modern world (which is, by the way, an outlook entirely foreign to primitive Christianity). And Christian Platonism is, indeed, anathema to the spirit of modernity. For this reason its continuous presence in the imaginations and religious beliefs of the Western mind has often been treated as a disease that must be purged by those who consider themselves as guardians and shapers of right thinking in Western modernity.

So before we can seriously look at modern theological objections to Christian Platonism, we need a careful understanding of what I will call the mythos of modernity, in which modern philosophy and theology is situated. The next chapter will unpack what I mean by the term "mythos," but briefly stated, "mythos" is the outlook on reality generated by the deep meaning orientating stories assumed in any given culture. For it is by key collectively believed stories that reality is creatively imaged and interpretively reflected in our minds. Part Two, then, seeks to uncover the mythos of modernity, notes its vested interests and its inherent limitations, and then evaluates modernity's antagonism to Christian Platonism in a manner that allows Christian Platonism to speak to us without it having to pass muster under the bar of the mythos of modernity first.

PART II

CHRISTIAN PLATONISM AND THE HISTORY OF WESTERN IDEAS

3

The Mythos of Modernity

Reality and the Size of Our Minds

In one of Shakespeare's famous plays there is a scene in which some of Hamlet's former schoolfellows flatter him about his breadth of mind. Hamlet's response shows that he is well aware of the dark political subtext to this flattery, but his response also demonstrates precisely the kind of conceptual expansiveness he ironically denies. Refusing the compliment that Denmark is "too narrow for [his] mind" Hamlet says, "O God, I could be bounded in a nutshell and count myself a king of infinite space."[1]

Here we touch on one of the reasons why Shakespeare's plays have such enduring power. Shakespeare, as a master observer of the human condition, well understood that in matters of right and wrong, final purpose, cosmic meaning, ultimate loyalty, etc.—all the things that really matter in the dramas of our actual lives—we live in a small and fragile world made comprehensible to us by conventional and functional reductions. There is no shame in this, and indeed, given the astonishing richness of reality, it could be no other way. But to Hamlet the safe boundaries of clearly understood reality had been radically damaged via his traumatic life experiences. With the walls of his safe metaphysical beliefs broken down, as it were, his mind was invaded by "bad dreams,"[2] which signaled to him a world much larger than his understanding could grasp. Compared with his friend Horatio, Hamlet is more accustomed to

---

1. Shakespeare, *Hamlet*, Act 2, Scene 2, lines 255–57.

2. The full quote from Act 2, Scene 2 above runs like this: "I could be bounded in a nutshell and count myself a king of infinite space, were it not that I have bad dreams."

43

finding reality bigger than his capacity to understand it. Thus Hamlet can say to Horatio "there are more things in heaven and earth . . . than are dreamt of in your philosophy."[3]

In reality the meaning furnishings of our mind are always constructed out of string and wax and whatever else comes to hand from the particular historical and cultural environment into which our existence throws us. Our small and cobbled together conceptual receptors of the wonder of reality do as best as they can to make some functional sense of the world. And most often, at least in a manner suited to our small and fleeting lives, we *can* make workable sense out of the world we live in. Yet what is "workable" as a functional and psychologically necessary understanding of reality is never true in any simple and complete manner. Even so, if our understanding of reality cannot be true in *some* manner, then reason and knowledge are both delusions.

In exploring the structures of our thinking about the nature of reality, one cannot avoid noticing that there are inherent limitations in trying to get to the bottom of what reality really is and what it really means. Probably no one better understood those limits in recent times than Hans-Georg Gadamer.[4] Yet Gadamer's awareness of the delicate, linguistically situated interpretive nutshells in which all our visions of reality are found does not lead him to conclude that our interpretations of meaning cannot have some relationship to truth. And if his explorations into the meaning of truth are to have any degree of valid meaning themselves, then *some* knowledge of truth *must* be both possible and communicable.

In approaching the truth about reality, two opposite impossibilities must be avoided. On the one hand, we must not treat any set of stated reality beliefs as obviously, immediately, and incontestably true. Interpretive complexity and the superabundance of reality in comparison with our comprehending capacities makes a simplistic "black and white" outlook on truth impossibly naïve.[5] We always reason from within a given

---

3. Shakespeare, *Hamlet*, Act 1, Scene 5, lines 168–69. Note, it is the appearance of a ghost in the daytime, which Horatio's philosophy could not map, that gives rise to this statement in the play, rather than the offense against heaven and earth of regicide, which so unhinged the young Hamlet. Yet unhinging and the inbreaking of the incomprehensible are intimately tied in this astonishing play.

4. Gadamer, *Truth and Method*.

5. And, as Kierkegaard points out, knowledge is never simply knowledge, but is always connected in one way or another with sin and faith. The acts of knowing and believing are done by actually existing people, and the central drama of any existing human life, Kierkegaard maintains, concerns the relation of that individual to

culturally and historically located conceptual nutshell, and that nutshell defines an inner space that is necessarily "smaller" than reality but which makes comprehension possible to us. On the other hand, we must not think that truth is entirely humanly constructed such that no reality belief can validly participate in *real* (i.e., not simply of our making) truth. That is, just because we can only think from within our nutshell does not necessarily mean that truth is not out there beyond our nutshell, or that some measure of truth cannot reach us through our nutshell. Indeed, our nutshells are part of reality and they only "work" in providing us with a comprehension and interpretation of the world around us because they have some positive relationship to that which is beyond them.

Let us, then, avoid a hubristic unawareness of the fragile and particular texture of all human knowledge, and let us also avoid the (ironically) absolute relativism of cultural constructivism. These two impossibilities stand like the pillars of Hercules, ready to wreck any metaphysical ship that would voyage into the vast ocean of a meaningful understanding of reality beyond this entry point. We must sail between these pillars. I think this can be done for if it cannot then it seems unavoidable that reasoning is either impossibly hubristic or entirely meaningless.

Sailing between these pillars is no simple matter yet Plato (though not all Platonists) does sail through them, and so do carefully calibrated forms of Christian Platonism. However, the dominant approaches to knowledge and truth within a contemporary Western context display a marked tendency towards conceptual wreckage on one or other of these rocks. Modernity has a powerful tendency towards a hubristic conception of the unmediated simple truth of a scientifically reductive understanding of the real—it does not appreciate that it reasons within a specific nutshell. Postmodernism, on the other hand, has a powerful tendency towards throwing out truth altogether—it reduces "truth" to the nutshell of the constructs of our specific culturally located worlds. In what follows I am going to argue that because both modernity and postmodernism lack a constructive and truth-carrying understanding of culturally situated "mythos," neither of them can get through these twin pillars. Further, it is precisely this lack and this inability to get out into a

---

God. That primary relation—which is the only "place" in which the human spirit *can* live—is always a dynamic of sin and faith, and that dynamic shapes knowledge and belief far more causally than knowledge and belief (understood propositionally—i.e., in abstraction from their existential context) shape faith and sin. See Kierkegaard, *Concluding Unscientific Postscript*.

place where metaphysical truth can have any real meaning that makes Christian Platonism seem an impossible fantasy to the modern cultural mindset.

Introducing "Mythos"

Let us now shift back from Shakespeare's analogy of the nutshell to the specific challenge of defending Christian Platonism in our times. To play with the strait of Gibraltar analogy one last time, there is no reasonable way of judging Christian Platonism by the standards of modernity because modernity is within the Mediterranean, unable to pass through the pillars of Hercules, and Christian Platonism is out in the Atlantic Ocean. So before we can properly address the philosophical and theological objections to contemporary Christian Platonism that modernity posits, we need to be aware that there is a much more basic sort of objection to what we are talking about than can be found on the surface of abstract reasoning. For even though it is not recognized as such, the mythos of modernity tells a totally different story about how things are and about what counts as believable reasoning than does Christian Platonism. This being the case, it is important to recognize that the background assumptions of our times, which frame reasoning itself and which define what is understood as valid knowledge to a modernist, have a powerful cultural and political bias against Christian Platonism.

"Mythos" as I am using the term here means an imaginative and collectively believed story about how things are which is assumed by the norms of the everyday way of life of any given human community.

Probably the most remarkable thing about the mythos of modernity is that it explicitly maintains that it has no mythos. Central to living within the modern Western life form is the strong conviction that there is nothing imaginative or story-like about how we see the world. We simply assume that our understanding of reality is all entirely factual and rational. Indeed, being factual and rational is—we believe—what makes us "advanced" and hence what makes our reality outlook superior to others in the past and in different civilizations. If we are happy modernists we are unquestioningly committed to the belief that we believe no myths and this distinguishes us from every obsolete reality outlook.

What I want to examine in this chapter is how the dominant culturally believed origins story of modernity is not only a myth, but it is also a myth that powerfully conceals the true origins of modernity. Further, I want to point out how this origins cover-up narrative sustains our deep belief commitment to a false story about how far superior we are to all previous cultural outlooks. Because we are not critically aware of the actual history of the rise of modernity we simply assume that modernity—as patently realistic and naturally advanced—simply replaced Christian Platonism by inevitable historical progression. Assuming this stance as we do it is natural that talk of any recovery of Christian Platonism in our times would be heard as advocating civilizational regress with the aim of taking us back to the dark and pre-scientific age of ignorance, irrational violence, ecclesial oppression, and superstition.

This chapter needs to be in this book because until we can find good reasons to be suspicious of the truth of the assumed narrative of cultural origins that underpins our modern way of life, no genuine alternative—such as Christian Platonism—will be deemed worthy of serious consideration.

The Song of Modernity

Culturally believed origins stories are not something that we consciously learn. They are more like songs that we have always had going in the background than things we read up for in a scholarly assignment. The more powerful they are, the less we notice them. The more they are simply the assumed background truths that everyone knows—cultural wallpaper if you like—the more entrenched and powerful they are in shaping how we live.

I remember first becoming aware of modernity's cosmogenic narrative when I studied philosophy as an undergraduate student. It was here that I realized that Western modernity has its own distinctive origins song. So—intentionally mimicking the form of the first few chapters of Genesis—let me sing you the song of the origins of modernity in the history of philosophy key in which it was first sung to me.

In the beginning there was myth. Reason brooded over the inchoate waters of imagination but found nowhere to alight. Then came the Greeks. These were—like all people at that time—merpeople who swam and lived in the Ocean of Imagination. But one of these Greeks, named Thales, swam over shallows where the ocean floor came near to the surface. Thales found that the touch of the ocean floor was solid and did not shift according to the currents of imagination. After much exploration, Thales even found a small patch of mud that stood up out of the ocean entirely, and with labored breath he dared to breathe the air of Truth and touch the ground of Reason.

The Spirit of Truth (Mathematics) was brooding over the waters of Imagination and found Thales. It dropped from the heavens a mangrove pod. Thales saw it go into the mud and take root. Over many generations the children of Thales tended the mangrove and it grew to be a forest. Soon dry land appeared such that philosophers—for so the descendants of Thales were called—could haltingly attempt to build a civilization of Reason on solid ground. But the early philosophers where still children of the Sea of Imagination from which they had come. The ancient Greeks were a quantum leap forward, out of the womb-like darkness and fluidity of *mythos* (myth) and towards the clear light and solidity of *logos* (reason), but they were not true philosophers. The high masters of antiquity—Plato and Aristotle—were still a hybrid breed, governed by many a speculative flight of fancy. Only the atomists and skeptics of ancient times were genuine foretastes of the birth of the true philosopher. For the philosopher—governed only and fearlessly by Truth and Reason—has no use for imagination and religion. The philosopher has no truck with speculative and superstitious fantasy wrought of the oceanic imaginative origins of the primitive human mind.

The classical philosophers evolved past the genuinely aquatic origins of our species, but they were more amphibians than true land creatures. Plato and Aristotle exercised enormous influence over the thought and imagination of Western civilization for nearly two millennia. As a result, not much of philosophical interest happens between the high classical period and what we now call the birth of modernity. However, something religious happened between Plato and Descartes that was to prove very important. A religion called Christianity appeared in an obscure corner of the Greco-Roman world and this religion saw itself as an enemy of pagan imagination. By a freak accident of history Christianity came to replace the pagan religious structures of antiquity at much the same time that classical culture collapsed. Thus, Western Europe became Christendom as it entered the Dark Age during which time religious superstition flourished and learning almost disappeared. Even so, three very important things happened in that dark period. Firstly,

Christian prohibitions against the worship of any created thing began to de-mythologize nature. Secondly, and most importantly, late
medieval Christian theologians discovered that unphilosophical
matters of doctrine and faith could be held to be fully separate from
matters of philosophical reason, scientific knowledge, and practical
action. Thirdly, the Reformation produced the peace of Westphalia
and paved the way to separating politics out from religion. After
these important non-philosophical developments the way was finally open for the speculative sea of religion and imagination to be
genuinely separated out from the practical, political, and scientific
land of truth and reason. Thus matters of faith were increasingly
shipped off shore to the realm of harmless subjective and personal
belief, and matters of scientific knowledge and rational thought
were finally set free to pursue objective truths in the solid, real, and
public arena, unhindered by religion and speculation. Ironically—
as it turned out—Christianity aided the birth of true philosophy.

So it was during the seventeenth century in Western Europe,
among groundbreaking thinkers like Francis Bacon, Galileo Galilei,
and René Descartes, that true (that is, modern) philosophy really
begins.

Early modern philosophers were courageous innovators who
made it possible for the Western mind to become free of the chains of
superstition and ignorance. But unlike ancient Greek philosophers,
their struggle was not against pagan imagination but against the
medieval synthesis of Christian doctrines with pre-scientific natural
philosophy, against church authority, and against dogmatic book
learning that refused to look at the real world. One must remember that the medieval universities were often set up by the Roman
Catholic Church and in medieval society the church, learning, and
politics were all terribly tangled up with each other. So the bold innovators of true philosophy had to fight not only against the church
and against civil power in the thrall of the church, but against the
upholders of academic status and power in the universities too.

The fathers of modernity inaugurated an intellectual age in
which the mythos not only of religious superstition, but of speculative metaphysical imagination as well, would finally be separated
out from scientific truth. The fathers of modernity also inaugurated
a political age in which religious authority would finally be separated out from political power. Thus was truth as demonstrable

proof separated from speculative fantasy and thus was heaven and all matters of religious belief separated out from knowledge and power in the real here-and-now earth. Finally, a true Age of Reason could be born.

Galileo signals one of the great watersheds in the birth of modernity. Using mathematics and observation, Galileo demonstrated that Aristotle's understanding of mechanics was faulty and that the church's view of the cosmos was simply wrong. Descartes employed his own form of skepticism in order to cast doubt on traditional natural philosophy and to demand absolute proof as the necessary ground of valid belief. Descartes' idea that only what an individual knowing human subject can be indubitably certain of provides a valid foundation for true knowledge demotes metaphysics as first philosophy and puts epistemology (the philosophy of knowledge) in its place, and this has been a signature of modern philosophy ever since. But arguably it is Francis Bacon who is the greatest herald of the modern age. Bacon is not remembered as a philosopher or a scientist, yet he planted the seed of a great idea that is central to the modern world. Knowledge gives us power over nature, thus the central criteria of deciding "is it true?" becomes "does it work?" Once this stance is accepted as valid, questions of metaphysics and theology are simply irrelevant to matters of public truth and technological power. Reason and knowledge can now be free from the restrictions and fantasies of speculative thought and religious power.

The dominant Anglo way of reading what comes next in Western intellectual history is that British empiricism and American pragmatism overcame the more European tendency towards abstract rationalism and speculative idealism, producing twentieth-century heroes of truth and reason such as A. J. Ayer and Bertrand Russell. But alas, in the latter half of the twentieth century a bunch of weird Europeans—Lyotard, Derrida, and the like—play incoherent linguistic games with the philosophical enterprise and introduce the virus of postmodernism into the English speaking world. This being the case, the Age of Reason may now be experiencing something of a decline; yet we still have the undisputable advances of scientific knowledge and technological power which are the gift of the Age of Reason.

Is the Origins Myth of Modernity True?

The above song is an inspiring and assuring story. The courageous heroes of truth and reason battle against the traditional bastions of superstition, ignorance, and oppression until, at last, the modern world that we know and love is born. We are the children of reason and freedom who are liberated from the caprice of nature by our science and technology. We now have no time for the magical and religious speculations of the past, speculations embedded in superstitious imagination (such as Christian Platonism). This story affirms our own nobility, valorizes our historical epoch's commitment to truth and reason, and assumes our obvious superiority to the past. There is only one problem with this song—it is almost entirely false. Just about every interpretive gloss embedded in the song I have sung you is debatable, and most of it is demonstrably false. Even so, the very way we live assumes this song's validity.

I will seek to demonstrate to you how false this story is by focusing on but two verses of the above song. The two narrative components I will focus on are like key pieces in a three-dimensional puzzle. If you take them out, the whole thing falls to pieces. So I will extract two key falsehoods of the mythos of modernity with the intention of making the background assumptions of modernity open to genuine questioning. If that can be done, then the Christian Platonist view of reality need not be simply dismissed because it is incompatible with the unconscious collective narrative assumptions about truth and reason that are integral to modernity.

The two false aspects of the myth of modernity that I will target are these: (1) philosophy is all about the triumph of logos (reason) over mythos (understood as imagined and false stories), and modernity is the age in which this triumph occurs; (2) modern philosophy has no debt to medieval theology.

Logos, Mythos, and Modernity

The idea sequence where classical Greek antiquity is the place where logos starts to replaces mythos, that mythos is imaginative fantasy tied up with irrational religion while logos is factual and scientific truth, and that modernity is the true age of logos, is just not defensible. There are a number of ways of pointing this out, but I will limit this section to a discussion of a few scholars of classical antiquity and some quick peeks at Friedrich Nietzsche and Johann Hamann.

Francis Cornford—an early twentieth-century classics scholar from Cambridge University—wrote a fascinating book titled *From Religion to Philosophy*.[6] Here he points out that far from philosophy (logos) being in radical and incommensurable competition with religion (mythos), logos arises out of mythos, but without leaving mythos behind. Logos is a transformation *within* mythos, not a replacement of myth by reason. That is, the very idea of logos—that the world that we experience is an ordered and reasoned unity that can be understood by our minds—arises out of a religious outlook. Christians should understand Cornford's central insight well as the prologue to John's Gospel famously identifies the divine Logos with Christ (John 1:1–18).

In the central trends of ancient Greco-Roman culture the relationship between philosophy and theology is essentially integral. This is because the most outstanding philosophers of classical times were the most outstanding theologians of that era. Plato essentially invented theology[7] and Aristotle saw no conceptual distinction between the terms "first philosophy" (what we would now call metaphysics) and "theology."[8] So the lines of continuity and inter-dependence between religion, theology, philosophy, and the life of virtue were well understood in ancient Greece, and Greek philosophy in general is profoundly integrative in these terms. This is the case even though the appearance of philosophical religion did indeed upset the apple cart of traditional Greek religion.[9] In terms of that tension the classics scholar Walter Burkert points out that one of Plato's primary agendas was to integrate personal religious piety with civic religion and philosophical inquiry. Plato was successful in this fusing of religion with philosophy, and this weld was a hallmark of dominant trends in Greco-Roman philosophy for the entire classical era. Burkert notes: "[In] Plato's *Laws* . . . the essential lines of the situation which was to hold for the next 600 years become visible: the conflict between philosophical

6. Cornford, *From Religion to Philosophy*.

7. "Since Plato there has been no theology which has not stood in his shadow." Burkert, *Greek Religion*, 321.

8. See Aristotle, *Metaphysics*, Book VI, chapter 1 (1026a 18–32); Book XI, chapter 7 (1064a 27–39).

9. Aristophanes explores this tension in his play *Clouds* as does Plato in—amongst other places—his dialogues *The Apology* and *Euthyphro*. For a fascinating study of Plato and Aristophanes on the matter of the complex dialectic relationship between traditional and philosophical religion in ancient Athens see Weierter, *Understanding Life and Death through Plato and Socrates*.

and traditional religion is denied."[10] For while classical philosophy was not uniform on the question of the relation of divinity to human reason, there is no disputing the fact that Plato's stance dominated the ancient philosophical landscape after him.[11] And Plato's approach to philosophy was profoundly religious even though it was, for theological reasons, dismissive of any literal interpretation of morally despicable stories about the gods. Thus ancient philosophy in the dominant Platonist key was very much concerned with theology and with the divine grounds of reason and truth. Philosophy for Plato was the pursuit of a high way of life that was a moral and intellectual discipline so that the soul would be prepared to leave the body upon physical death.[12] Indeed Plato defines philosophy as a preparation for death: a preparation that involves the practice of dying to all those things that would hinder the soul in its eternal journey towards the Good.[13]

Pierre Hadot notes that if one belonged to a school of philosophy in ancient times, this was far more akin to the way of life of religious orders—governed by exacting spiritual exercises—than it is to the kind of academic interest in different abstract arguments, as is typical for the professional philosopher today.[14] Further, E. R. Dodds deftly points out that Greek philosophy was profoundly open to that which escapes rational capture.[15] All this is to say that a modern understanding of reason—as formal logic, as pure, clear, secular, and non-religious truth, as reductively scientific knowledge, and as decidedly incompatible with dogmatic theology—is an entirely modern invention that does not have its origins

10. Burkert, *Greek Religion*, 337.

11. It is not correct to maintain that a naturalistic Aristotle represented a serious alternative to the more theologically inclined Platonist metaphysical sensibility in antiquity. Gerson points this out well in his landmark text *Aristotle and Other Platonists*. And while the Skeptics, the Cynics, the Atomists, and different continuations of pre-Socratic sophism certainly rose and fell in periodic popularity, the civilizational impact at the level of basic reality assumptions was with Platonist, Neoplatonist, and finally Christian Platonist metaphysical convictions. For an accessible overview of the classical period see Brunschwig and Lloyd, *Greek Thought*.

12. Giving close attention to the fact that ancient philosophy was a *lived form*, not—as we would now understand it—an "academic" pursuit, D. C. Schindler has discovered that a fascinating interpretive key for reading Plato's dialogues is to notice that Socrates often embodies the matter being investigated. See Schindler, *Plato's Critique of Impure Reason*.

13. Plato, *Phaedo* 64a.

14. Hadot, *Philosophy as a Way of Life*. See also, Hadot, *What is Ancient Philosophy?*

15. Dodds, *The Greeks and the Irrational*.

in ancient Greek philosophy. That is, the central understandings of Logos in ancient times were almost exactly *not* like modern reason. This is most decisively evident in that the dominant schools of classical Greek philosophy believed things about the nature of reality that a modern understanding of "pure" logic and "objective" science could not possibly provide.

Lloyd Gerson notes that one of the defining characteristics of antiquity that separates it from modernity is that the ancients believed that *meaning was prior to perceiving*.[16] Thus the stance often assumed in antiquity was that eternal and divine truths alone constituted genuine knowledge whereas sensation-dependent perception only ever attains the status of a revisable and somewhat unreliable belief.[17] This is neatly the opposite of typically modern understandings of valid truth and solid reasoning. To us moderns, only tangible phenomena and an appreciation of the value neutral, meaning neutral, mathematical regularities of physical phenomena constitutes true knowledge. Anything to do with meaning, value, and divinity is—to us—mere belief. (We will return to this later, for it seems at least plausible that the ancient way of thinking about meaning and truth is far more obvious and far more philosophically defensible than the modern notion.)

Underlying the modern story about the origins of valid philosophical insight is a distinctive re-telling of ancient philosophy as a primitive forerunner of non-theological modernity, coupled, as we shall see, with a willful ignorance of how medieval Western theology deeply shapes modernity. So the accepted cultural meta-narrative of the origins of modern truth and reason—i.e., the long passage to a Western triumph of

---

16. To clarify, Aristotle maintains that as regards the process of knowing things, nothing is found in the intellect that is not first perceived; and yet, meaning and purpose and intelligibility is already in what we perceive. That is, the priority of meaning over perceiving is not a temporal priority within the process of coming to know things, rather it is a priority of being (an ontological priority) within the nature of reality itself. We perceive meaning and reason in the world because it is already there before we perceive. Thought, intellect, meaning—these realities make perceiving possible and make human reasoning about the intelligible truth of the cosmos possible. It makes no *sense* to Aristotle to think of some brute meaningless reality that is simply there. Reality is always meaningful and intelligible, thus Divine Reason is the most basic feature of reality, and thus our capacity to reason is why we can perceive reality for what it really is. In this sense, thought is the grounds of perceiving, even if perceiving is the means to thought in the temporal process of coming to know things.

17. Gerson, *Ancient Epistemology*.

non-religious logos over dark and ignorant religious mythos—is itself a "myth" (in the derogatory sense) without a basis in historical truth.

Yet it is Nietzsche who makes the remarkable claim that the very notion of validly interpreted historical truth is essentially mythic, and that mythos is *always* prior to logos—and modern logos is no exception.

If this all sounds hopelessly relativistic and obviously false in relation to the cold hard truths of science, like Newton's laws of motion, do not switch off here. Stay with me, for my argument goes through Nietzsche rather than remaining with Nietzsche. Even so, Nietzsche has important things to tell us about the unavoidability of mythos for any culture.

Friedrich Nietzsche was a brilliant nineteenth-century scholar of classical languages and literature. As a language specialist and a penetrating scholar of ancient culture he was particularly sensitive to the fact that all thinking and all human action is only meaningful to us because of words. But words are very fragile and malleable things. Their meanings are a function of culturally situated use, and all cultural and historical situations are contingent and shifting artifacts of imagination, desire, and power, and provide us with no fixed or objectively factual grounding in truth. Any reasoned thought about "objective truth" is thus a self-deception because it must of necessity rely on words shaped and interpreted by culture and by the contingencies of one's particular community, life, and times. Contingency is the inescapable context for all human ideas, thus human ideas simply do not have the power to be universally and eternally valid (and anyone who tells you they do is selling something).

Nietzsche maintained that the desire for certain truth is a crutch that seeks to provide the illusions of security and necessity in what is in fact the radically insecure and contingent situation of all human life. Those who embrace this situation well are those who do not let the artificial and inevitably constructed cultural claims of right and wrong, of truth and of reliable knowledge, delude them. Those who are free fly above the cultural expectations of their society and take responsibility for generating their own meaning in their lives out of their own imagination and out of the vital forces of life, will, and power that stir within them.

So to Nietzsche all truths are contingently generated within culture and language. Thus "knowledge" and "truth" are derived from imagination and poetry and there is nothing more basic than myth to culture. Thus, logos and every claim to knowledge of how things *really* are (as if things had essential and eternal natures rather than continent and transitory natures) is an illusion created out of human weakness and driven by

the vain desire to gain mastery over the contingencies that we find ourselves within. It is misplaced hubris to think that we could somehow pull
ourselves up by our own contingent culturo-linguistic bootstraps into the
realm of universal and eternal truth.

Now the point of mentioning Nietzsche at this juncture is that
his thought has had a powerful influence on what we now call cultural
studies, the sociology of knowledge, and hermeneutic philosophy. These
disciplines all find that it is now very hard to understand the cosmogenic
song of modernity as anything other than a cultural myth itself. And a
bad myth at that, for a staggering feature of the story of modernity is the
idea of progress. But are we really so much further advanced than the
ancients just because we can fly planes? Freud and Picasso think not. Not
a few very serious psychologists, artists, and social anthropologists tend
to think—along Nietzschean lines—that culture is a sort of grand cop-
ing mechanism that flexibly and artfully responds to the basic social and
individual givens of our frail and transitory existences. One cannot say
that one culture is more advanced than another, that one set of cosmic
placement and reality definition stories is more true than another. All
meanings—including the meanings of the truth claims of modern science—are now often understood as contingent side effects of historically
embedded culture.

Nietzsche's arguments have considerable force and his influence is
not surprising. But I am not trying to persuade you that radical cultural
constructivism is true (and of course, such a claim would be self-defeating as a truth claim anyway). At this point, let us swing back a hundred
years before Nietzsche to another language and culture theorist, but one
whom I find even more fascinating than Nietzsche: Johann Hamann.

Hamann had a deep appreciation for the "oh so human" nature of
language and culture, and of the impossibility of thinking about human
thought without reference to its inescapable cultural and linguistic context. This can be briefly illustrated by reference to Hamann's relationship
with his contemporary and friend, Immanuel Kant. In 1781 Kant—a central figure in modern philosophy—published the first edition of his now
famous *Critique of Pure Reason*. In response to this fat and densely reasoned tome Hamann wrote a brief piece, which he titled *A Meta-critique
of the Purism of Reason*. (Even so, because Kant was Hamann's friend, this
meta-critique was not published in Hamann's lifetime.) Hamann's meta-
critique of Kantian "pure" reason is a simply devastating assault on the
pre-eminent achievement of eighteenth-century Enlightenment thought.

Kant thinks modern science and logic can provide us with a description of the world that is superior to all other types of claims to valid knowledge. But Hamann points out that Kant has forgotten that his description is crafted out of *words*, and words that get their meaning from inherited and culturally situated use. Even in Kant's own very careful, very powerful philosophical writing, there is no *pure* reason.

I mention Hamann here for an interesting reason. As pointed out above, Nietzsche's appreciation of the cultural and linguistic context in which all meaning is mediated to us and interpreted by us is now fairly well understood to place an inescapable "No" on Enlightenment pretensions to cultural progress and the attainment of simple truth via the modern scientific outlook. This Hamann also illustrates, considerably before Nietzsche's time. Yet a significant reason as to why Nietzsche's understanding of cultural hermeneutics is acceptable to late modern and postmodern thinking, and Hamann remains obscure, is that Nietzsche was a self-proclaimed enemy of Christianity and Hamann was a Christian.[18]

Hamann believed that language, culture, art, imagination, and tradition were not *simply* contingent human constructs, though they certainly are that, but these are also the interactive media—interactive between Humanity and God—of revelation. For this reason Hamann, at the same time that the Germanic trend in historical critical biblical interpretation takes off (which gave us Liberal Protestantism, which in turn inspired many of the great atheist thinkers of the nineteenth century), denounced the idea of a rational interpretive science of textual analysis being "objectively" applied to sacred writ. The fragile tissue of revelation—a tissue of

18. It is clear that there are two possible ways of being "postmodern." There is postmodern thinking that is a continuation of what John Milbank calls the secular reason of modernity. This way is persuaded, like Kant, that no true knowledge of transcendent meaning is possible, but unlike Kant this stance recognizes that all meaning constructs are equally untrue given that the contingencies of culturo-linguistic interpretation can never be risen above when one thinks, believes, speaks, and writes. The other type of "postmodernism" is one that finds divinity acting within human language and culture, but here divine truth is never reducible to the human media in which it is partially manifest. This is the path that Hamann, Kierkegaard, and Milbank, for example, take. "Postmodernism" in continuation with the secular reason of modernity must falter on unavoidable self-contradiction. For if it is true that no truth is possible, then this stance must also not be true. So only the second form of postmodernism can use an appreciation of the contingencies of language and culture in order to say anything meaningful. For true meaning that is not simply a culturally solipsistic imaginative construct is here possible because there is a dialectic relationship between the non-human divine truth and the constructed world of human language and culture.

tradition, of culturally situated and existentially enacted meanings, of the stories of specific people and events—is the very medium through which God gives us the Scriptures. And Scripture is always interpreted within that medium so no abstractly "pure" and "objective" science of interpretation is possible. The Spirit of Truth blows where it wills and cannot be contained in some rational and methodological box. Hamann revels in this. God situates his revelation to us (and it is a revelation to an interpretive and practicing community, situated within culture and language) in this manner in order to pour scorn on our hubristic pretensions to "stand over" his revelation to us with our oh-so-human reason and our oh-so-human knowledge. We will be hearing but not understanding, seeing but not perceiving, if that is our approach to divine revelation. For the "foolishness" of hearing the Word of God is only granted to those who will understand (stand under) his revelation in an attitude of obedient and receptive humility.

It is Hamann's understanding of how revelation operates *within* language and culture that separates him from Nietzsche's hermeneutics of ever-contingent linguistic and cultural constructivism. To Hamann the breath of God within human language and culture, and particularly within the Scriptures, is why Hamann does not think we can either finally "crack" the truth open in terms of the pretension of mastery latent in human knowledge, *or* simply generate our own myths.

But let us see where Hamann and Nietzsche agree and where they disagree. Mythos—as a richly imaginative store of pre/super-rational culturo-linguistically embedded meanings—is seen by both thinkers as the grounds of human logos. That is, human reason is not the grounds of truth and any human picture of truth is grounded itself in something more basic than itself. But to Nietzsche logos is always a sort of false consciousness, for there can be no knowable essential meaning in the contingent and ever-changing realm of becoming in which we live. So to Nietzsche logos is always a derivative form of mythos, and both are inexplicable contingent realities that do not speak of anything beyond themselves. So in Nietzsche's view both mythos and logos are tools that can be themselves imaginatively manipulated and then used to construct a very broad range of life possibilities. To Hamann, however, that which grounds both human imagination and human reason is Divine Logos. The true meaning of reality—on which we depend and out of which we are derived—does not jump through hoops for our small human intellects or limited human imaginations. But our small intellects and limited human imaginations can grasp some measure of real (divine) truth even so.

Two points are important to make here in relation to the modern cosmogony about the supposed triumph of philosophical logos over religious and imaginative mythos. Firstly, Hamann's stance has yet to be taken seriously as a powerful and inherently credible alternative to a Nietzschean understanding of the cultural contextuality of human meaning. John Betz's stunning book *After Enlightenment* is a significant intellectual exploration showing us the way to that sort of thinking. Secondly, if Hamann and Plato are right about human language and meaning being a fragile and delicate media for our partial comprehension of divine truth, then there can be partially true myths, and cultural myths can partake deeply in truth. Myth only means "not true" to a literalist naturalism, which has no theological understanding of how imaginative artistic inspiration actually works (i.e., to those already committed to the modern mythos). And it just might be—as C. S. Lewis was firmly convinced—that myths can partake in far *more* truth than human logos ever could.[19]

Imagination touched by the divine light of inspiration may not be as instrumentally useful as modern science, but it is likely to go a lot further in the direction of wisdom than any "purely" rational approach to value, meaning, and ultimate purpose. And even with regard to science, Nietzschean cultural constructivism cannot see its truth, thus—ironically—only a "mythic" view of the divine grounds of reason and creation can see science as partially revealing real truth. But it takes a degree of piety, even in scientific knowledge, to remember that we must not confuse science—the humanly constructed knowledge icon—with that divine reality that it sacramentally participates in, for such would be to fall to the idolatry of worshiping our own knowledge constructs as if they were capable of mastering ultimate truth. Thus a Hamannean understanding of the contextuality and inherent humanity of all human knowledge constructs is sensitive to the real interpretive fragility of our understanding of truth, but without sacrificing the idea of truth itself, which any serious form of cultural constructivism (to its own undoing) must do.

To sum up this section, the modern worldview is just as imbedded in mythos as any other worldview. Collective imaginative narratives are not optional extras that cultures may or may not have; they are inherent to human culture and linguistically expressed human reason. As such

---

19. Lewis' most fabulously inspired imaginative reasoning in this direction is, I think, *Perelandra*.

mythos always gives rise to and shapes the understanding of reason (logos) that any given cultural life form largely accepts. However, if contingent and entirely humanly constructed mythos is all the access to "truth" that we can have, then we have no access to truth, and then it cannot be *true* that human mythos is all the access to truth that we can have. Thus pure constructivism is self-refuting. For this reason it is profoundly irrational to maintain that an appreciation for the mythic as the grounds of reason in every culture precludes the possibility of mythos-grounded logos being some sort of medium of divine truth that is not simply contingent. That is, if truth is real and at least in some measure knowable, and if reason is a valuable tool in understanding truth, then some myths will be more true than others, even while it remains the case that truth as culturally expressed is always shaped in some way or another by contingencies and contextual relativisms. Even so, whether this hope for truth and reason is valid or not, the modern cosmogenic story about the triumph or logos over mythos to the complete displacement of mythos is itself a myth, and an inherently unbelievable myth.

But why did *this* origins myth arise for modernity? Or, to ask the same question another way, what is the true origin of modern logos if it is not this story of the gradual triumph of rational, scientific, non-religious logos over superstitious, imaginative, made up mythos? To this we now turn.

Modernity is Medieval

The other key falsehood about the myth of modernity is the tacit claim that nothing much of philosophical importance happens between Greco-Roman classical philosophy and Descartes. This is particularly misleading because the true story of the birth of modernity is a medieval story. Indeed, medieval *theology* is the real womb of modernity, and what is distinctive about this womb is that it is such a decisive rupture with the classical Western tradition that it can make no believable claim to have any real continuity with ancient philosophy.

Modern logos is a product of late medieval thinking, and this thinking re-invents the idea of what reason is, of what knowledge is, of what the relationship between philosophy and theology is, and of what philosophy itself is, in ways that are genuinely new. So, ironically, unless we can understand how medieval modernity actually still is, we will not be able to appreciate why it is so strongly biased against Christian Platonism. But

modernity has a very distinctive kind of medieval heritage, a very Franciscan heritage shaped powerfully by the subtle thought of Duns Scotus
and the radical thought of William of Ockham. How modernity arises
from this type of medieval theology is something we will now briefly
explore.

The classical Greco-Roman civilization slips irrevocably into the
past in the year 529 AD.[20] After this date the classical world and its imperial majesty fades to black and Western Europe is left with only the
memory of antiquity's lost glory. Thus the sixth century is often called
the beginning of the "Dark Ages" by modern historians, for here the high
culture, the military glory, and the unified system of language, power,
and commerce of the classical era gives way to the beginnings of medieval Christendom.

But what is dark to those who pine for what was lost with the passing of ancient imperial Rome was something of a new dawn for the early
architects of Christendom. Yet continuity with the past was not simply
lost with the arrival of a new era. In particular, the church maintained
continuity—largely through the monastic movement—with what was
accessible in Latin of the learning of the classical past. The emphasis of
monastic learning at this time was on biblical knowledge and the lives
of the saints and had little interest in the high philosophical learning of
the now gone classical era. Even so, the theology of Augustine of Hippo,
the pre-eminent Latin Christian thinker of late antiquity, was also foundational to the new Christendom. So whilst the period from the sixth
century to the eleventh century was not even a shadow of the imperial
civilization it replaced, yet this is a fascinating period where continuous
invasions of pagan barbarians were integrated into Christendom because
of the vitality of the monastic movement and the Celtic missionaries.
Thus Europe was Christianized at its core, not under the blessing of the
classical Roman Imperium, but during the "Dark Age" of civilizational
collapse and foreign invasion. Christendom is a much more grassroots
and spiritually grounded movement than we often give it credit for. The
living inner light of post-imperial Christian faith was in fact a bright and
attractive flame during the "dark" early centuries of Christendom.

By the twelfth century the fortunes of Europe finally overcame the
misfortunes she inherited with the collapse of classical civilization. And

20. Pieper, *Scholasticism*, 16–22.

her fortunes revived through the church for it was the church that saved Western culture from disappearing forever.

The period of the High Middle Ages was an astonishing time in Western cultural history. This was the era of the founding of the West's universities, the re-discovery of ancient learning, the rise of wealthy cities with their powerful merchant classes, innovation in crafts, the flowering of art and music, the flourishing of new Western military and pre-nationalist aristocratic powers, and it was an era when the glory and power of the Roman Catholic Church oversaw all.

Modernity's intellectual institutions and the traditions that produced modern knowledge were born in the medieval era; the political forms of life we now take for granted are formed out of institutions that evolved from medieval origins; our legal system still has connections to medieval canon law; the wealth of the medieval merchant cities undermined feudalism and produced modern cities—and yet modernity does not see itself as historically embedded in medievalism. Why?

Highly significant in the dynamics that underpin the cosmogenic mythos of modernity is the need, as Picasso put it, to kill our fathers. The Roman Catholic Church fathered the Western University, sponsored learning, legitimated political power, and its theologians set up the very framework of the modern world. But we cannot admit that the church caused the modern Western world to come into being, rather we must think of modernity arising in strident rebellion against the power, patronage, and beliefs of the church. This is our bold and independent adolescent cultural mythos. But if, as John Milbank argues, modernity is a medieval theological idea, the entire standard narrative of the formation of the modern world as I originally sung it to you is a deception.[21]

I will endeavor to very briefly tell you the counter story of the medieval origins of modernity along the lines of John Milbank's powerful argument.

Aquinas and the Relation of Reason and Faith

The pivotal thinker of the High Middle Ages was the Dominican friar Thomas Aquinas. Aquinas was a great synthesizer who managed to integrate much of the newly re-discovered writings of Aristotle into a philosophically rich Christian theological framework. This was a phenomenal

21. See Milbank, *Theology and Social Theory.*

intellectual achievement, for the kind of communally practiced, scripturally embedded, and spiritually disciplined understanding of Christian orthodoxy that Thomas accepted from medieval Christendom was rightly seen to be of a very different sort of intellectual milieu to the pagan and naturalistic pre-Christian Greek philosophy of Aristotle. However, as the great medievalist Etienne Gilson notes, Aquinas' astonishing integration of orthodox Christian belief with Greek philosophical reasoning proved to be so finely nuanced as to be, historically, highly fragile.[22] For the fact is that Greek reason (including what we would now call science) and Christian faith appeared to many of the university professors of the thirteenth century to be such different sorts of knowledge pathways that they become almost irreconcilably separated out. Thus the origin of the modern Western notion that philosophy (reason) and religion (faith) are fundamentally different sorts of things is properly traced to the year 1277, not to some supposedly ancient struggle between mythos and logos. For in 1277, a few years after his death, crucial features of Thomas' integration of Aristotelian philosophy and Christian theology were condemned by Stephen Tempier, the Bishop of Paris.

Thomas had integrated medieval Christian faith with ancient Greek philosophy by following the long-established Platonist intellectual tradition of putting the wisdom of divine truth above the always-derived powers of human reason. Yet so convinced was Thomas that divine wisdom and valid human reason could not contradict one another—for there are not two truths, truth is a unity—that he was entirely fearless in exploring the learning of the pagan philosopher Aristotle. Where Aristotle's philosophy appeared to contradict Holy Writ or the teaching of the church, Aquinas either pointed out that the contradiction was not in fact real, or showed where Aristotle was wrong by appeal to other intellectual authorities, to reason (logic), and to Scripture as intelligently and orthodoxly interpreted. Yet this expansive and fearless capacity for integration is evidence of a very wide-ranging intellectual power, and people of the intellectual stature of Thomas come only rarely to any given civilization. Indeed it is no surprise that the Bishop of Paris was not convinced that the learning of the pagans would not lead the scholar hungering after the dazzling pagan knowledge of the past away from the truths entrusted to the church, for the bishop had concrete evidence that this in fact had happened at the great university of Paris. So the condemnation of 1277 signaled the advent of what was eventually to seem like a fundamental fork

22. Gilson, *History of Christian Philosophy in the Middle Ages*, 325.

in the road for scholars: either stay with the church (the pathway of faith where reason is firmly situated underneath dogmatic faith and ecclesial authority) or follow philosophy (the fearless and independent pathway of reason, which had no interest in doctrine or ecclesial authority).

But the situation was not at all polarized in the thirteenth century, even if the Bishop of Paris saw things in fearful and shrill terms. The problem of the appropriate integration and delineation of "faith" and "reason" was an inescapable feature of medieval university life from 1277 on and Thomas' integration would not long remain officially blacklisted. Indeed, it is was not high but late medieval theological developments that came to justify the decisive division between faith and reason such that the autonomy of philosophy from theology became the defining reality given to secular modernity by medieval theology. Here we need to briefly examine Duns Scotus and William of Ockham—the true fathers of modernity.

Scotus and the Univocity of Being

Duns Scotus was a fourteenth-century Franciscan scholar. Two of his brilliant innovations are foundational to modernity.[23] One is an innovation in metaphysics; the other is an innovation in epistemology.[24] These next few pages are going to be quite a head crunch as I endeavor to quickly explain what these innovations mean and how radically they depart from the classical and patristic traditions of thinking about reality and knowledge. If it does not all come clear at this stage do not fear as we will circle back to these ideas as the argument of this book unfolds.

In metaphysics, Scotus invented the idea of the univocity of being. At first blush the term "univocity of being" sounds impossibly abstract

23. In what follows I provide a very brief outline of what is a hotly contested stance amongst contemporary scholars interested in the relationship between Duns Scotus' thought and the emergence of the modern era. All parties interested in this matter see Duns Scotus as highly influential in shaping a number of modernity's fundamental ideas about being, knowledge, will, and politics, but whether he is seen—in his historical *effect*—as a hero or a villain is a matter of intense debate. The stance I take here largely adheres to the "Scotus is a villain" side of the "Scotus wars" as it seems unavoidable to me that his particular form of Aristotelian epistemology and his theology regarding the being of God both play a key role in the manner in which proto-modern trends in the West become cut off from key aspects of Christian Platonist epistemology and ontology.

24. Epistemology is a field of philosophy that explores the perennial questions "what is knowledge?" and "how can we know the truth of what we think we know?"

and obscure, but it is actually a remarkably simple idea. Assuming a Scotist stance, when I say, "this book is a real thing" and when I say "my
friend is a real thing," what it means for something to be real has the *same*
meaning, even if a book and a person are very different types of things.
That is, the meaning of the phrase "is a real thing" is uni-vocal (spoken
in one voice, i.e., always of one meaning). Crudely put, "is a real thing"
equates to the notion of "being," for being is the property that every real
thing shares ("being" is the quality of "is-ness," if you like). So to say that
"the cup is a real thing" is similar to saying that "the cup is performing
the action of being in the real world."[25] Scotus insists that unless the very
idea of being has a stable meaning, then coherent philosophical thinking
about reality completely unravels.

This may all seem pretty straightforward and uninteresting, but look
at what happens when you apply this idea to God. If I say that God is real
in the same way that I say the book is real or that my friend is real, then
"being" (realness if you like) is independent of or "bigger than" God, and
God becomes one being among other beings (albeit a very different type of
being from other beings). Both of these notions are radical departures
from the long tradition of Christian Neoplatonist metaphysics, which
envisioned reality itself as multi-layered and composed of different orders of being nested within one another, all nested within God. That old
ontological[26] outlook held sway in Western theology from Plato to Paul
to Augustine and to Aquinas, but Scotus abandons it with his univocity
of being idea.

Two key components of pre-modern Christian Neoplatonist metaphysics are radically attacked by Scotus' univocity of being innovation.
Firstly, the univocity of being innovation is a rejection of the Augustinian
stance that maintains God *is* Being. To Augustine God alone is real in
himself, and the reality of creation is a reality that is given to it by God.
This notion of the fundamental distinction between created reality and
God's reality is implied by Augustine's understanding that God created
the cosmos out of nothing. Hence, any created thing's reality is a derived
and dependent reality, a reality of a very different nature to the reality of

25. Abstractions, ideas, and phantasms also have being in that they exist (at least)
in our minds and in the Mind of God. So in medieval thought there is a distinction
between those things that have being in matter and those that do not. There is no sug-
gestion in Scotus that only material things are real.

26. "Ontological" is derived from the Greek word *on*, which means, in English
"being." So ontology is reasoning about being.

God. Augustine maintains that for any created thing to be real it must be in an ongoing dependent relationship with the fount of all real existence, God himself. So a creature's reality—be it a rock or a person or a ray of light—is not something the creature owns and generates in its own right, but is a wonderful gift of participation in the Life and Reality of God himself. This idea of the ontological participation of all created beings in the Being of God means that because Being is fundamental to my own being, I am most intimately enfolded in God, and I am most intimately in communion with all other created beings who are also grounded in the Being of God. This is the vision of the great chain of being and the community of all creation in the Being of God himself. This vision of an ontologically nested reality fundamentally dependent on God is lost if being is univocal and God becomes simply *a* being (albeit an infinite being) sharing the same property of reality that creation has.

Scotus radically shifts from the metaphysical vision that Aquinas upheld. Agreeing with Augustine, Aquinas thought that we never directly know what true Being is in Itself, for God is *not* "a being" within creation. The existence of all created beings is dependent on Being Itself, but God has no such dependence on Being, for he *is* that very Being on which all beings depend for their actual existence. Yet, while we cannot comprehend Being itself, we can understand what it means for *a* being to be real, for any created being is real because of its participation in the life and reality of God. Saint Paul, quoting Epimenides, puts it like this: "[God] is not far from each one of us. 'For in him we live and move and have our being'" (Acts 17:27–28). So to know what Being is in Itself is to know what God is in himself, and this is beyond the capacity of human knowledge because all of our knowledge is dependent on the Being of God, not the other way around. Even so this does not leave God's Being in total darkness as far as our knowledge is concerned. The very idea of revelation insists that we *do* know God even though God is the foundational *I Am* (Being Itself) upon which all of creation depends for its existence. But our knowledge of God is only partial and only as he makes himself known to us in a relational, participatory, loving, and analogical manner. To Aquinas, we do not know God in the way that a scientist rationally and quantifiably knows a compound. Nor do we know God in the manner in which a conceptual grammarian knows the precise definition of a term. For how can the derived and created human mind stand over and comprehend the uncreated reality of God, the source of all derived reality?

To Thomas, we use the word "being" analogically when we speak of God. Aquinas had a strong respect for what could not be said about God,[27] so he maintains that our creaturely understanding of being can never apply to the uncreated Reality of God. Even so, the reality of created things speaks analogically of the Reality of God, so it is not as if the idea of "being" as used in relation to creation has no relation to God. Thus, holding to Augustine's intimate identification of God with Being, Aquinas rejects both a univocal and an equivocal conception of being.[28] In contrast, Scotus' univocity of being idea rejects the Augustinian understanding of God as primary Being Itself (as distinct from the secondary and derived being of all creation), as well as the Thomistic approach to understanding being analogically.

Secondly, the univocity of being makes the notion of "being" solidly meaningful, but removes God from the sphere of any sort of rational understanding. It works like this. For Scotus we do not participate in the Being of God, for our being is the same sort of thing as God's being. If we are real and God is real then the difference between God and us is not a difference in being, it is a difference in type of being. For Scotus, we are finite beings but God is an infinite being. What Scotus is seeking to do by positing an absolute difference between God (who is an infinite being) and any finite being is to preserve God's standing as above the necessities of human rationality. The idea that an entirely philosophical understanding of God—an understanding where reason alone grasps who and what God is—is one Scotus powerfully opposed. So God, as infinite being, is not limited to our understanding of rational necessity. Thus God's will is to us entirely arbitrary. We cannot determine what God will do or what he is like through any exercise of human reason. And if God decrees that some human act is moral, it is his will that makes it so,

27. See Pieper, *The Silence of Saint Thomas.*

28. To describe a word such as "being" as having a univocal meaning means that "being" always means the same thing whenever we say it. Here the word "being" has only one meaning in all of these clauses: "the cat's being," "God's being," "the being of Beauty," "the chair's being." To describe a word such as "being" as having an entirely different meaning when applied to creatures as when applied to God is to use the word "being" in an equivocal manner. That is, "being" here has two entirely separate meanings, depending on whether we are talking about God or about creatures. To describe the word "being" as analogical when applied to both God and creatures is to posit a derivative relation between the creature's being and the Being of God, such that there is a real connection of meaning between these two contexts of the word "being" but it is not a univocal connection, just as it is not an equivocal disconnection.

and not any unfailing rational necessity that stands "above" God's infinite freedom. In fact, the key attribute that Scotus is seeking to protect here is the sovereignty of God's *will*, for God is the ultimate being of power and freedom (even if he is not Being Itself). This is the genesis of a very important notion that is a crucial feature of modernity: voluntarism. But we will come back to that later. The point here is that to Augustine the first attribute of God was love, not will. And love is a type of intimate knowledge, and has its own rationality, even though love cannot at all be reduced to formal reason. The God who is love is a God whom you can relationally rely upon, whom you can relationally understand, even if no person is ever reducible to the categories of understanding. But in Duns Scotus' theology, God is infinite and unbounded *will* and is thus pro-foundly a-rational in the terms of a human understanding of necessary reason, or a human understanding of reliable relations. We now have the problem of how a finite being of limited will and power could be related to an infinite being of unlimited will and power, particularly once the idea of ontological participation is denied. Scotus gives us an inscrutable "irrational" God of arbitrary will and unlimited power (and perhaps you thought Calvin did that!).

Scotus and Representational Knowledge

In epistemology, it is Scotus who comes up with the idea that human knowl-edge is representational without being ontological.[29] This is a crucial depar-ture from approaches to knowledge where a participatory understanding of being is central to every act of knowing. That is, where I participate in the Being of God, I am grounded in the very fount of reality, and to the extent that I understand things I understand features of God-sustained reality that are—like my own being—given to reality by God. So when I perceive a tree, my understanding of the tree is possible because the tree and I are co-creatures whose being is grounded in God. That is, the tree and I are in

29. Scotus' thinking on representation is grounded in Aristotle's understanding of the process of perception. Scotus does not invent the idea of phantasms in the mind that are representations of the external perceived world. Yet Scotus' innovation is to think the representational aspects of perception through without the assumed meta-physics of ontological participation undergirding perception itself because being is now a discrete property of all existing beings, rather than the grounds of communion with God that informs the process of knowledge. That is, Scotus is able to separate epistemology from ontology in a manner that is basic to the rise of the modern ap-proach to knowledge.

communion; there is a deep ontological bond between me and the tree and any created thing. So when I know the tree it is the intelligible essence of the tree, which is gifted to that tree by God, that I understand. As God gives all creatures their form—both as generic entities (i.e., a tree) and as specific individuals (i.e., this *particular* paperbark gum tree)—who and what anything is, is firstly a function of its ontological relation to God and its reception of the intelligible form from God that gives that thing its specific attributes. To the Christian Neoplatonist tradition, God is the ontological foundation not just of being but also of knowing. So whenever I have any true knowledge what I have is a relational, ontologically grounded, communion-based knowledge informed by the Logos of God. But not so for Scotus.

For Scotus, something's being is entirely separate from our capacity to know it. I, as a self-contained being, represent any object of knowledge in my mind, and *it is my representation, not the thing itself, that I know.* This is the modern understanding of knowledge, and the modern world is entirely reliant upon this for its view of reality.

So Scotus gives modernity univocity (my individual particular being is fully adequate as a measure of all being), voluntarism (pure will is fundamental to human nature, for humanity is made in God's image), an inscrutable God (thus religious devotion is an entirely different sort of enterprise to rational and practical endeavors), and knowledge as representation (the knowing subject surveys representations of the objective world within his own mind). These are all entirely medieval theological concepts, but modernity would simply not exist if these concepts were not taken for granted by us. Modernity also drew deeply on a philosophical innovation known as nominalism. Yet before we can appreciate what nominalism is (even though modernity assumes a nominalist understanding of reality), we need to have a rudimentary understanding of what is often called Plato's "Theory of Forms" and a working knowledge of the "problem of universals." After introducing those notions we will take a quick look at the thought of William of Ockham and the nature of nominalism as it was bequeathed to modernity via his thought.

Plato's "Theory of Forms" and the Problem of Universals

Trying to briefly outline Plato's "Theory of Forms" is a perilous activity. For the fact is, there is no single "Theory of Forms" presented in Plato's dialogues. The conceptual subtlety, suggestiveness, self-criticism, and narrative complexity of the way Plato approaches the intelligibility of reality is not captured by "proof texting" a few things Plato says about forms as if that is a water-tight account of what Plato means by the Greek words *eidos* (idea) and *morphe* (form). Indeed, the lack of access to nearly all of Plato's dialogues in the early Middle Ages has a lot to do with why a simplistic and inadequate understanding of Plato's forms was then prevalent, and why that outlook was so savagely debunked by the sharp wits of Peter Abelard.

Very, very crudely, then, this is something like what Plato means by form. The world as we immediately experience it seems composed of matter and form. That is, not only are tangible things made out of something (matter), but they are all structured in specific ways (form) such that they are something in particular (a rock is not a bird, a man is not a ray of light). The structure, the operational logic, the intelligible essence expressed in all existing things is the form of each particular thing. Even so, we notice that there are families of things that share common characteristics. So it seems like it is not only individual things that have form, but there are macro-forms that families of individual things derive their common intelligible essence from. Thus the idea (*eidos*) of Man is a form that all particular human beings have in common.

Plato also notices that particular men come into and go out of existence, yet the idea of Man does not come and go with the birth and death of particular men.[30] So it seems that any particular in-formed and en-mattered thing is not a permanent reality, so it does not exist in the strong sense of the word. Things that go in and out of being—things that become and un-become—are not enduringly real. Really real things, it seems to Plato, are eternal, unchanging, and universal. The idea of Man, for example, seems to endure a-temporally while particular men are born and die. Thus universal ideas (such as the idea of Man, which is common to all human beings) and unchanging mental truths (such as the mathematical relation between the sides and angles of all right angle triangles) are *more* real than the particular en-mattered expressions of eternal and intelligible forms.

High forms (universal ideas) are also perfect to Plato, whereas every expression they have within matter is transitory, subject to contingency, and incomplete in (at least) that it does not endure forever unchanged. Hence, that which the mind grasps about the universal and ideal essence

---

30. Actually, Plato argues that all mortal men must have non-material and eternal souls. So particular men and women as en-mattered souls come in and go out of existence, but the intelligible essence of each particular person is not subject to becoming and unbecoming.

which is partially revealed in any temporal expression of form in matter is more real than the temporal expression of that matter-form complex that one has sensory access to.[31]

Even mundane things made by us have some sort of ideal blueprint that the fabricator follows that makes them recognizable as particular types of objects. Hence, the universal idea "Table" is a mental reality in which all particular en-mattered tables intelligibly participate. But forms, be they of mundane objects or of high qualitative realities—such as Beauty, Truth, and Goodness—are not themselves things in the world. Forms are a-temporal, a-spatial sources of intelligible essence. That is, they are the spiritual powers of being generating the intelligible meanings that are expressed in the tangible world. To Plato, these spiritual powers are extra-mental realities that inform all en-mattered things. That is, these "ideas" do not originate in our minds even though they can be apprehended by our minds. To Plato intelligible essence is a deep feature of reality, it is not something subjectively generated within our consciousness and then projected onto a meaningless objective cosmos.

The "problem of universals" concerns the relation of particular things to universal categories. What is the relation between Socrates as a particular man, and Man as a universal category. The complexities of trying to understand how particular en-mattered beings might be related to ontological powers that confer intelligible essence is labyrinthine, and Plato was well aware of that complexity. We will not enter that region here. All that I will mention here is that there is a very neat solution to those complexities, and that is to treat universals as words—as functions of our language rather than features of reality—and to simply reject the Platonist idea that there actually are ontological powers conferring universal essences in reality. That is the nominalist solution, which we shall now look at via the great father of Western nominalism, William of Ockham.

31. This does not mean that Plato despises the body, or matter, nor does it mean that he finds particularity inherently unreal. Even so, it is not hard to see how Plato has often been read as upholding a dualism between mind and matter such that mind is real and matter unreal. The manner in which Christian Platonism modifies anti-matter dualist tendencies in Plato will be explored in chapter 5 of this book, for the incarnation of God within matter, space, and time (the realm of flux and contingency) exalts matter and historical particularity within Christian Platonism and gives it quite a distinctive character in relation to other forms of Platonism that were available to the ancient world.

Ockham and Nominalism

William of Ockham, like Duns Scotus, was a post-Aquinan medieval Franciscan theologian, but nominalism has a much longer history than fourteenth-century theology. The history of nominalism is one that is centrally concerned with separating itself off from the Christian Platonist metaphysical traditions of Western culture.

In the sixth century AD Plato's academy in Athens was shut down by the Eastern emperor, and though the traditions of Christian Platonism continued to develop in the East, there was now no non-Christian living institution supporting Platonist thought accessible to Europe. Further, rigorous philosophical thought largely falls by the wayside in the West from the sixth century. At the close of the classical era monasteries preserved commentaries and translations of a very small part of Plato and Aristotle's writings, usually in Latin translations. So through the early Middle Ages—apart from the stunning exception of John Scotus Eriugena in the ninth century—nothing much was going on in what we would now call philosophy, and there was very limited access to the great philosophical heritage of the West.

Then there was Paris and Peter Abelard. By the late eleventh-century Paris, now a wealthy and secure city, was rapidly becoming the center of a European revival of learning. Peter Abelard was this new center of learning's brightest young star. He was a man of dazzling intellect and a master of public debate. He set up his own school and students flocked to him from all over Christendom. He was a brilliant logician and an original thinker. He was also a ruthless and often insulting debater who used every tactic at his disposal in (always) winning an argument.

At that time the thinkers who saw themselves as learned in philosophy held Plato and Aristotle in high regard, yet with very little knowledge of their work and even less knowledge of the subtleties of their arguments. So those who saw themselves as followers of Platonist metaphysics held that the forms of universal ideas—such as the idea of Tree—were super-concrete "things" that existed in some transcendent "place." These were called Realists. Abelard opposed them by many a powerful argument, and against medieval Realism he claimed that a universal concept like "tree" or "human" or "green" is a name (*nomen*) that is useful and necessary for speaking and thinking, but is not an ontological entity, a thing, which has a real and separate existence from our language. So a nominalist is someone who thinks universals are *names* but not *things*.

Further, the nominalist holds that the only things that exist in concrete reality are individual objects. Abelard thought that the Realist belief in ontological orders of being in which particular beings exist was the result of falsely reifying purely linguistic meanings.[32]

So nominalism, as a powerful linguistic response to the medieval understanding of the ancient "problem of universals," was around from the beginning of the High Middle Ages; William of Ockham did not invent it. Yet Aquinas, in the thirteenth century, won back intellectual respectability for the idea of ontological participation, and he won this back after Aristotle's full corpus was available in the West and with a very astute mind sensitive to logical argument and philosophical subtlety.

Aquinas could not simply drop the idea of ontological powers of being as Abelard had done because Aquinas was a very fine student of Augustine and Pseudo-Dionysius.[33] It seemed to Thomas that the crucial Augustinian doctrine of the original deep harmony of creation, the Neoplatonist metaphysics of communion and its epistemology of participatory comprehension, and the theological significance of paradox, symbolic meaning, and analogy in language and in reality, were right. Thus, though Thomas well appreciated that Abelard was right to find early medieval Realism logically and conceptually incoherent, this did not mean that ontological participation itself was wrong.

Ockham, with his English proclivity for logical linguistic analysis, leads a powerful return to the full nominalist stance after Aquinas. Whilst Aquinas did not simply fade away during the late middle ages, it is a fascinating but little-studied feature of Western intellectual history that nominalism became the dominant intellectual stance in the philosophy and theology characteristic of the proto-modern era. Nominalism is, for example, largely assumed by the Reformers of the sixteenth century.[34]

Late medieval nominalism has two important foci—a metaphysical focus and a political focus. Metaphysically, nominalism maintains

32. To "reify" means to treat an abstract idea or a linguistic term as if it is a concrete and real thing.

33. The anonymous sixth-century Syriac writer we now call Pseudo-Dionysius wrote under the assumed name of Dionysius the Areopagite (see Acts 17:34). Via Latin translations by John Scottus Eriugena, his high patristic and Neoplatonist theology came to have a powerful influence on Western medieval theology.

34. One of the striking significances of this was a re-framing of the notion of sacramentality in Roman Catholicism and Protestantism, and a virtual loss of the notion of sacramental participation in ecclesial forms born modern in the seventeenth century, such as evangelical Protestantism. See Boersma, *Heavenly Participation*.

that *only individual things exist in reality*. There are no non-material and universal essential forms in which individual things participate.[35] This is the default metaphysical assumption of modernity. But politically, nominalism is also at the heart of the very modern idea that there are sharp lines that separate out individual real things from the realm of religious authority.

William of Ockham was a key political player in a serious dispute between his religious order—the Franciscans—and the Pope. The details of this situation and the fascinating complexities of William's stance cannot be explored here, but the end result of this situation is that William of Ockham became a powerful voice in late medieval Christendom advocating limiting the authority of the church to explicitly spiritual matters. Religious authority came to be seen as functioning legitimately only when it operated within the sphere of discretely religious and spiritual matters, a sphere strongly separated out from "real world" political, economic and legal matters.[36] That is, nominalism—in breaking the Augustinian/Thomist link between the Being of God and every particular created reality—separates out religion and the church from the ordinary real world. This has the end effect of creating the idea of a second tier of super-reality—the supernatural—that is of an entirely non-earthly nature. It is this supernatural sphere that secularism considers as the discrete realm of the church. In contrast, the first tier of reality becomes the un-spiritual realm of tangible nature which is the "secular" realm of politics, economics and science, and this is *not* the sphere of church authority.

Politically, the evolution of the idea of the discretely supernatural, as a realm fully separate from the natural realm, has deep roots in late

---

35. Actually Ockham is more nuanced than this. He maintained that one could not know if there were or were not ontological powers of being, but where one did not need to posit them, then one should not posit them.

36. It is astonishingly ironic that the aim of Ockham's long war with the Pope was to get the Pope to continue to own the properties that the Franciscan's used. The Pope's refusal to do so, and the manner in which he forced the Franciscans to become property owners, made it clear to Ockham that the Pope was a heretic who defied the Scriptures, who ignored sacred doctrine, and who made all manner of invalid logical assertions in a vain attempt to legitimate his obviously un-Christian outlook on wealth and power. So it is simply fascinating that under-girding the birth of modern secular politics, with its separation of church and state, is the Franciscan commitment to the radical spirituality of Christ-like poverty. And, indeed, the fabulously wealthy and militarily powerful Pope did not engage Ockham's very careful arguments from Scripture and reason, but simply refused to accept that the church had no legitimate place in the realm of wealth and power.

THE MYTHOS OF MODERNITY 75

medieval theology and philosophy. Modernity is still thoroughly medieval to the extent that this astonishing innovation is accepted largely
without question by modern people, be they religious or not.[37] Thus was
the tangible cosmos ontologically disenchanted, and a new approach to
political and technological power and to religious authority follows naturally on that development.

The Medieval Architects of Modernity

The great architects of modernity were Duns Scotus and William of Ockham
even though these figures hardly appear at all in the cosmogenic song of
secular and scientific modernity that we moderns now simply assume. The
mythos of our very way of life is one of a total break from medievalism—we
are modern, *not* medieval. In reality, however, it was medieval theologians
who gave us univocity, voluntarism, an inscrutable God, knowledge as
representation, nominalism, and secularism. All of this is set in place long
before René Descartes, Francis Bacon, and Galileo Galilei were born. All
the seventeenth-century fathers of modernity do is put these late medieval
ideas into practice in such a way that the structure of the high medieval way
of life can no longer support it. So modernity is actually the life form that
fits the theology of the late medieval theological innovators whose ideas
we have briefly sketched. That is, the reality assumptions and operational
givens of the modern way of life rest on our collective belief in late medieval
theology. As one famous theorist put it, "we have never been modern"[38] if by
"modern" we mean something fundamentally in antipathy to medievalism.
In fact, modernity is a species of medievalism.

A Level Playing Field

The aim of this chapter is not so much to defend the contemporary credibility of Christian Platonism, but to disclose the back-story behind why
any defense is going to find it very hard to get a fair hearing. I have tried
to locate the mythos of modernity as the prime site of this difficulty, and I
have tried to show how this is a particularly hard nut to crack because we

---

37. See Dupré, *Passage to Modernity*, for a fascinating account of the origins of
the notion of "pure nature," the idea that nature is entirely natural and exists in some
discrete plane from the "supernatural."

38. I quote here the title of the fascinating book by the French social theorist Bruno
Latour. Latour's argument is very different to the one I am making here, but I think his
text's title can aptly be appropriated to sum up what I am saying.

moderns typically believe that mythos is something that belongs to other civilizational worldviews, but not to us. We—scientific and technological modernists who live in our "rule of law" liberal and secular democratic consumerist societies—only believe what is factual and reasonable about the nature of reality. Anyone who thinks reality is other than ontologically univocal and other than how a nominalistic and naturalistic (whether this includes a supernatural parallel universe or not) secular perspective sees the world, is obviously talking about fairies or Santa, or some other magical make believe myth that a child might imagine before they know any better. So confident are we of the indisputable truth of our latent, unconscious, civilizational reality assumptions that it is simply too embarrassing and childish to take metaphysically incompatible outlooks about reality seriously. (This is particularly so for highly educated modernists, and amongst them, particularly so for professional philosophers.) Any self-critical truth-seeking engagement with our deeply cherished late medieval ontological orthodoxies is simply not to be countenanced. Viewed in the "natural" light of our civilization's assumed reality beliefs, Christian Platonism cannot possibly be viable now.

Thus it is necessary to point out that modernity has its own mythos—as do all cultures—and that logos is always derived from mythos, for mythos is more basic than logos as far as human culture (the inescapable interpretive lens of all truth discourse) goes. For this reason it was necessary to show up the most central features of the real conceptual origins of our culturally assumed modern metaphysics—certain trajectories within medieval theology—because it is these unstated historical innovations that are the grounds of the central objections to Christian Platonism. If those grounds are accepted as the valid terms of the playing field on which the contest between nominalist modernity and Christian Platonism will be played out, then there can be no fair contest and the obvious victory of modern realism over Platonist "idealism" and Christian "supernaturalism" (even though Platonism is not Idealist and Christianity is not supernaturalist) will be a false victory over a mere caricature of Christian Platonism.

Even so, it is by no means a foregone conclusion that Christian Platonism will defeat univocal secularized nominalism on a more level playing field. Any real contest is not going to be a walk in the park for either side. However, before we can engage that contest we must address a basic theological question: does the notion of *Christian* Platonism makes sense or not, from within Christianity?

In the next two chapters we will transpose our explorations into a more biblical and theological key before addressing whether Christian Platonism can stand against the objections of modern philosophy. Since modern theology (and modern approaches to biblical scholarship) has the same set of mythic framings as modern philosophy, this chapter on the mythos of modernity must be born in mind as we evaluate the strongly negative view modern Western Christian theology typically has towards Christian Platonism.

4

Platonist Ideas in the New Testament

This chapter sketches a short outline of how some important statements in the New Testament align with one of the central ideas about the nature of reality found in Plato's dialogues. In order to do this I will be "proof texting" both the New Testament and Plato. Whilst I hope this chapter will prove to be a useful contribution to the argument of this book, I am very aware that this exercise has some very clear limits and is fraught with perils.

The first reason why proof texting is of limited value here is that Christian Platonism is not actually closely tied to Plato's texts. The nature of the bond between Christian Platonism and Plato's dialogues is far deeper than textual alignment, and far freer than any tight doctrinal coherence between the dialogues and the New Testament. Indeed, getting to the underlying metaphysical commonalities that connect Plato to the New Testament worldview is what the following chapter is centrally interested in. Even so, there are some obvious textual alignments that are readily apparent, so we will tentatively explore one of them in this chapter.[1]

Secondly, when comparing texts from different milieus that have both been translated and have both undergone long and separate processes of historical transmission, there is no end to how complex and speculative unpacking the simplest resemblance can get if you try and textually dig down to the supposedly original meanings. Thus, for the

1. There are also, of course, some obvious textual, theological, cultural, socio-sexual, and religious dissonances between Plato's dialogues and the New Testament. We shall not explore these dissonances here, but when we come to distinguishing between Christian Platonism and other forms of Platonism in the ancient world, the manner in which Christian Platonism does *not* align with certain features of the dialogues will be noted carefully.

sake of brevity and with a somewhat ironic nod towards Luther, I am going to proceed by assuming that there is at least an approximate and reasonable "plain meaning" that can be appropriated in both Scripture and Plato.[2] Yet an approximate and reasonable meaning is as far as I can go.

For thirdly, and most seriously, I am aware that proof texting the Bible to show a tight conceptual point is far more subject to distortion than proof texting Plato's dialogues to unveil a contained doctrine of Forms (as deeply problematic as *that* is). For the whole council of Scripture is remarkably rich in its God-breathed depth. The Christian doctrine that the canonical Scriptures are inspired (which I accept) means that the living, divine breath of the Scriptures—the very Spirit of God—cannot, finally, be tightly captured in tidy conceptual formulations. In this sense Scripture and the core doctrines of the church are always prior to, and always exceed, our systematic theologies.[3] This is not to say that clear truths cannot be drawn from the Scripture,[4] nor is it to suggest that every

---

2. I say "ironic" here because interpretation is indeed a deep process, and it is a process often aided by a careful study of contexts and transmissions. Even so, and with Luther, but because of a theology of Christ as Logos, I do think that meanings are not endlessly looped in closed hermeneutic circles. If one takes reasonable care then I think it is not too problematic to discover a reasonably clear obvious meaning in most texts we read, including the Bible and Plato's dialogues. The risk for the modern textual sciences of literary criticism and for certain irrealist flavors of postmodern sophistry is to find things so interpretively complex as to lose any clear meaning, and to make such extensive speculative projections from the slimmest of historical and stylistic indications as to end up with an interpretation that is completely defined by the lens of the interpreter. In modern literary scholarship, this lens also often assumes that there is no God-breathed process in any text or cultural production, that meaning *is* entirely enclosed in hermeneutic circles, and that one must assume a secular and functionally materialist metaphysics if one is to gain a "realistic" understanding of the meanings and modes of production and transmission of any text. I do not know of any compelling reason to take any of those interpretive assumptions as valid.

3. See Hamann's "Biblical Reflections" in Smith, *J.G. Hamann*, 117–38. See De Lubac, *Paradoxes of Faith*, 227–28.

4. I recall tutoring an undergraduate theology class in a subject titled "What Christians Believe." This particular week we were reading a complex display of theological brilliance that endeavored to show us that the doctrine of the Trinity was all entirely rational. The previous week we had been looking at Jesus' teaching on loving one's neighbor. In comparison with our reading in high-powered theology, it was crystal clear what Jesus actually wants us to do in following him. In a flash of inspiration one of my students observed that "Christian teaching is very hard to do but easy to understand, whereas Christian theology is easy to do (anyone can sit down and crunch ideas) but very hard to understand."

age does not need its systematic theologians. Yet complex and contextually provisional interpretive maneuvers are always required for the historically situated theologian to do her job well. So, with considerable trepidation, and without getting engaged in the many points of interpretive contention that could be brought up, let us briefly look at a few New Testament texts in order to show their broad sympathies with Plato.

The Apostle Paul on Seeing Reality through a Glass Darkly

In 1 Corinthians 13, the great love chapter of the New Testament, Paul explains that unlike knowledge, love is perfect.[5] Paul explains that "Love never ends . . . our knowledge is imperfect and our prophecy is imperfect; but when the perfect comes the imperfect will pass away" (1 Cor 13:8–10).[6] The implication is that if we embrace the way of love now we participate in some partial manner in the abiding perfection of the Divine Love that has always fully understood us. Further, we have this hope that one day we too will be perfected in that Divine Love. The future horizon of perfection that Paul is here directing us to is what New Testament scholars call eschatological.[7] That is, the Christian hopes for the end of the present age and for the arrival of a radically different world order to be established by the return of Christ at some unknown time in the future.

5. Paul uses the word *teleion* in 1 Cor 13:10 to express the perfection of love. *Telos* in Greek means completion, end, purpose. Whether Paul's usage bears more resemblance to Aristotle's understanding of teleology or to Plato's understanding of teleology is a point worth considering. This cannot be explored here, but for historical and textual reasons I go with Plato here, as to him *telos* reflects cosmic order as governed by the Mind of God, in contrast to what he reads as the more or less mindless contingencies of merely physical causation. In Paul, along Platonist teleological lines, the perfection of love is that it realizes the eternal intentions of God for the cosmos in contrast to the knowledge that operates within the realm of mere contingency and flux, the realm that cannot reach such perfection, the realm of that which is transient and passing away.

6. All biblical quotes in this chapter are from the RSV unless indicated otherwise. Note here the priority of the ontological over the epistemological. This is a feature of the ancient worldview in general and of the New Testament and Platonist thinking in particular. This is strongly in contrast with the modern priority of epistemology over ontology, often to such a degree that metaphysics is replaced by epistemology.

7. The Greek word "eschaton" means "last," as used in John 6:44 where Jesus explains that he will raise up those whom the Father has drawn to him on "the last day." So the eschaton is the conclusion of this age and the beginning of a new age of eternal life to come, that very age Paul anticipates in 1 Cor 13:10.

There is a clear contrast here between the pre-eschaton and imperfect cosmic age in which we presently live (that is passing away), and the future arrival of an already spiritually abiding perfection, ushering in a new cosmic order of reality that will not pass away. Before the eschaton, then, two orders of reality are in current operation: the present, fallen, and passing age operating at one level, and the eternal, abiding, and heavenly reality of God operating at another level. These two orders are very different in kind, yet our transient and imperfect age is deeply dependent on eternal reality for its very existence and for the coherent harmonies and inherent meanings of its created nature. Indeed, these two orders are only apparently separated by the temporal sequence that distinguishes the present from the future as viewed from within the perspective of time. Notice how Paul describes the relationship between that which is temporal within the present age and that which is abiding in 2 Corinthians 4:18: "We look not to the things that are seen but to the things that are unseen; for the things that are seen are transient, but the things that are unseen are eternal." As we see in 2 Corinthians 5:1–10, Paul associates our mortal life with the realm that is seen, transient, and imperfect, and our future life, after we have physically died, with the realm that is unseen, perfect, and eternal. Even so the relationship between the temporal and the eternal is not one that is contained within temporality itself: to the contrary, time is enfolded within eternity.

Significantly, the Hebraic eschatological perspective of the New Testament does not denigrate time, even while it does find the transience that is now integral with fallen nature to be a corrupted feature of the cosmos. Time, as seen in the days of creation, is good, and on the seventh day—the Hebraic culmination of creation—time becomes the most holy sacrament of the eternal Shalom of God.[8] In the narrative opening Genesis, the original creation is without death such that the disintegrative chaos of transience is inserted into time at the catastrophe of the Edenic fall. Thus, the eschatological Day of the Lord in the New Testament is not the abolition of time, but it does entail the redemption of time itself such that death with its sorrow and transience is removed from the redeemed created order (Rev 21:4). The New Testament vision of the final redemption of all things does indeed entail the annihilation of transience, but it does not entail our translation into a-temporal eternity.

---

8. See Heschel, *The Sabbath*. See also Chesterton, *The Man Who Was Thursday*.

The passage in 1 Corinthians 13 that I want us to zone in on is verse 12: "For now we see in a mirror darkly, but then face to face. Now I know in part; then I shall understand fully, even as I have been fully understood." The *image* here is that we only see the coming eschatological truth of things—which is the sacrament of the real and eternal truth—indirectly in the mirror of immediate experience. By fixing our inner gaze on those eternal truths that are darkly indicated by the mirror of our tangible experience, we walk by faith, in the way of love, within this present and passing age.[9] The kingdom of heaven in its cosmos-redeeming totality is not yet fully visible and has not yet fully arrived. However, being a function of the eternal perfection and unlimited goodness and power of God Himself, this unseen yet-to-be-revealed truth is actually incomparably *more* real than the realm of immediate experience, which is transient and passing away. Study 1 Corinthians 13, study 2 Corinthians chapters 4 and 5, examine Colossians 1:15–20 and Ephesians 6:10–12 and you will see that I am not reading anything into Paul that he does not actually say or imply. Paul really does think that there is a spiritual dimension to reality that is more real than the tangible realm manifest to our material and transient bodies. This eternal spiritual reality is primary and the transience of the present, mortal, and suffering[10] order of the immediately experienced cosmos is a derivative and fallen product of that primary reality.

The relationship between the visible transient world and invisible eternal truth that Paul maintains here is common to all the New Testament writings and is not just a distinctive feature of Pauline literature. Hebrews 11:2, echoing the prologue to John's Gospel, notes that "the world was created by the word of God, so that what is seen was made out of things which do not appear." Jesus, talking to Nicodemus explains that "no-one can *see* the kingdom of God unless he is born again . . . [because] flesh gives birth to flesh but spirit gives birth to spirit." (John 3:3, 6, emphasis added, NIV.) Jesus uses parables because he wants us to see past the tangible and transient surface of things and to the spiritual and eternal truth that is partially embodied in material things. Jesus continuously challenges one and all to have eyes to see (Matt 13:15; Mark 8:18; John 9:39) and ears to hear (Matt 11:15; Mark 4:9; Luke 8:8) so that we might discern what he is really saying and understand the true meaning of what

9. Note 2 Cor 5:7, the walk of faith is not the walk of sight.

10. Rom 8:18–25.

we see him do. Clearly what Jesus means by this is that our vision of the glory of the Lord and our comprehension of the Word of God is manifest *through* what we see and hear, but only to those who are spiritually open to the ultimate truth, which cannot be contained within the immediate realm of direct tangibility. The eyes that see only the mirror of transient nature, the ears that hear only audible sounds, these are spiritually undiscerning eyes and ears that block the revelation of God from entering the inner spiritual sanctum of their being and filling them with the very life and truth of God. (See 1 Cor 2:14–16; Rom 1:18–23.)

For example, in John 9 Jesus heals a man born blind in order to manifest the abundant love and the healing grace of God, but all the religious authorities "see" is that Jesus breaks the Sabbath when he performs this miraculous work. Jesus notes, "For judgment I came into the world that those who do not see may see, and those who see may become blind" (John 9:39). We see here that the realm of transient tangible experience functions as a dark mirror through which the spiritually discerning eye can gain a glimpse of eternal and ultimate truths. Yet equally, the one to whom the Word of God comes, or to whom the glory of the Lord has been made momentarily visible, can refuse to see what the mirror of our tangible experience really indicates. We can choose to only see the reflecting surface itself or we can read the meanings found on the apparent surface of things wrongly. Particularly in John's Gospel we notice that time and again the pattern of Christ's preaching is that the word of God is spoken into someone's life, and this word then becomes healing, spiritual transformation, and revelation to those who respond with belief, but judgment to those who respond with unbelief. The world of our tangible experience is such that it allows for both possibilities such that spiritual dynamics are the final matter concerning what people see rather than simply that which is immediately and demonstrably there. This is because to the New Testament outlook on reality, the realm of immediate tangibility is never just nature in the modern sense, it is always nature as reflective of a larger, more solid, more real spiritual realm. This in no way denigrates the material realm—indeed, the incarnation is the strongest affirmation of the goodness of temporal materiality it is possible to think of—yet there is a clear dependence of what is visible and temporal on that which is invisible and abiding.

The prologue to John's Gospel reverberates on this point deeply; the eternal Word of the Unseen God is the most fundamental creative and sustaining origin of all that exists—be those existing powers and beings visible or invisible. Here the visible world, which is physical and temporal, exists in a derivative relationship to the invisible world, which is spiritual and eternal. The unseen is more real than the seen.

In sum, the New Testament maintains that the Word of God is the non-material source of all that is tangible in the cosmos, that eternal realities are primary and material realities are derived from and dependent on primary reality for their existence, and that the realm of immediate tangibility is not the ultimate realm of reality. Thus, if we are to "see" reality as it really is, we cannot see it with our physical eyes. We must see it by a process of spiritual discernment which is a function of our receptivity to divine illumination.[11]

Now let us turn to Plato. And recall, Plato writes four centuries before Paul.

Plato on Seeing Reality through a Glass Dimly

The *Phaedrus* is a dialogue of Plato's which—in some regards like 1 Corinthians 13—is concerned with love[12] and with the unseen truth that is more basic than the appearances that are manifest to us by our sensory

11. Note the recurring theme of divine light and divine illumination particularly in Johannine literature; e.g., John 1:9 "[Via the incarnation] the true light that enlightens every man was coming into the world."

12. Paul is explicitly concerned with *agape*—charity, selfless giving love—whereas in the *Phaedrus* Plato seeks to understand *eros*. *Eros* is sexual and desiring love, which, in the context of classical Athens, is typically homoerotic and pederastic. However, things are more complex than the jarring polarities that seem apparent between Plato's *eros* and Paul's *agape* that one first encounters when reading the *Phaedrus* if, like myself, you have a conservative Judeo-Christian understanding of sacramentally appropriate sexual relations. The kind of desiring love Plato thinks most fitting to the one who is interested in *eros* is to desire the highest things. Socrates as exemplifying this higher love is completely un-interested in physical eroticism, which is treated by Socrates as an insubstantial shadow of high *eros*. The potential to harmonize features of Plato's teaching on *eros*—where the highest human desires are always for the divine realities and for the Good Itself (God)—with the New Testament understanding of *agape* are implied, for example, in Pope Benedict XVI's encyclical *Deus Caritas Est*. Note also, Catherine Osborne's text on Plato's *Symposium*, titled *Eros Unveiled; Plato and the God of Love*. This is a must read for anyone seeking to understand the subtle and insightful nuances of Plato's explorations of *eros*. Overall, Plato profoundly appreciates the spiritual horizon to human sexuality such that any merely sensual eroticism is essentially unable to satisfy that which drives erotic desire and thus becomes sordid by stimulating ever more unsatisfiable need the more mere sensual desire is indulged. In our day of explicitly sensualized and relentless hyper-erotic stimulation, Plato's insights into *eros* could arguably do us a lot of good.

appreciation of the world. In the central poetic image of this dialogue Plato depicts the soul as a charioteer driving two winged horses.[13] Part of our nature—a noble winged horse—desires the high and glorious eternal realities it remembers from before it was embodied. The other part of our nature—an ill-bred winged horse—is not easily managed by the soul and in this mortal life it only desires shameless satisfactions for material needs and pleasures. Due to the combination of noble and base motivational powers the soul must master, the soul has quite a job in seeking to steer the chariot of his life in a manner that is worthy of an undying spiritual being. Even so, the soul will be judged after its mortal passage and if it has allowed its ignoble motive powers to over-ride its noble powers, or if it has never truly known the noble in its pre-born flight, then the passage of the soul within mortal embodiment will be a degrading voyage of spiritual poverty and that soul will be punished accordingly.

Bearing in mind Paul's description of us apprehending the true nature of reality through a dim mirror, note the below passage from *Phaedrus* 250b. Interestingly, whilst true reality is beyond the temporal field of transience for both Plato and Paul, in Paul there is a future realization for the eternal reality to be actively anticipated within time, whereas in Plato there is a pre-born vision of divine reality to be recalled and responded to in the here and now:

> all [embodied] souls do not easily recall the things of the other world . . . they may have lost the memory of the holy things they once saw. . . . For there is [comparatively] no light of justice or temperance or any of the higher ideas which are precious to souls in the earthly copies of them: they are seen through a glass dimly; and there are few who going to the images, behold in them the realities, and these only with difficulty.[14]

I have used Benjamin Jowett's translation here because he used the phrase "through a glass dimly" which has obvious literary allusions to 1 Corinthians 13:12. But it is not the case that Paul is here quoting Plato.[15] Even so, Jowett is not at all mistaken to use a turn of phrase similar to that used by the King James Bible in translating very much the same idea we

13. *Phaedrus* 246a–250c.

14. As translated by Jowett, *The Dialogues of Plato*, vol. 1, 456.

15. You can find the Greek original of the *Phaedrus* in volume 1 of Plato's dialogues in the Loeb Classical Library. In the Loeb's English translation by Harold Fowler, what Jowett renders as "through a glass dimly" is rendered by Fowler much more literally as "through the darkling organs of sense."

find here in Plato. For in Plato's analogy of the divided line (*The Republic* 509d–511e) the transient tangible world is seen as a dim reflection of eternal spiritual truths, and these higher truths cannot be apprehended directly by any tangible medium *because* these higher truths are *not* transient but are eternal. So the lower participates in the higher, but no knowledge of the higher reality underpinning all immediate perception can be had in the terms of our supposed knowledge of the transient realm of immediate sensation.

Plato and Paul use different images and different turns of phrase to say much the same thing about the spiritual nature of ultimate reality and the fragile and derivative nature of tangible reality. In this Paul is not plagiarizing Plato, rather this illustrates the fascinating fact that both Plato and Paul share the same basic outlook on the nature of reality. Walter Wink gives us a very helpful outline of what he calls "the ancient worldview"[16] that is, I think, common to both Plato and Paul. Wink explains that the dominant, assumed metaphysical worldview of ancient times finds the immediate realm of tangible perception to be intimately entwined with the spiritual realities in which reality itself is grounded. So the tangible realm is seen as a partial reflection of the spiritual realm and hence all physical things are never simply physical, but are incomplete and passing functions of spiritual powers, intelligences, ideas, values, meanings, and authorities, which are the real source of the dynamics of our immediately perceive reality contexts. Significantly, this does not entail a dualism between the physical and the spiritual, for there is no possibility here of the physical being in any way viable without its dependent relation to the spiritual.[17] To the ancient worldview, the material could not be comprehensible, ordered, or meaningful were it not for its participation in the spiritual. Plato is probably the greatest thinker

16. Wink, *Engaging the Powers*, 3–10.

17. Note, Wink defines "the ancient worldview" as one where the physical is entirely integral with the spiritual. This is not the only spiritually orientated worldview of ancient and other times, thus Wink distinguishes "the spiritualistic worldview" from the "ancient world view." The spiritualistic worldview sees spiritual reality as the only reality such that matter is either an illusion or inherently bad (opposed to and corrupting of spirit). Whilst Gnosticism and some forms of Neoplatonism certainly did embrace such an outlook, the outlook of Plato's dialogues to embodiment is far more subtle than any gnostic polarity between body and spirit can justly appropriate. Significantly, the New Testament outlook upholds the goodness of the body and of material creation, and thus sits within an ancient worldview rather than a spiritualistic worldview. Clearly, orthodox Christian Platonism also embraces this integrative understanding of the spiritual and the material.

of antiquity who most fully articulates this ancient spiritually dependent worldview, and he thinks its implications through very deeply. So the idea in 1 Corinthians 13 that eternal and unseen realities are more real than our knowledge of tangible things is not firstly a Platonist stance, yet it is a stance that both Plato and the New Testament accept.[18]

Moral Realism

Very briefly, another common outlook assumed by both Plato and the New Testament is that moral truths have a divine source. This stance maintains that even though normative customs and conventions vary with time, place, and culture, yet the source of what makes one act right and another act wrong is not ultimately culturally relative, but is derived from what C. S. Lewis calls "objective value."[19] As discussed in chapter 2 of this book, we saw that the *Republic* entirely rejects the idea that morality is simply a product of customs concerning which there can be no truth or error. In the metaphor of the sun (*Republic* 508a–509b) Plato draws a parable between eternal Goodness and the physical sun, for the sun is the tangible reflection of the Divine fount of all life and reality in our immediately sensed experience just as Goodness is the source of all life, being, and intelligibility in reality. To Plato morality is seen as of divine origin and of directly reflecting the divine nature. To the writers of the New Testament, the Law of God—which includes a clear moral code—is given by God, and as such this Law has great glory, and reflects the nature of God. So the mode by which what philosophers call "moral realism" (belief that moral truths are truths about reality, not simply socially constructed norms) comes to Plato and to the New Testament in different modes, and yet again, clearly both Plato and the New Testament are singing from the same song sheet concerning the grounding of morality

---

18. The Greek word for faith has—in general—a very different technical meaning in Plato than it has in the New Testament. In classical Platonist epistemology faith is a very low form of knowledge, tied to the realm of tangible reflections, and not a real knowledge of eternal truths. Even so, there is a lot more in common between the New Testament understanding of faith and the Platonist understanding of high knowledge than this terminological opposition would superficially indicate. Very briefly stated, the manner in which things not seen are considered to be *more real* than things immediately seen is common to both the New Testament outlook on faith and to the Platonist notion of high knowledge. Where they differ, however, is that history embedded in tangible reality is the chosen medium of divine revelation in Christianity and such a medium is somewhat disdained in high Platonist epistemology as inherently inadequate to the task of revealing eternal truths.

19. Lewis, *The Abolition of Man*, 11.

in God. Plato and Second Temple Judaism and the New Testament writers all share the same sort of spiritually dependent and divinely given outlook on morality. Here the existence of eternal moral realities are more basic to reality than are the transient attempts to express those truths that different types of cultural norms produce.

Worldview Dissonance

It is worth considering how easy it is for modern readers of the New Testament to misread or simply miss the assumed metaphysics of the New Testament. Our modern worldview typically assumes that the physical cosmos is a self-contained and entirely material reality, sealed off from the discretely supernatural realm of the spiritual.[20] Functionally, within modernity, there is no practical difference between the assumed realisms of a materialist non-Christian and a "supernaturalist" Christian—to both the here-and-now world operates within an entirely natural, entirely non-spiritual realm as known by objective science. In contrast, Jesus, Paul, John, and Plato all consider the material world to be fundamentally dependent on eternal meaning (Logos) and value (the Goodness of God); for them it is simply inconceivable to consider it as a discretely and self-contained material reality.[21] To Plato, the realm of tangible appearance would simply not be sensible or comprehensible were it not for eternal forms being transiently expressed in space and time. Further, to Plato, if we did not have minds wrought and formed of spiritual reality we would not be able to comprehend the ever-present traces of eternal Reason as expressed partially within time. To Plato

20. Wink finds two metaphysical outlooks to be at home within modernity. There is what he calls the materialistic worldview where the spiritual is considered non-existent, but there is also an outlook that Wink calls the theological worldview. This theological worldview maintains that there is a supernatural realm fully independent of the natural realm. According to Wink "Christian theologians . . . acknowledging that this supernatural realm could not be known by the senses . . . conceded earthly reality to modern science and preserved a privileged 'spiritual' realm immune to confirmation or refutation—at the cost of an integral view of reality and the simultaneity of heavenly and earthly aspects of existence" (Wink, *Engaging the Powers*, 5). Wink's book is fascinating in part because he sees the connections between our modern metaphysical and cosmological assumptions (which, by the way, are radically incompatible with biblical metaphysical and cosmological assumptions) and our operational assumptions about political power and day-to-day realism.

21. Interestingly, George Berkeley's (1685–1753) disbelief in "pure matter"—matter without meaning, without value, without the sustaining and creative Mind of God to give it being—is in clear sympathy with the ancient worldview assumed in the Christian Scriptures.

what we now call scientific knowledge would not be possible without divine order and value being expressed in nature. Even so, the medium of time and matter is inherently transient, so the eternal and real truths partially and provisionally expressed through time and matter are not themselves temporal and material. To Paul in 1 Corinthians 13:12, knowledge firmly situated within the tangible immediacy of the present age—compared to the eternal Love of God—is inherently transient, inherently provisional, and without ultimate signification. But to Plato, "knowledge" that is passing away is not actually knowledge—even if it is a provisionally useful and instrumentally powerful belief. For how could you really *know* something that is not eternally there to know?

If you think about the "grace and nature" controversies of modern theology you will quickly notice that these controversies could not arise within a broadly Platonist outlook on reality. In ancient terms one might think of nature as space, time, and matter and of grace as order, value, purpose, and meaning. In those terms nature is the medium for the partial expression of grace. But notice, within this outlook there is no way in which it is possible to conceive of nature as other than fundamentally graced. How could you have matter without form, how could you have facts without meaning, how could you have objectivity without value, how could you have time without eternity, how could you have thinking without reason? For to Plato, everything expressed in space, time, and matter is a derived and ongoingly dependent creation of the divine Reason that emanates from The Good.

To both the New Testament and Plato, the visible world, which is physical and temporal, exists in a derivative relationship to the invisible world, which is spiritual and eternal. Here the unseen is more real than the seen. Here the realm of the seen is only comprehensible and ordered because of its intimate yet incomplete and derivative dependence on the unseen. Bearing these commonalities in mind we will now look more closely at modern objections to the manner in which Platonist thought and Christian faith were developed together by some of the great thinkers in the early centuries of the church.

5

How Christian is Christian Platonism?

Even though there is no shortage of sympathy between the New Testament and some central Platonist ideas, modern Western Christians often find the idea of Christian Platonism immediately suspect. Much of this suspicion is more the product of the distinctive epistemic and metaphysical incompatibilities that exist between modernity and Christian Platonism than it is a function of a carefully supported negative evaluation of how Christian Platonism came into being and what it actually entails. In what follows we will now do some historical spadework to dispel ignorance around how Christian Platonism arose and what its distinctive features as *Christian* Platonism are. There is a lot of ground to cover here, so things may seem a little piecemeal as we skip along and segue from one thing to another, but all the history and ideas touched on here are necessary to build up a working overview of the relationship between early Christianity and Platonist thinking.

Foolishness to the Greeks

An obvious objection against the very idea of Christian Platonism should be brought up first. Surely, one might reasonably think, the Christian gospel is very far from being compatible with the Greek philosophical thought of Plato. Only one New Testament writer was (according to the traditional view) Greek, and even though Luke wrote about one quarter of the New Testament, all the other New Testament writers were Jews. And, of course, Jesus was a Jew from rural Nazareth, a tradesman and a wandering teacher, not a Greek philosopher or an academic of any kind. In fact, on a number of occasions the Greeks get short shrift in the New Testament. Jesus explicitly insults a culturally Greek (*Hellēnis*) woman (Mark 7:26–27), Paul notes that the divine wisdom of the cross is foolishness to Greek philosophy (1 Cor

1:18–25), and Luke makes fun of the Athenians as idle dilettantes who are always dabbling in the latest speculative fashions (Acts 17:21). Indeed the decidedly un-academic Galileans who are the core disciples of Jesus show a parochial Jewish bias against the cultural compromise of their cultic leaders in Jerusalem who are depicted as resentfully enmeshed in the machinations of their Gentile overlords. The New Testament seems embedded in a back-water yet defiant Galilean outlook, which is not surprising considering the self-authorizing religious independence and radical zeal of their Nazarene leader.

For these sorts of reasons it is quite easy to read the New Testament and get the (false) picture that Jerusalem was the center of the ancient world and that the Gentiles—Greeks and Romans—were depraved and pagan outsiders to the world of the gospel. This would be a false view because the impact of the Greek language and the Greco-Roman cultural milieu on the New Testament is very deep. Indeed, that Christianity flourished after the effective end of Judean Christianity with the destruction of Jerusalem in 70 AD is testimony to how readily comprehensible the Christian faith was to the non-Jewish Greco-Roman world. By the time the Gospels are written (remember, it is Paul's letters that are the earliest writings in the New Testament) Christianity was already predominantly Gentile.

Then there is Paul himself. The remarkably learned and dynamic Paul of Tarsus (an important Hellenistic[1] city located in modern Turkey) is a key figure in the Greco-Romanization of early Christianity. Hence today there is considerable interest in whether Paul invented Greco-Roman Christianity, and whether this Pauline Christianity was in fact a radical rupture with the very Jewish and Galilean nature of the original

---

1. *Hellas* is the word the classical Greek historian Thucydides uses to describe the place where *Hellenes* (that is, Greeks) live. Thucydides explains that well before classical times there were distinct tribes living around the Aegean Sea, but there was no common sense of cultural identity among them. Apparently Hellen (a man, and not Helen of Troy) was the first person to provide some sort of unifying inter-tribal sensibility to the region and this is how *Hellas* became a notion roughly meaning Greece. After Athens had fallen from its short imperial golden age (that is, after the time of Thucydides) the Macedonian conqueror Alexander the Great created a huge empire, and Greek cultural sensibilities were exported into Africa, Asia, parts of the Mediterranean basin, and Mesopotamia. So the period of ancient history from Alexander to the rise of the Roman Empire is often called the Hellenistic era. Even so, the educated classes of Imperial Rome spoke Greek and the love of Greek culture was a powerful feature of the Roman imperium, so Hellenism comes to mean the influence of Greek culture in the ancient world in a rather broad sense.

Jesus movement. Yet, the assertion of fundamental discontinuity between Christ and Paul does not seem justified. With scholars such as N. T. Wright, I see no reason to find Saint Paul a radical religious innovator who re-works both Christ and Christianity and makes the strange little Galilean sect into a world religion.[2] For whilst the early Jewish Christian communities in Judea certainly had different communal and ritual signatures to their Gentile brethren, the lines of continuity between Jewish and Greek Christians were much deeper than were their differences. An important feature of their continuity was simply the larger Greco-Roman milieu in which all the inhabitants of the ancient world lived. Let us briefly explore some of the features of this broader milieu that are inextricable from the New Testament writings.

The Greek Language and the New Testament

The Greek language is aboriginal to Christianity. One could even say that in linguistic terms, Christianity is a Greek religion. This fact in no way diminishes the Judaic context of Christianity in the New Testament era, and there can be no doubt that Judaism at that place and time certainly had its highly distinctive religious and political signatures within the larger Greco-Roman world. Yet there are at least three reasons why we must not under-estimate the extent to which Greek language and culture shaped the very assumptions and life world of first-century Judea.

Firstly, the impact of Hellenistic culture was over three centuries old by the time Jesus of Nazareth began teaching (longer than modern Australia has been in existence). Secondly, the history of little Judah's relation to Greek Imperialism after the conquest of the Persian Empire by Alexander the Great in the fourth century BC was explicitly culturally invasive, and at times, violently and sacrilegiously so. In this context the survival of Judaism required some fairly expensive forms of cultural accommodation to Hellenism by Judaism. Thirdly, the centrality of textual proficiency to Second Temple Judaism meant that then, as now, Jews were very comfortable in a high culture that was transmitted largely by texts. Jews in the Diaspora, and often in Jerusalem too, were remarkably literate and were often fascinated by the learning and wisdom of the Greeks. And numbers of the Greeks, too, had considerable fascination with Jewish religion. But let us here stay focused on the linguistic impact of Hellenism on Judaism.

2. Wright, *Paul*.

The Septuagint is a collection of Greek language sacred writings written largely by Alexandrian Jews containing translations of the Jewish Scriptures. The Septuagint was written over a period of time probably from about 250 BC to 100 BC and was the Bible that was primarily used by the first Christians in Judea and probably exclusively by early Christians in the larger Greco-Roman world. And, of course, the New Testament is written in koine Greek, the common language of Greco-Roman civilization east of Rome. So the Greek language is basic to the very fabric of the cultural world in which the early church lived. Further, the Greek language was the language of empire (educated and aristocratic Romans spoke Greek) and of learning so it was the bridge that connected the disparate peoples of the empire with the power and knowledge that undergirded that empire.

For the above reasons, you can take the Christian Bible out of the Greek language and translate it, but you cannot take the Greek language out of the Christian Bible if you really want to understand its shades of meaning and the context in which its words have their original meaning. And with a language—often very subtly—comes a certain range of cultural assumptions, and even a certain range of ideas and outlooks that are the unstated background to meaningful communication. Let us see if we can find some important traces of very Greek ideas in the background outlook of the New Testament.

The New Testament and Greek Beliefs and Ideas

Alexandria was a key Greek-speaking Egyptian city noted for its dynamic Jewish engagement with Greek intellectual culture. Philo of Alexandria—a contemporary of Jesus of Nazareth—provides us with an obvious bridge between a distinctly Jewish appropriation of Greek intellectual culture and a key term that John in particular uses in the Christian New Testament. Specifically, one of the ways Philo connects Jewish religion with Greek philosophy is via his distinctive gloss on the word *logos*.

At this point we need to re-introduce "logos." This expansive Greek word means "word," "reason," "logic," and "explanation." When the ancients used this word philosophically it often has a cosmic reach wherein the order and intelligent purposes of the cosmos speaks to our minds via the language of reason. To Anaxagoras, for example, that there is order in the cosmos is indicative of a Divine Mind communicating to us. Here it is divine Reason that generates the coherence and beauty of the cosmos.

Reason is thus divine, and we mortals are seen as receiving communications from the Divine Mind whenever we perceive a rational structure, an intelligible essence or a meaningful purpose in the cosmos.

If you recall chapter 3, the origins song of modernity likes to contrast logos as reason with mythos as fantasy. Now that we are embedded in a secular and functionally materialist modernity our conception of what reason is tends to also be secular and functionally materialist. This conception of reason contrasts neatly with a modern conception of religion. We tend to think of philosophy as an exercise in hard-headed and logical reasoning as applied to the scientifically verifiable material world. In sharp contrast we tend to think of religion as being concerned with scientifically un-testable and subjective beliefs, with imaginative speculations concerning regions beyond matter, and with a somewhat embarrassing pre-modern credence towards the miraculous. So, within the mythos of modernity, *real* philosophy rises by shaking off the magical mythos of religion.

As we have noted, the genesis narrative of modernity tends to read ancient pre-Christian philosophy as the beginning of the shaking off of religion in the passage towards rational and scientific truth. However, as scholars like Cornford and Jaeger powerfully argue, this is an almost entirely disingenuous reading of ancient philosophy. In the ancient world, Logos is a profoundly religious idea and religion and philosophy were intimately entwined.[3] Indeed, this is a very sensible and natural way of looking at the world.[4]

---

3. Cornford, *From Religion to Philosophy*; Jaeger, *The Theology of the Early Greek Philosophers*.

4. I use the words "sensible" and "natural" intentionally here. Sensible means that which our senses make immediately apparent to us. The world as we actually sense it is embedded in order and is experienced by us as meaningful in its own right. From time out of mind till the modern era, this order and meaning was seen as being divinely gifted to reality. This is the natural and original perspective of humanity. In this sense, then, modern naturalism is an entirely un-natural innovation. In modern naturalism the order in the cosmos is considered to be a function of random and mindless chance, and does not evidence any Divine Mind gifting the very fabric of reality with providential order. Cosmic order and coherence are astonishing mysteries to modern naturalism, but they are also completely opaque mysteries. To modern naturalism, meaning is not an objective feature of material reality but is a subjective interpretive gloss we project onto meaningless reality. How we can take anything we think as having any valid meaning is entirely unclear to me if this stance is actually believed. To the ancients, cosmic order and meaningful thought are basic features of reality, and features that connect us intimately with the Divine.

Philo, reading the Septuagint, found Isaiah 55:11 to be very philosophically interesting. This passage is about the Word (Logos) of God being the means by which God accomplishes his will. Thus Philo equates a Greek notion of cosmic Reason with the active will of the God of Abraham, Isaac, and Jacob. In this way Philo seeks to wed Jewish religion to Greek philosophy. Hellenic Jews who followed Philo's trajectory quite naturally came to connect the "Then God said . . ." passages of Genesis 1 with the Reason/Word of God as the ever-active foundation of all created existence. When John equates the Logos of God with the means by which the cosmos was created, this is recognizably a Hellenistic Jewish move. Indeed, John's notion of God creating all that is through his Logos is hardly conceivable outside of the Jewish Greco-Roman cultural milieu in which the New Testament is written. It is not simply Hebrew or Greek, as if the dividing line between the two were sharp, but *both*.

John, however, is not simply synthesizing Greek and Hebrew thought. The radical nature of John's equation of Jesus of Nazareth with the eternal all-creating Logos of God is one that has, indeed, powerful dissonances with both Greek and Jewish ways of thinking about ultimate concerns.[5] Even so, the way in which the very words and background ideas of the Greco-Roman world are the raw materials out of which the strikingly original Christian revelation is fashioned cannot be denied.

At this point we should back up considerably and outline how Middle Platonism arose, and how the cultural milieu in which the New Testament was written was deeply influenced by Platonist assumptions.

5. The notion of the creator of the physical world as a divine craftsman—as seen in Plato's *Timaeus* 28, 29—makes obvious sense to the Greek theological mind, but not the idea that this cosmic architect is God. Certainly God would not become enmattered. To the Greeks matter is a chaotic entity that must have order and meaning imposed on it. So the great craftsman who shapes the chaos of unformed matter into an intelligible cosmos does so by replicating—as best as his material will allow—the genuinely eternal forms of divine reality. A sharp dualism between eternity, as the divine unchanging realm of the Real, and the everlasting, as the work of Reason within the physical cosmos, is upheld in most high Greek theological thought. The Christian idea that the eternal Word of God, who *is* God, is the creator of the temporal physical cosmos is not a notion that could easily arise out of Greek theology. And here the essential otherness of God from us, as upheld by Judaism, is clearly more at home with the classical Greek theological outlook than with the incarnational theology of Christianity.

From Classical Antiquity to the Cultural World
of Middle Platonism

The broadly dominant Greco-Roman philosophical era in which Christianity was born is called Middle Platonism. Middle Platonism, however, starts several centuries after the life and times of Plato.

In the history of Greek thought, Plato and Aristotle define the high classical era of the fourth century BC, but what happens next is complicated. In simplified terms, after Plato died the academy he set up became a center of very technical and specialized "academic" intellectual pursuits, and these pursuits were increasingly focused on what could *not* be justifiably said, known, or done, rather than what could. By the third century BC Plato's academy was showing many of the signature characteristics of what we would now call scholarly research, and, as a result, was showing less of the signature characteristics of a spiritually formative community of dialoguing souls seeking to improve the world and prepare themselves for eternity. Put less charitably, one could say that once the inspiring charisma of Plato was gone, arcane skepticism rapidly moved in. Likewise, through a bizarre set of historical contingencies, the original research that Aristotle started in all sorts of fields of knowledge and action continued for only a few generations and was then effectively sidelined from the scholarly world until the first century BC. By that stage the dominance of the more religious and metaphysical interests of Middle Platonism overshadowed a revived interest in Aristotle's scientific and logical works, thus they were considered of second order importance when compared to Platonist reflections on the immortal soul and divine transcendence.

The late fourth and early third centuries BC not only saw the rise of academic skepticism and the fading of Aristotle's influence, but also the emergence of two new important schools of thought. One of these was Epicureanism. Epicurus was an atomistic materialist. He believed that only matter and void exist, so all beliefs in divinity are superstitions. Being very this-worldly Epicurus maintained that the only good that we can know is pleasure. However, Epicurus' hedonism was decidedly not a justification for sensual indulgence, for his school aimed at tranquility and the absence of pain. Stoicism was the other important school of thought to arise at this time. Stoicism is a life practice of careful reasoning, of detachment from unhealthy and immoral passions, and of rational and calm acceptance of the inevitable determinates of nature, such as death. By the second century BC many educated Romans found Stoicism a very attractive way of approaching reality and morality. So the period between the high age of classical philosophy and Middle Platonism was a complex and innovative era, yet in comparison to Plato's academy and Aristotle's Lyceum, philosophical pursuit itself had a somewhat diminished spiritual vitality and its institutional guardians became increasingly esoteric and abstract. The result of this was that the academic successors of Plato's school more or less argued themselves into rarefied obscurity in relation to the larger cultural concerns of their times. Middle Platonism, on the other hand, was a culturally timely revival of a religiously vital and "dogmatic" form of Platonism.

"Dogmatic" here means the opposite of skeptical. That is, a "dogmatic" Platonist believes that there are things about transcendent truth that—via revelation and in practice—we really *can* know, even though such knowledge remains inexpressible in mundane demonstrable terms. This is in direct contrast with the highly skeptical Platonism of the Middle Academy and the mitigated skepticism of the New Academy that historically preceded Middle Platonism. These academic Platonists denied that anything could be known that transcended the inherently non-truth-disclosive limits of human "knowledge." In other words, nothing could be known.[6]

At this point it is worth giving some attention to the use of this term "dogmatic Platonism" in recent scholarship, for its powerful contemporary currency is traceable, unsurprisingly, to that remarkable critic of all things Christian, Friedrich Nietzsche. "Dogmatic Platonism" in Nietzsche's lexicon had, of course, a fiercely derogatory designation because he believed it marked the central fall into fantastic delusion that has plagued Western culture ever since Plato. And on that front Nietzsche

---

6. How then, one might wonder, could skeptical Platonists really be Platonists? Frederick Copleston notes that "Plato had held that the objects of sense-perception are not the objects of true knowledge, but he was very far from being a Sceptic, the whole point of his Dialectic being the attainment of true and certain knowledge of the eternal and abiding" (Copleston, *A History of Philosophy*, volume 1, 414). This reading—which I think highly persuasive—does indeed situate Middle Platonism within the ambit of Plato's philosophy and the Academic Skeptics outside of that ambit. So while the skeptics may decry Middle Platonism as "dogmatic" and hence anti-philosophical, certainly the Middle Platonists did not see themselves as anti-philosophical or anti-Platonic/Socratic. Even so, skeptical academic Platonists did see themselves as genuinely Platonic in that Plato's central dialogue on (or against?) epistemology, the *Theaetetus*, does show—among other things—that neither perception-based knowledge nor criteriological justifications for knowledge can get you true knowledge.

sees no distinction between Christianity and Platonism.[7] However, Middle Platonists did *not* see themselves as unphilosophically "dogmatic," but rather maintained that the central teachings of Plato were not skeptical, and that Plato strongly opposed skepticism because it promoted exactly the sort of relativistic sophistry and moral indifference that the academic skeptics advanced.[8] Middle Platonism saw itself as a revival of real (that is "Old") Platonism. And, in distinction from academic skepticism, Middle Platonism gave its adherents something that (to use a modern phrase) people could "believe in." That is, Middle Platonism adhered to substantive insights about the soul, divinity, goodness, transcendent reality, etc., which does indeed make it "dogmatic" by the standards of skepticism,[9] though here the use of words is obviously complicated. For Plato has as much to say against mere opinion and mere appearance (that is "*doxa*") as any skeptic, yet clearly, he maintains that truths that are beyond the realm of perception and contingency are indeed knowable, and clearly (to again use a modern turn of speech) Plato "*believes*" in these higher truths.[10]

It must also be noted that *doxa* and its cognates have a very different evaluation in Hellenistic Judaism and in Christianity than they have in high classical philosophy. The Greek word *doxa* means opinion, appearance, hearsay. Yet *doxa* is also the root from which we get the English words

7. Nietzsche, *Beyond Good and Evil*, ix–x.

8. Plato, *Sophist*.

9. Technically, Middle Platonism stands in opposition to skeptical *epoche*—the suspension of judgment. *Epoche* was the means by which the skeptics sought to attain the state of *ataraxia*, the tranquility of total indifference to all those contestable things that cannot be reasonably decided (i.e., everything). So the opposite to this skeptical stance should really be characterized in terms of *propolemeo* (interested engagement) and *taraxe* (unrest) as befits the one who does not suspend judgment and is prepared, like Socrates, to strive and suffers for the truth. Clearly this is how Plato sees the role of the philosopher in the famous analogy of the cave in the *Republic*. For the philosopher *returns* to the cave and faces the inevitable rejection, slander, and hatred that is levied against those who try and set the comfortable prisoners of illusion free.

10. Here Gerson's wonderful text *Ancient Epistemology* should be consulted. For Plato did not think that things you believed were the same as things you knew. To Plato the things you *believed* were inherently tied to sensory knowledge and the secondhand opinions of others, and the things you *knew* could only be grasped by a direct spiritual exercise of the intellect. That is, those things that we Modernists would now call matters of belief—concerning God, the source of value, the source of beauty, etc.—were to Plato matters of knowledge, and those things we see as matters of knowledge—the atomic weight of a carbon dioxide molecule, the news, etc.—were to Plato obviously matters of belief.

doctrine, dogmatic, orthodox, and doxology. In classical philosophical thought, "opinion" is a very low and unphilosophical type of belief, far beneath "knowledge." This being the case, it is intriguing to note that Christian "doctrine" was always seen as an inherently positive and truth-anchoring feature of every true thought for Christians. That is, in direct contrast to the prevailing non-Christian philosophical understandings of *doxa*, Christians equated *doxa* with *the manifest "appearance" of the glory of God*, and hence doxology is the appropriate worshiping response to the strangely tangible revelations of God breaking into human history. To the Christian, then, the revelation of God is solidly clothed in singular and apparently contingent spatio-temporality. This way of thinking is far too unspiritual for a "high" Greek understanding of theology.

Clearly the origin of this positive Christian understanding of *doxa* is the Septuagint's translation of the Hebrew word *kāvod*—the manifest (that is apparent) glory of the Lord—into *doxa* and its cognates. By prioritizing the manifest revelation of God in Jesus—thus in history—over all other truth claims, Christian Platonism always sees the doctrines of the church as more authoritative than the brilliant thoughts of Plato. Thus it always *interprets Platonic philosophy through the lens of Christian doctrine*. This, more than anything else, distinguishes Christian Platonisms from non-Christian Platonisms.[11]

Back to non-Christian Middle Platonism. Whether Middle Platonism is a "dogmatically" degenerate religious aberration of philosophy or the restoration of genuine philosophy after a skeptical decline is not important here. What all interpreters agree on is that the cultural climate of the period in the history of Western ideas known as Middle Platonism is centrally concerned with the fusing of the horizons of religion and philosophy. Further, this period births the next and last period of classical philosophy, Neoplatonism. In relation to the fusing of divine revelation with human thought, Middle Platonism and Neoplatonism are in full agreement. For by the first century BC the dominant culturally living approach to philosophy that most ordinary educated Greco-Romans were interested in was what we—thanks to Nietzsche—now call "dogmatic."

---

11. Indeed, it is the role afforded to believing historically transmitted reports of the triumph of Christ over the grave that made Christianity so hard for philosophically minded pagans of the second and third century to take seriously. E. R. Dodds' study of this time period brings this out beautifully with this wonderful quote by Julian: "There is nothing in your [Christian] philosophy beyond the one word 'Believe!'" (*Pagan and Christian in an Age of Anxiety*, 121).

The above can be well illustrated by another fascination movement of Greco-Roman learning during the Middle Platonist time period called Neo-Pythagoreanism. The pre-classical mystical philosopher and holy man Pythagoras is famous to this day for his theorem on the proportions of right angle triangles. However, ratios, music, and numbers were profoundly mystical to Pythagoras and his followers, and he was also a strict vegetarian because of his belief in the immortality of the soul and its re-incarnation. Pythagoras established a religious community at Croton that was especially interested in musical modes, cosmic logic, and aesthetic disciplines. Initiates of this community vowed to keep their central teachings about cosmic order secret (and they were highly successful in this silence too—we have no idea what these teachings are).[12] Middle Platonism was a period in which the long-disappeared Pythagorean mysteries were sought for and wherein Pythagoras' mathematico-religious community was lovingly romanticized. Coupled with Aristotle's fascination with nature and Ptolemy's groundbreaking astronomy, the worship of Divine Reason via a study of the heavens during Middle Platonism was a common expression of the fusing of religious, philosophical, mathematical, and scientific approaches to nature and meaning in this era.

Middle Platonism is commonly dated from Antiochus of Ascalon in the early first century BC to Plotinus in the early third century AD. Antiochus rejected the sophisticated arguments of skepticism that were advanced by his academic teachers. The academics maintained that nothing is absolutely certain, yet Antiochus pointed out that without firm convictions no rational guide to life is possible. For it is rationally self-defeating to assert that nothing can be asserted, no matter how subtly you hedge this stance. Antiochus was also eclectic. He wished to show that well-thought-out Academic, Aristotelian, and Stoic thinking all pointed in the same direction (what we now call "dogmatic" Platonism). This tendency of underlying Platonist convictions to provide a framework that was able to incorporate key elements of Aristotelian and Stoic thought into itself is characteristic of Platonism throughout the rest of the ancient era.

Because of historical transmission, today the most well-known figure among the Middle Platonists is Plutarch (45–120AD). Plutarch's main interests were theological and ethical. Plutarch was a priest at the temple of Apollo in Delphi and in opposition to Stoic materialism and

12. Catherine Osborne's fascinating and highly accessible little book *Presocratic Philosophy* gives a wonderful introduction to the remarkable world of the pre-Socratics, Pythagoras being among them.

Epicurean atheism he adhered to ideas about God and religion that were in clear continuity with the dialogues of Plato. Being so closely affiliated with the oracular tradition of Delphi, it is no surprise, then, that Plutarch was a strong philosophical defender of the practice of prophesy. Plutarch also developed an idea about matter being the cause of evil within his Platonist system that would prove very significant in what we now call Greek dualism. We will come back to this later. At present it is important to note that a significant trend in Middle Platonism developed that saw the passions of the mortal body (the flesh) and matter itself as opposed to the life of the eternal soul. Such an outlook is not absent in Plato, but in Plato it is not developed into a systematic cosmic doctrine.

If you recall chapter 3 of this book, you will remember that the mythos of modernity tends to view the history of genuine philosophy as skipping from classical Antiquity (i.e., Plato, Aristotle, the Skeptics, the Stoics, the Atomists, and the Epicureans) directly to Descartes. Everything that is mainstream in between these two epochs (and most of what happens before classical philosophy) is simply not thought of as philosophy *because* it is so integrated with religion and theology. As I hope that I have pointed out, the idea that philosophy *must* be discrete from theology and religion if it is to be genuine philosophy is a central "doctrine" of the mythos of modernity. Right here, it does not matter whether this doctrine is true or not, but the obvious manner in which everything from Middle Platonism to early modern philosophy is considered muddled and full of speculative superstition bears witness to the fact that the longest period of Western intellectual history on record is indeed profoundly affected by the Middle Platonist fusing of the philosophical with the theological. Neoplatonism, the dominant philosophical period after Middle Platonism, is in straight continuity with this integral manner of approaching theology and philosophy, as is Medieval Christian philosophy after it.

Plotinus in third-century AD Alexandria marks the end of Middle Platonism and the start of Neoplatonism ("neo" means new). Plotinus sought to synthesize Plato's metaphysics with Aristotle's logic and ethics and Plotinus' distinctive theology. Yet Plotinus' Neoplatonist synthesis was not a rejection of trends in Middle Platonism but rather a radical development of them within a distinctly non-Christian and highly intellectual direction. "Pagan" Neoplatonists after Plotinus were often explicitly interested in forwarding a hard-hitting intellectual alternative to the rise of a vital and intelligent Christian Platonism, as seen in Alexandria with figures such as Origen. As Plato readily lends himself to a theological and religious approach to philosophy the question of the times was not *whether* Plato and religion should be integrated, but *which* religion was adequate to the task, or whether an entirely new Platonist religion could be crafted to that end. Plotinus' followers are the last flowering of explicitly non-Christian monotheist Greek theology, yet this trend does not survive. Christian theologians subsequently largely subsumed important features of Neoplatonism. But this is outside our immediate scope.

Here is what these shards of intellectual history means in relation to the context of Hellenized Judea and Galilee in the first century AD. The high intellectual culture of classical antiquity had profoundly shifted the religious ground underneath those who had status and power within the Greco-Roman world. Pagan polytheism could no longer be simply believed, even though the sensibilities of that era remained highly religious. Hence, the cultural world of that time was very interested in complex forms of symbolically interpreting and theologically re-framing the pagan polytheism of pre-classical times. Further, because traditional Greek religion was not centralized and did not have a systematic theological unity, the Hellenists became increasingly interested in exploring other religious traditions (such as Judaism and Zoroastrianism) that were more amenable to the systematic categories of Greek philosophical theology. Broadly speaking, from classical times forward Greco-Roman culture displays a fascination with theology that was a function of the collapse of traditional paganism in a cultural context where public life without religion was inconceivable.

The reason why you do not see a move towards what we would now recognize as a secular way of life in the ancient world is that for time out of mind religion had been integrally related with political power and authority and was a key means of integrating subjugated peoples into a unified empire. Religion and divinity as integral with public life was thus a central arena for the working out of very practical and hard-edged matters of power, money, law, and morality. So not only were philosophers and the educated holders of status and power interested in theology, religion, and philosophy, but so was everyone else, even slaves.

Perhaps the notion of "economics" is a roughly culturally equivalent idea in contemporary society. That is, very few of us are professional practitioners or educated initiates in one or more of the dominant economic doctrines of our times. Very few of us work in the spheres of power where economic theories—as handled by elite specialists—are used to shape the larger way our society functions. Even so, everyone knows something about economics and has some opinion about "the economy," because it is the key discourse of power and authority in our times (and equally, it is the functional means of integrating subjugated people into the structures of power we could call global consumer society).

In sweeping terms then, the spirit of the times was one where religion and politics were integral and all pervasive in the operational assumptions of the cultural form of life, and in this context philosophical high culture took theology very seriously. This meant that philosophical ideas concerning God were of a broad background interest to people generally at this time. Further, due to the commerce and the imperial structures of the Greco-Roman world being deeply shaped by Greek language and high culture, seepage from the dominant Greco-Roman worldview even into the back-blocks of Galilee was inevitable.

A curious feature of modern intellectual specialization is that classical philosophy scholars and Christian biblical scholars often have little to do with each other. Dedicated scholars of classical and antique philosophy are often little interested in Christian and Jewish theology and texts, and dedicated biblical scholars often have little interest in classical philosophy. So the manner in which classical thought is alive within Christian texts—such as those that comprise the New Testament—is often simply not seen. However, scholars who work across both fields cannot help but see the deep and obvious links.[13] These deep links are there, in the very spirit of the times. And, indeed, these links have been clearly seen by the foundational scholars of modern biblical studied, but they are typically read as corrupting links rather than constructive links. Let us see why.

Liberal Biblical Scholarship and Middle Platonism/ Neoplatonism

The modern secular scientific outlook, which has a complex and interesting relationship with the ancient skeptical outlook, functionally recognizes (and revels in) the order in our perception of the universe, but, if really pushed, it leaves as undecidable the big metaphysical question of whether that order is *really out there* or is simply a function of our thoughts and perceptions. That is, because "knowing"—understood in terms of logical relations and methodically testable observations—is the grounds of science,

13. See, for example; Ferguson, *Backgrounds of Early Christianity*; Eric Osborn, *The Beginning of Christian Philosophy*.

questions of ultimate "meaning" are simply not an object of knowledge at all. Here meaning exists in the subjective realm of belief and interpretation, not in the objective realm of scientific knowledge. Knowledge is only about how facts *appear* to us and how we can make *use* of the world that so appears; there is no true or false knowledge concerning what the facts *mean*. In other words, the interpretation of the meaning and ultimate nature of observable phenomena is not itself something science can do and hence not something that can count as knowledge within the outlook of modernity.

Now because we link a scientific understanding of our experiences of the phenomenal world with a true understanding of reality, this means that we are tacitly agnostic regarding the question of whether there could be any true meaning to what is real at all. For this reason, the New Testament could not have been written in the modern scientific age. The broad culturally assumed meta-outlook of scientific realism—where "knowing" is the only valid path to truth and "meaning" is a matter of subjective belief and interpretative preference—is entirely foreign to not only the New Testament, but to the broader cultural assumptions of Greco-Roman antiquity in the first century.[14] Now, perhaps, you can see how Genesis 1, Philo of Alexandria, Plato, Aristotle, Middle Platonism, St. John, and Jesus all stand on the other side of scientific modernity's knowledge-based understanding of truth. There is not a word of the New Testament that does not assume that divine meaning is the ultimate cause and sustainer of everything we can know about reality, and that a human understanding of truth that is valid is a function of some sort of gratuitous divine to human relationship. For this reason how one interprets *meaning* is a question of truth or error, and knowledge framed in terms of "objective" logic and tangible sensations is entirely secondary. G. K. Chesterton, reflecting mercurially, points out that this outlook was not just followed in Antiquity but also "the Middle Ages (with a great deal more common sense than it would now be fashionable to admit) regarded natural history at bottom rather as a kind of joke; they regarded the soul as very important."[15] Truth is here inherently situated in terms of metaphysical meaning, and scientific knowing only concerns truth in a derived and trivial manner. No one puts this better than St. John: "In the beginning was the Word" (John 1:1).

The ancients had an almost precisely opposite understanding of what is primary and what is secondary when compared to the metaphysical

14. Here again I would refer you to Gerson's text, *Ancient Epistemology*.
15. Chesterton, *Heretics*, 175.

and epistemological priorities assumed by modernity. To the ancients there is a priority of the metaphysical over the physical, meaning over use, quality over quantity, truth over facts, wisdom over knowledge, and divine initiative over human curiosity. This set of priorities is a cause of amazed and annoyed frustration to many a modern scholar looking back on the spirit of the times that prevailed in the Greco-Roman world during the New Testament, the Late Antique, and the medieval eras. Listen to the great liberal biblical scholar Adolph von Harnack as he rails against Neoplatonism:

> Not as a philosophy and not as a new religion did Neoplatonism become a decisive factor in history, but, if I may say so, as a frame of mind. The feeling that there is an eternal highest good which lies beyond all outer experience and is not even intelligible, this feeling, with which was united the conviction of the entire worthlessness of everything earthly, was produced and fostered by Neoplatonism. But it was unable to describe the content of the highest being and highest good, and therefore it was compelled to give itself entirely up to fancy and aesthetic feeling. Therefore it was forced to trace out "mysterious ways to that which is within," which, however, led nowhere. It transformed thought into a dream of feeling; it immersed itself in the sea of emotions; it viewed the old fabled world of the nations as the reflection of a higher reality, and it transformed reality into poetry . . . it wove the delicate veil which even today, whether we be religious or irreligious, we ever and again cast over the offensive impression of the brutal reality [of simple facts;] it begat the consciousness that the blessedness which alone can satisfy man is to be found somewhere else than in the sphere of knowledge.[16]

Interestingly, whilst Von Harnack wryly observes that even someone as practically and religiously intelligent as Porphyry could not escape the delusions of Neoplatonism because "the spirit of the age works almost irresistibly [and to that spirit] religious mysticism was the highest possession of the time,"[17] yet nowhere does Harnack consider that the modern spirit of his time might be equally irresistibly at work in his evaluation of that very different era.

Harnack here sees very clearly the profound difference between the spirit of the times in metaphysically foundational and

16. Harnack, *History of Dogma*, Volume 1, 409–10.

17. Ibid., 418.

divine-wisdom-centric antiquity and physically foundational and human-knowledge-centric modernity, but so certain is Harnack of the validity of the priority of knowing over meaning—as a true modernist— that he shows no awareness of how deeply shaped his negative evaluation of the spirit of Greco-Roman antiquity is by the spirit of *our* times. But whether his evaluation is valid or not, this very modern thinker well sees that the spirit of the ancient world was inherently theo-centric and this was as true of Middle Platonism and Neoplatonism as it was of popularist rural Galilean teachers of miraculous charisma.

Plato clearly sees divine reason, mind, purpose, value, and meaning as the true foundations of reality and as what should be of most central concern to lovers of wisdom (philosophers). Plato clearly sees the realm of tangible perception and historically contextual human action as dependent for their very intelligibility and existence on a higher divine reality. And, as Harnack well grasped, this does indeed mean that Plato is not as interested in what we now call science as he is in theology and ethics. Unsurprisingly, Plato's theology and ethics is certainly *not* a function of his understanding of scientific knowledge (it is not modern theology and ethics). And *this* worldview assumption of the priority of divine meaning over human knowing—an assumption upheld by the cultural ballast of the "spirit of the age"—is native to the New Testament. This New Testament worldview assumption is in full agreement with a Platonist outlook and in radical discord with the modern understanding of the priority of human knowing over all meaning beliefs.

The modern interpretive lens profoundly distorts the New Testament. For example, the key New Testament notion of "faith" is entirely incomprehensible if approached in a modern manner. Mark Twain best explicated the modern understanding of faith by explaining that "faith is believing what you know ain't so."[18] That is, only that which is tangible and mathematically mappable is real to a modernist, so anything to do with God or any transcendent source of meaning or tangible reality is— in the final analysis—a profoundly irrational act of willful imagination in order to make oneself believe something you know ain't so.

In the New Testament, however, faith is a body, heart, and mind commitment that is a function of receptivity to revelation, which has its origins in what is beyond that which the merely tangible can generate. Faith arises precisely in response to a revelation of what is *really* so.

18. Mark Twain, *Following the Equator*, see the opening of chapter 12.

The convergences between Platonism and New Testament thought, given what Harnack calls "the spirit of the age," is in no manner surprising. Yet it must be stated because, particularly after Harnack, the assumption that Platonism in conjunction with ecclesial power is a toxic perverter of the primitive Jesus movement is now very well established in the reflexes of modern theologians. We will examine that outlook in more detail shortly.

Gospel Treasures (Taken from the Greeks)

There are significant and obvious ways in which Jesus of Nazareth, the New Testament, and the primitive Christian faith directly lift key concepts from the Greco-Roman world. As pointed out earlier, Judaism and the Greeks had a lot to do with each other well before the first century AD, and this "to do" was not simply at the level of cosmological theology. Imperial power and Hebraic religion were in continuous engagement prior to and during the life of Christ, and Christianity draws heavily on imperial political concepts that are also, in the spirit of that age, theological concepts. The claim that the message of salvation is a gospel (*euangelion*) is a straightforward appropriation of the imperial edict; the theology of the kingdom of heaven (*basileia tōn ouranōn*) is in clear defiance of the authority of the very visible kingdoms of the earth; and the claim that Jesus is Lord (*Kurios Iesous*) is an obviously defiant statement of relativization against the claim—backed up by violent power and imperial cultus—that Caesar is Lord; the very idea of church (*ekklēsia*) is a Greco-Roman notion drawn from civic politics. Take these very Greco-Roman ideas out of Christianity and, well, you lose Christianity. Christianity is deeply, perhaps inextricably, shaped by its original Greco-Roman as well as its Jewish cultural context. Or, as Hamann would have it, the apparent contingencies and temporal framings of this particular historically situated revelation are the media God chooses to reveal himself to us in. The very contingencies and specificities of "oh so human" history are in fact far more than they appear to be, yet—amazing wonder!—without ceasing to be genuinely contingent and historically situated meanings.

Given the extent to which key theological understandings in Christian faith are lifted from the Greco-Roman world, and given a "spirit of the age" where theology, philosophy, and politics were obviously fused, it is no surprise that as soon as Christians start engaging with Greco-Roman high culture, not a few of them find an obvious ally in the dialogues of Plato. However, the story of the origins of Christian Platonism proper is not as easy to recount as we might suppose.

Early Christian Platonism

The story of the relationship between early Christian faith and Middle
Platonist philosophy has far more complexity and nuance than is usually
admitted. None of the un-nuanced overview accounts fit the reality. Simple
opposition (what has Athens to do with Jerusalem?) is true to some degree.
Simple integration (pagan Platonism is Christian theology hindered only by
historical ignorance of Christ) is true to some degree. Popularism (Christianity is Plato for the masses) is true to some degree. The incremental transformation of Christian faith by Platonic philosophy, doctrinal definition,
and centralized ecclesial power (Christian faith is colonized by Platonist
theology and ecclesial power) is true to some degree. And yet each of these
views are incompatible with each other as total accounts. The fact is that
the complex historical relationship between the development of Christian
theology, ecclesial authority structures, and Christian engagements with
the high culture of the Greco-Roman civilization does not allow for any
simplistic account.

I will point towards a more nuanced understanding of the rise of
early Christian Platonism by quickly outlining what is valid and what is
not valid in each of the un-nuanced narratives portrayed above.

1. What has Athens to do with Jerusalem?

The two phrases for which the Afro-Latin Christian Tertullian is now largely
known by are these:

> What indeed has Athens to do with Jerusalem? What concord
> is there between the Academy and the Church? What be-
> tween heretics and Christians? . . . Away with all attempts to
> produce a mottled Christianity of Stoic, Platonic, and dialectic
> composition![19]

> . . . the Son of God died; it is by all means to be believed, because
> it is absurd. And He was buried, and rose again; the fact is cer-
> tain, because it is impossible.[20]

19. Tertullian, *Prescription Against Heretics*, VII
20. Tertullian, *On the Flesh of Christ*, V

However, if these statements—divorced from their argumentative context—are all that you know about Tertullian, then you do not know Tertullian.[21]

Tertullian is a fascinating and enormously influential figure of second- and third-century Afro-Latin Christianity. I think it not unreasonable to compare him with Kierkegaard from more recent times. For both are easily mis-construed as irrationalists—and nothing could be further from the truth—because they polemically and brilliantly oppose what is taken for reason by the sensible people of their times. Both find the Christian Scriptures to contain the most powerful force of truth, both insist on the practice of Christian life—lived truth—as being the pathway to valid theology and philosophy, and both are highly polemic thinkers who revel in paradox, passion, insulting witticism, and both laugh at philosophical systems.

Tertullian has as his polemic targets the heretic Marcion and various gnostic sects. As the influence of Middle Platonism was very strong in both Marcion and Gnosticism, it is not surprising that Tertullian associated the "wisdom of the Greeks" with the fount of all heresy. Marcion could not reconcile the God of the Hebrew Scriptures with the revelation of God via Christ. Marcion identified "God" in the Hebraic Scriptures as the evil demiurge of Middle Platonism, who creates matter and is thus full of the base passions of this lowly realm. This demiurge, Marcion maintains, is not the properly divine God that Jesus reveals to us. Hence, civilized and rational Greeks could believe in the Christian revelation only if they clearly disassociated it from its Hebraic origins and the base materialism of claiming that Jesus was God in human flesh. Thus, to cleanse the Christian revelation of characteristics unworthy of Greek theology, Marcion jettisoned the Old Testament, denied that Christ was God incarnate, and developed his own restricted canon of New Testament writings so as to have a Christian faith that was compatible with the dignity and eternal impassibility of a purely spiritual Greek divinity. That is, Marcion set the non-Christian and culturally respected criteria of reason in his day as the bench mark by which the Hebrew and Christian scriptural revelations were to be judged and accepted, vetted, or rejected (sound familiar?).

Tertullian will have nothing of this. If the vetting of divine revelation by the inconclusive and merely speculative fashions of Greek

21. See Eric Osborn, *Tertullian, First Theologian of the West* for an excellent introduction to this fascinating ancient theologian.

philosophy is "reason," then Tertullian embraces absurdity. Tertullian's argument, however, is dripping with irony and is a powerful critique of what Marcion thinks of as "reason." For it seems clear to Tertullian that if you were merely dreaming up your own rational theology then of course you would not embrace the Christian revelation. What this demonstrates to Tertullian is that "rational theology" is an entirely human invention, not a revelation of God at all, and as a merely human production it has no truth, and hence no true rationality, in it. For the truth of Christian faith depends not on whether it makes sense to our tiny minds or not, but on whether it really is the revelation of God. One is not reconciled to God by any human work—least of all by mere arguments and conceptual system—rather, it is the active work of God reaching out to us that saves us. Thus the real evidence for the genuinely divine nature and true authenticity of the Christian revelation cannot be decided by whether it is compatible with Greek philosophy or not, but is to be found in the life-transforming power of the Holy Spirit in the Christian church. Such an outlook was well accepted in ancient Christianity, as is attested to in the famous phrase of Minucius Felix: "We don't speak great things, we live them."[22]

The matter that Tertullian is firmly establishing here—at the wellspring of Latin theology—is the priority of the active work of God over the receptive work of humanity in all matters of fundamental truth. And here he is in full agreement with the apostolic teaching traditions of the church, even though the texts of the New Testament were not yet formalized into a defined canon at the time of his writing. Valid human reasoning is thus seen as a derivative function of the active divine gift of saving and transforming truth, and never is this causal relationship to be reversed without catastrophic hubristic failure. Reason can only succeed as a function of divine gift as demonstrated existentially. (This too is Kierkegaard's central message.)[23]

So, then, does this mean that Tertullian is an irrationalist hater of reasoning and a blind dogmatist, and that early Latin theology maintained that a corrupted and heretical Christianity diluted by Platonic speculations can be the only outcome of any attempted Christian engagement with Greek philosophy?

22. Minucius Felix, *Octavius*, as found in Bercot, ed., *We Don't Speak Great Things—We Live Them*, 65. This quote continues, "We can boast that we have attained what the philosophers so earnestly sought for, but were never able to find."

23. Simpson, *The Truth Is the Way*.

Firstly, Tertullian was a highly educated Roman who was a powerful and original thinker of considerable note. Indeed the Latin word *ratio* (reason) is one of the most common nouns in his corpus.[24] If "Athens" symbolizes learning and argumentation formed by Greco-Roman high culture, then Tertullian himself had much to do with Athens. Further, as Augustine cautioned, Tertullian's sharp and evocative wit produced many memorable and humorously insultingly denunciations, but we should not take Tertullian's powerful rhetorical flourishes, deployed in specific polemic contests, as straightforward and general statements of truth.[25] Given Tertullian's target—specific teachings by Marcion, which were the result of interpreting Christian doctrine through the lens of pagan Middle Platonism's flesh- and matter-denouncing doctrines and entirely spiritualized theological concepts—his blanket denunciation of all things Greek and philosophical makes good *polemic* sense.

In the later development of orthodox Christian Platonism the priority of scriptural revelation and the existential and community practice of Christian life over abstract concepts, and the affirmation of the *flesh* of Christ and the *goodness of matter* Tertullian so powerfully puts forward, is the interpretive lens through which the wisdom of Plato is appropriated. In this regard Tertullian is a significant formative presence in the later development of orthodox Christian Platonism. Once Marcion was no longer a rival to catholic orthodoxy, once Gnosticism had faded with the demise of the occult and esoteric fascinations of the age of anxiety in which it flourished, once doctrines of Christ's incarnation and an affirmative understanding of material creation were fully accepted by the church, then the reasons why "Athens" was off limits to Tertullian no longer applied. Yet Jerusalem was *always* prior to Athens for orthodox Christian thinkers, as is most clearly illustrated in their attitude to *doxa*. The Septuagint translation of "glory" for "*doxa*"—depicting the historically and tangibly manifest appearing of God—was carried into Christianity in such a manner that the doctrines of the church always held

24. Tertullian, *Treatise on Penance*, see note on *ratio* on page 137. There is debate as to whether "ratio" has a Latin legal meaning in Tertullian to the exclusion of any Greek philosophical implication, or not. Certainly Latin theology in general is more shaped by legal thinking than Greek theology in general. But whether Tertullian has a sort of prejudicial disdain for all things Greek—including philosophy—because he is a Latin or not, clearly he is a not only a powerful rhetorical polemicist, but a powerful reasoner. His many treatises are fine examples of persuasive reasoning.

25. This is my gloss on a short and humorous reference to Tertullian by Augustine in the *City of God*, book 7, chapter 1.

greater authority than the highly brilliant speculative contemplations of the great Greek thinkers. Tertullian won this battle decisively for Christian orthodoxy.

In sum, Tertullian's insistence on the incompatibility of Athens and Jerusalem is the strongest form of cautioning he can give us against the criteria of Greek philosophy becoming the hermeneutic lens through which the Christian revelation is interpreted. For if the mind of fallible and sinful humanity seeking God stands over the revelation of God seeking and redeeming humanity, then nothing but cunning and deceptive corruption (i.e., normal religious and intellectual hubris) can be expected.[26] However, if the priority of God's revelation to humanity is upheld, and if the receptivity to the transformative power of that divine initiative is upheld, then "to the pure all things are pure" (Titus 1:15). Certainly this is what Origen thought. Origen (an Alexandrian) thus believed that the Christians should "despoil the Egyptians" of their treasure (Greek philosophy) after the template of the Hebrews being given gifts when they left Egypt in the great exodus (Exod 12:35–36).[27] In this Origen follows Irenaeus' Christian interpretation of the exodus wherein the spoils of the Egyptians represent that which the Christian gains from the surrounding civilization and then employs to the worship and glory of God. Irenaeus, quite credibly, claims this interpretation is of direct apostolic lineage.[28] And if the interpretive priority Tertullian so staunchly defends is upheld, why should not both Tertullian and Origen be compatible?

2. Christianity Is True Philosophy

Justin Martyr—older than Tertullian, and admired by Tertullian[29]—is famous to us through his apologetic defenses of the faith and his martyrdom. He was a Greco-Roman Palestinian and a philosopher, both before and after his conversion to Christianity.

Justin, writing in the second century, maintained that Christ is the very Reason (Logos) of God. Hence, Christ pre-existed his birth in

---

26. Here again Kierkegaard is very akin to Tertullian. For Kierkegaard there is no knowledge that is existentially independent of either the error and hubris of sin or the humility and truth of grace. See Kierkegaard's *Concluding Unscientific Postscript* for a powerful exposition of the epistemological significance of sin and grace.

27. Origen, *Letter to Gregory*. That is, Gregory Thaumaturgus.

28. Irenaeus, *Adversus Haereses*, V, 30.

29. Tertullian, *Adversus Valent.*

Palestine, and, as John taught, is the fount of all creation. As there is no other true Reason than Christ, then everyone who ever heeded reason heeded Christ.

> Christ is . . . the Logos of whom every race of men have been partakers. And so anyone who has lived by reason was really a Christian, even though he was called an atheist. For example, among the Greeks there were such men as Socrates and Heraclitus. Among the barbarians, there were Abraham, Elijah, Hananiah, Mishael, and Azariah, and countless others. Anyone who lived apart from reason and killed those who lived reasonably actually opposed Christ—even though they lived before Christ's human birth.[30]

Justin, possibly as an inheritance from Hellenistic Judaism, held that the uncanny theological continuities between the God revealed in the Hebrew sacred texts and Plato's philosophy was probably a function of Plato borrowing from Moses! Interestingly, Walter Burkert has shown that Greek culture was indeed strongly influenced by the great Near Eastern civilizations that pre-date classical Greek antiquity, yet there is no modern scholarship that gives any credence to the idea that Plato read (or could have read) Moses.[31] Even so, classical Greek theology in a Platonist key is often monotheistic and upholds the moral purity and eternal and transcendent nature of divinity, in direct contrast to any literal belief in the morally depraved and "oh so human" mythic actions of the gods.[32] Leaving spurious speculations concerning historical causation to one side, it is clear that the conceptual links between Platonist theology and the Hebrew and Christian understandings of God were not seen as mere historical accidents to early Christians. For if Christ as the incarnate *Logos* of God was not simply a narrowly Christian "belief" but a real truth, *the* Truth no less, then Christ being the cause of any truth apprehended by Greek philosophers—and *all* truths, and *any* valid intelligible meaning— was no surprise. This gives a brash and incredible air of hubris to early Christian apologists in the ears of their learned non-Christian hearers.

---

30. Justin Martyr, *First Apology*, VIII, in Bercot, ed., *We Don't Speak Great Things— We Live Them*, 100

31. Burkert, *Babylon, Memphis, Persepolis*. Augustine too thinks the idea that Plato learnt from Moses to be highly unlikely. See Augustine, *City of God*, VIII, ch. 11.

32. The gods were immortal but not eternal in ancient Greek thinking. The eternal divinity above the immortal gods is the proper object of classical Greek theology.

Justin, addressing the Roman Emperor Antoninus Pius and his son Marcus Aurelius no less (!), claims that, "On some points we teach no differently than the poets and philosophers you honour. On other points, our teachings are more complete and more divine."[33] Justin is so bold as to claim that, "it is not that we hold the same opinions as these philosophers, but that these, and so many others, speak in imitation of us."[34] This sort of claim is, on the face of it, quite laughable, in that Christian scholarship and philosophy as such was almost entirely undeveloped at this point in time. If you compare the intellectual and scholarly quality of Justin with his near contemporary Sextus Empiricus, Justin—wearer of the philosopher's gown though he was—is a rank amateur in comparison. Yet, clearly Christian scholarship grows out of this conviction that the Christ-event is the decisive revelation of God breaking into human history, and thus the only genuinely valid portal to understanding truth in *any* and *every* field of knowledge and evaluation. And, if it is indeed true that Christ is the divine Word of God incarnate, then there is nothing illogical or hubristic about this stance.

When we look just a bit further on in Christian history we see the rise of first-class scholars and thinkers—such as Origen of Alexandria—and while they do indeed have a staggering grasp of learned Greco-Roman intellectual culture, they still see the world through this remarkably Christo-centric lens. This is the beginning of the high age of Eastern Christian Platonism, and its intellectual stars are, to this day, very bright. But even in the West it is Augustine who claims that "the true philosopher is the lover of God"[35] and goes on to affirm Plato as a true philosopher who had profound "insight which brought him so close to Christianity."[36] Certainly by the fourth century we are now dealing with Christian thinkers who are genuinely great thinkers. Even so, it is important to note that the basic stance of Justin—that it is the revelation of Christ and the ongoing movement of the Spirit of God in the community of Christians that is the fount from which truth arises—is staunchly maintained by the high thinkers of patristic Christian Platonism.

In sum, early Christian thinkers often found deep grounds of commonality between aspects of Greek philosophy and what they recognized

33. Justin Martyr, *First Apology*, chapter 10; in Bercot, *We Don't Speak Great Things—We Live Them*, 108.

34. Ibid., 112.

35. Augustine, *City of God*, VIII, 1.

36. Ibid., 11.

as truth from within their Christian understanding of reality. Further, early Christian thinkers retained their stance within Christian orthodoxy to the extent that they used the ruler of Christian revelation to measure the truth claims of philosophy, and not the other way around. This does not mean that a narrow grid of Christian doctrine filtered their appreciation of all thinking and science; rather, the guidance they received from revelation was seen as a means of liberating the life of the mind to fearlessly follow the *Logos* of God wherever he should lead.

But . . . does the dogmatic foundation to Christian thought, the firm belief in the Gospel narratives as told by common people (which anyone moved by the remarkable story could grasp, be they educated or not), make the entire edifice of Christian thought little more than a catchy popularist mythology? Is Christianity a culturally timely combination of the "low" and "common" nature of the basic Gospel narratives with a simplistic gloss of the worldview and "high" spiritual sensibilities of the Middle Platonist spirit of the age? Does Christianity meet the felt needs of the larger post-mythological pagan culture that was still desperate for religious anchors, but without the demanding and elitist intellectual trappings of non-Christian Greco-Roman philosophy? Does the dogmatic interest in the soul and a transcendent God combined with the new community form of Christian *koinonia* simply find the cultural conditions right to take off? Is Christianity a popularist and mythological form of Platonism for the common people?

3. Christianity is Platonism for the Masses

In his preface to *Beyond Good and Evil*, Nietzsche famously noted that Christianity is Platonism for the people.[37] Hegel pre-figured this line of thinking and Heidegger continued it in the twentieth century.[38] And, indeed, history does show a strong swing in the early church towards Neoplatonist thinking at around the same time as a large up-take of "the people" of the Roman Empire moved into the church in the fourth century. Unlike the very intellectually demanding Platonism of non-Christian philosophical thinkers—from the academic tradition of skeptical detachment to the high religious sensibilities of Plotinus' school—the intellectually simple doctrines of Christianity meant that un-educated people could have the

37. Nietzsche, *Beyond Good and Evil*, x.

38. See Hegel's "Lectures on the History of Philosophy" of 1896; see Heidegger's "Introduction to Metaphysics" of 1935.

high notions of absolute goodness and the immortality and perfection of their souls without a lifetime of study and exacting aestheticism.

The important question at stake here is not so much "is Christianity Platonism for the masses?" but *in what sense* (if any) do the popularist "Platonist" features of Christianity *explain* what Christianity is? For there can be little doubt that entry into Christianity was remarkably egalitarian regarding class, race, gender, status, and education (Christianity is, after all, a universal—in Greek, *katholikos*—religion), nor can there be much doubt that Christian doctrine does indeed reflect some strikingly similar understandings of God, of the soul, and of reality as can be found in Plato.[39]

Nietzsche's reading finds that the desire to see past appearance into reality and the desire for perfection, which the immediate world does not offer, are the core aspirations of Platonism. This refusal to give ultimacy to the immediate, and thus this denial of the ultimate reality of the contingent, the transient, the embodied, the imagined—this "other worldly" focus on some perfect "beyond"—is, to Nietzsche, the very nub of delusional Platonist dogmatism, and *this* desire is put within the reach of uneducated ordinary people by its various Christianized institutional forms. So to Nietzsche, Christianity being Platonism for the masses does indeed explain the nature of Christianity—it is a popularist delusion. More precisely, the granting of this desire to the masses explains the attraction of Christianity; the erotic femininity of Christianity.

The other side of this outlook explains the internal dynamic of Christianity as a function of what Nietzsche called "the will to power." In exchange for the people being given access to the larger rituals and institutions admitting them to belief in a (false) promise of idealized perfection, the church gets power over the masses. In important regards the critique of Christianity put forward by Feuerbach and Marx prefigures the

---

39. Scholars do contest all these points but I think more often than not the desire to see differences (which really are there) overshadows the real areas of similarity (which are also there). The "Platonic soul," for example, is often (badly, by the way) characterized as a non-material entity that is released from its physical bodily prison on death and then returns to its native purely spiritual heaven of perfect ideas. Clearly the Christian notion of bodily resurrection without re-incarnation or pre-existence is very distinct from some of the mythic suggestions Plato has offered regarding what might happen to our soul after death. Yet both Platonism and Christianity hold that we *do have* a personal spiritual essence that survives physical death. Many philosophies and religions do not share this broad understanding of the soul with Christianity and Plato.

Nietzschean fascination with the immediate and tangible power-dynamic of the practices of embodied life as the only "sincere" reality revealed in any structure of belief. So to Nietzsche the nature of Christianity is thus explained as the generation of a delusional populist mythos of ideal perfection for the real purpose of the expansion and protection of very tangible (economic and violent) expressions of ecclesial power.

This broadly Nietzschean interpretation of "the essence of Christianity" has lodged itself deeply in the larger intellectual culture of what Milbank calls modern secular reason. Unsurprisingly, this perspective plays a significant role in nineteenth- and twentieth-century modern theology in general and Protestant liberal theology in particular. This is not surprising because, in Scotist and Ockhamean fashion, modernity's movement away from metaphysics to epistemology, its move away from divine Being to human knowing *must* reverse the polarities of our cultural outlook on reality. Now, in modernity and postmodernity, "the real" *is* the apparent; then, the transcendent was the ground of the apparent and only the reality of that ground could give substantiality to the apparent. But even within its own terms, Nietzsche's "explanation" of Christianity is not convincing.

Here I would ask you to cast your mind back to the brief discussion of Nietzsche and Hamann in chapter 3. If Nietzsche is genuinely persuaded that *all* meaning is exclusively apparent, entirely contingent, and nothing other than imaginatively generated mythos, then this must also apply to his own account of the essence of Christianity, and that account is then clearly seen as but a screen for *his own* will to power. If we are to consider reasoning as a valuable truth-seeking tool (something Nietzsche cannot do) then there are two consequences to this stance.

Firstly, there can be no "objective" way of deciding that the beliefs of Christianity are any more delusional than Nietzsche's preferred poetic alternative. Conversely, how could the belief in "ideals" be false if no belief can be true?[40] Suspicion is a worm that eats itself. In other words, one must abandon the truth-revealing capacity of reason if one accepts Nietzsche's reasoning, but then one would not be accepting his reasoning

40. The point I am making in these two sentences is that "false" is a notion tied to a bivalent conception of "truth." False makes no sense if there is no true. If one abandons bivalent truth itself—as Nietzsche seems to be attempting—then all "knowledge" and "meaning" claims becomes poetic assertions, and then the idea that *any* claim could be false is meaningless. But then the poetic assertion that there is no bivalent truth is itself an act of unreasoned will such that there can be no Nietzschean *reason* why Platonist ideals are false (or true). Here we touch a virulent voluntaristic irrationalism.

on the grounds that it was reasonable, but simply because one liked his willful imaginative assertion. Then, of course, if you ditch reason, there is no reason why belief in transcendence is false, it is merely that you do not like that belief and would rather imagine a different reality. But this is to abandon reasoning as such and to revert—in the final analysis—to arbitrary will and violent power.[41]

Secondly, the vitriolic stance against Christian religion that this outlook supports cannot escape the charge of resentment.[42] The Nietzschean nihilist resents the cultural and political power that the Christian imagination exerts over Western culture and simply wills to replace it with a nihilistic culture of power that is more amenable to its own imaginative desires. Simone Weil well saw that the dynamic of resentment in Nietzsche is an inversion of his stated claims. To Weil, that Christianity is a religion of slaves is undoubtedly true,[43] but it is the powerful who resent the weak on whom their power must depend, and all too often it is not the weak who resent their powerful oppressors. For the great ones are only great in relation to the not great whom they stand out from and on whom they stand. No great one is genuinely great out of their own splendor. They must have viewers and a stage apart from themselves in order to be great. And as they would never worship any other than themselves, they despise those who worship them, yet they need their worship as a function of their own greatness. Christianity—where creation is an originary harmony, a gracious act of divine joy, love, and goodness—espouses the radical inversion of the agonistic religio-mythic power structures that

41. Plato gives a very careful exposition of how the failure to believe in reason as truth-disclosing results in violent tyranny in book 2 of *The Republic*. This does not mean, of course, that there is any simple pathway from reason to truth, as Plato well understands. But our reasoning as a human function within a divine *Ratio* can save us from mere violent power, and can help us as we seek divine truth, be it ever-beyond our grasp (though in the seeking we are placed within Truth's grasp). David C. Schindler very beautifully expounds this face of Plato in chapter 1 of his stunning book *Plato's Critique of Impure Reason*.

42. When Christianity is a religion of respectable status quo small power, then it can easily bear little resemblance to the Christian texts and then the Nietzschean critique of it as a comforting self-delusional cover for the will to power has, indeed, often got real teeth. In the spirit of Psalm 140, Christians should happily accept being struck by Nietzsche's hammer to see if our faith—existentially and culturally—does ring hollow and is an idol of our own making. That task is fully in line with the ministry of the Old Testament prophets and with the essence of Christianity understood as a prophetic movement that radically challenges power and idolatry.

43. Weil, *Waiting for God*, 67.

emerged with the rise of the great ancient agrarian civilizations.[44] The prophetic imagination is the eschatological imagination of the weak and the oppressed, not for power over their oppressors, but for life without oppression for all.[45] This is a profoundly subversive understanding of power and Weil understands this very well. Stanley Hauerwas, influenced by John Howard Yoder, also understands this well.[46] Of course, the church, like any human institution, readily succumbs to the false "realism" of a Babylonian understanding of power and religion, but this is something recognized as a failure by its own doctrines and sacred texts.

Where "Platonism" means belief in transcendent Reality that relativizes the transience, contingency, injustice, moral relativism, violence, and mortality of human existence understood in exclusively immanent terms, then yes, Christianity *is* a type of Platonism. Even so Christianity (and also Plato) does not despise the immediate nature of immanent human existence; indeed, the incarnation gives human immediacy its great dignity within Christian faith. But the immediate is never understood as merely immediate for either the Christian or the Platonist. And this does indeed distinguish it from Nietzsche and from any who believe in the early modern idea of "pure nature," where the immediate and immanent is real in its own terms, and is really the only reality we can meaningfully talk about. But Nietzsche can offer no *reason* why there is only immanence without appealing to something beyond mere contingency (reason). So the manner in which thoughtful argument must shatter in the hands of those who use it in the name of a realism of unmitigated immediacy—of embracing the reality of mere appearance—divides reason from immanence and upholds a profound irrationalism of mere will and merely willful imagination.

In fairness, reason cannot disprove ir-reason on ir-reason's terms, but neither can ir-reason destroy reason on reason's terms. If you trust ir-reason you will go to Nietzsche; if you trust reason you will go to Plato. If you trust in Christ as the divine Reason of God, you will go to Christian Platonism. But there can be no *reason* why a Nietzschean ir-reasoned understanding of Christianity as Platonism for the masses explains what Christianity itself is.

44. See Ricoeur, *The Symbolism of Evil*, 175–98.

45. See Brueggemann, *The Prophetic Imagination*; Jürgen Moltmann, *Theology of Hope*.

46. Hauerwas, *The Peaceable Kingdom*; Yoder, *The Politics of Jesus*.

4. Christian faith is Colonized by Platonist Theology and Ecclesial Power

Robert Banks' wonderful study *Paul's Idea of Community* is an enthralling scholarly work that beautifully describes the socio-cultural world in which Paul and the churches he planted lived.[47] The Christian communities Paul fostered were "organic" home fellowships. Teaching was important from the word go, but the vitality of these churches was to be found in the way of life they lived and the fruit and gifts of the Spirit divinely exercised in their midst—centralized doctrinal controls, established rites and liturgies, over-arching institutional supports and hierarchies and the wealth, power, and high culture that goes with it were just not there. In short, all the usual replicating and controlling institutional structure of the established religion that Christianity became were not aboriginal to it. Three hundred years after Paul all the trappings of an established religion with centralized hierarchies and tight doctrinal definitions has evolved out of this Pauline beginning.[48] So is this move from Paul to Eusebius a perversion of the original Christian faith? Or is it even more degraded than that? For Paul is already a long way from the parochially Jewish Jesus of Nazareth, whom the Greco-Roman world traveler Paul never met (in the flesh). Is the original Jesus movement colonized firstly by Paul, then by a centralized teaching body who defined correct faith dogmatically and set up governing structures to enforce teaching uniformity, which the emperor then takes over to further his own imperial ends? Does this colonization incorporate Platonic doctrines and Greco-Roman notions of power and authority that are in radical antithesis to its original nature? Is Christianity of the fourth century simply unrelated to Jesus of Nazareth?

The manner in which the followers of Jesus became the Christian religion is indeed a story of profound change. However, whether it is the change either of corruption or of development is a matter that contemporary early church scholarship does not seem to allow an answer to: it

---

47. Banks, *Paul's Idea of Community*.

48. George Lindbeck's fascinating study *The Nature of Doctrine* makes a very persuasive case that doctrine plays a key regulating function within the historical life of the church, where doctrine establishes conceptual boarders and shapes practices of life within those boarders in a manner that enables a defined way of life to be both preserved, replicated, and developed. Lindbeck sees this function in entirely positive terms whereas the opponents of doctrine see this same function in entirely negative terms. Whether doctrine is essentially regulatory and whether the regulatory function of doctrine is good, bad, or in itself neither good or bad, are very big questions that deserve considerable attention.

is *both*. Theologically—if the Holy Spirit indeed indwells the real flesh of fallible and not-yet-perfected Christians—it must always be both. But here one's approach to orthodox Christian doctrine cannot help but provide a hermeneutic lens on how one reads this amazing and complex history. For if one believes that Christ was the Son of God who did rise from the dead and whose Spirit is the life of his church, then the fact that the church is a partnership of fallible people and divinity means that no corruption is *simply* corrupt, and no development is *simply* divine. But if one does not believe that Christ is the risen Lord of heaven and earth and if one believes that the only valid way of understanding the development of any human institution is in terms of what it must have in order to increase its power and control, then "religion" viewed as an entirely human enterprise does not provide any meaningful distinction between corruption and development.

As fascinating and important questions about the development of the church are, we will go no further here but remain focused on the relationship between Platonism and Christianity.

We have argued that a broadly Platonist understanding of reality is assumed in the New Testament, and so the gradual uptake of more explicit doctrinal formulations with some Platonist signatures is not out of keeping with its original sources. The replacement of prophetic ministries overseen by *pater familiar* elders with teaching bishops modeled on a mono-episcopate and "monarchic" conception of ecclesial power structure does occur as doctrine develops and as the institution becomes more organized. But again, the question is whether this correlation explains the role of Platonism within the development of Christian doctrine and power, or not. Viewed through a modern interpretive lens where only things that can be measured and comprehended as "natural" are real, then mere political and institutional necessity does provide us with a total explanation of the development of doctrine and ecclesial authority structures. But, of course, to view things in this manner is to *presuppose* the only possible answer that you are ostensibly "looking" for. If you view this question through an ancient epistemic lens—where meaning is prior to knowing, where divinity is prior to humanity, and where our human knowing and acting always participates (to some degree) in that which is ontologically prior to us—then the vision of immanence is not lost but it is explicable only in the light of the transcendent.[49] That also is

---

49. Of course, to say that anything is "explicable" in the light of transcendence is an impossibility within a modern interpretive outlook, for here the very idea of

inescapably the New Testament outlook, and—I submit—no Christian understanding of reality can maintain its connections with New Testament source of this religion without rejecting a modern reductively naturalistic explanation of the nature of the church.

In sum, it is the case that doctrinal definition sharpens at the same time as Platonist conceptual categories become part of the vocabulary of the early high culture of the ancient church, and this also occurs at the same time that ecclesial authority structures develop as modeled after Roman imperial notions of order and hierarchy. What these historical facts explain—or whether they are an explanation at all—depends on which interpretive lens you wear when viewing this development. The modern interpretive lens—very popular with highly academic German Protestant trends in biblical interpretation from the late eighteenth century to the late twentieth century—is unquestionably foreign to the broadly assumed worldview and mainstream life forms of the ancient church. The modern interpretive lens thus stands over the early church and presumes to know what was *really* happening, as seen from the historically distant perspective of a reductively scientific view of reality where knowledge is prior to meaning. From our interpretive modern vantage point we also assume that explanations are not only entirely naturalistic, but that there is no phenomena that cannot be reduced to a naturalistic explanation in principle. This perspective *cannot* be believed by Christians who wish to remain Christians. Take the priority of divine act over human reception and the priority of divine meaning over human knowing out of Christian faith, and you lose historical continuity to the orthodox Christian community of belief and belief-formed practice.

Modern theologians in Harnack's trajectory express a powerful desire to get back to the real historical Jesus, who was an extraordinarily inspiring man with some remarkable moral teachings, but certainly not the miracle-working Son of God who died for the sins of the world and physically rose from the dead. This academically respectable outlook believes the truth discourse of what is possible as defined by modern science and reads all accounts of the "super-natural" within "nature" as fundamentally deluded. Hence this outlook seeks to escape all the

explanation is rigorously naturalistic and definitionally "beneath" our understanding. This reflects the Latin derivation of the word explain (*ex* from *planus* the plane) implying a far-seeing view of an intelligibly flattened panorama where everything is made clear beneath our gaze. Contrasted with this is Plato's image of the sun as the source of intelligibility that we cannot look *at*, but can only see *by*.

superstitious and political corruptions of that remarkable event by the church and its officially sanctioned doctrine. But this is simply another version of Marcionism. This stance wishes to interpret the meaning and validity of the history of the Christian religion through the non-Christian scientistic truth lens accepted as respectable to the larger intellectual culture of secular modernity. No Christian should accept this account of the rise of Christian Platonism, for this would amount to throwing out historical Christianity in order to have some modernity-framed, reconstructed, speculative fiction of a historical Jesus.

Conclusion

We are now some way towards re-considering the reflexive disdain for Christian Platonism as seen by self-consciously modern theological perspectives. The development of Christian Platonism did not happen as a foreign invasion of Greek philosophical ideas into a discretely Jewish primitive Jesus movement. Rather, Judaism was profoundly influenced by Greco-Roman thought and culture before the New Testament era; the New Testament is written in Greek and its key terms are informed by the Septuagint; the New Testament is saturated with the worldview that synthesizes religion and broadly Platonist philosophical concerns that was common to its age, and; key Jewish readings of Greek notions of *logos* and *doxa* are original to Christian faith and are firmly carried into Christian orthodoxy. Further, while gnostic sects and Christian heresies did indeed embrace Middle Platonist dualisms (e.g., the idea that matter is evil and spirit is good) the Christian doctrines of the incarnation and of the goodness of creation entirely prevented this outlook from gaining access to orthodox Christian theology and orthodox Christian Platonism. In short, there seem to be no valid theological reasons why Christian Platonism should be viewed as anything other than as nascent to original Christianity and as entirely orthodox.

We have seen that Christian Platonism is Christian before it is Platonist. On the goodness of material reality (in the doctrine of creation), on the goodness of human flesh (in the doctrine of the incarnation), on the work of God within the human realm of history, Christian Platonism flies directly against other forms of Platonism that flourished in late antiquity. Further, the extent to which Plato's philosophy and Christian doctrine align is seen as evidence not of cultural conditioning, but as a function of the work of God through, yet beyond, culture and history. The coming of Christ to that specific point in space, time, and culture is understood to be no merely contingent accident but as specifically chosen by God.

So Christian Platonism is genuinely Christian, and Christian orthodoxy is significantly Platonist in some of its key cosmological, moral, and metaphysical stances. But, if all this is true, why did Christian Platonism fall so conspicuously from favor in Western theological thinking, and—more seriously—from Western culture as it was embedded in Christendom? This is the question we shall explore in the next chapter.

6

So What Went Wrong?

At this point in the book I think we have done enough background digging to realize that the deep-seated antipathy that modern Western philosophy and theology reflexively has towards Christian Platonism may well tell us more about modernity and nineteenth-century progressivism than it tells us about Christian Platonism. Further, I hope that it is clear that we can now no longer simply *assume* that Christian Platonism is obviously a bad and dead idea that is a travesty to both philosophy and theology. However, I would not be writing this book if it was not broadly assumed by academics and the spirit of our times that Christian Platonism, as a viable and serious philosophical stance, has (thankfully) long since been superseded.

So, historically, what went wrong? If Christian Platonism is, as I am claiming, such a good idea, and still retains a powerful lodging place in the Western mind (even if "only" in the realm of imaginative narrative), why is it largely considered to be a complete non-player for serious philosophical attention now?

In this chapter I am going to attempt to define more adequately what Christian Platonism actually is, and then I am going to sketch a very brief overview of the historical fall of Western Christian Platonism from intellectual respectability. And here I will argue that one of the big reasons Christian Platonism is in the cold today has much to do with accidents of history and the fickleness of the currents of intellectual fashion. Yet, there is also a profound shift in basic cultural attitudes towards truth and knowledge that has a strong, almost irresistible attraction to us post-seventeenth-century Westerners, and this shift makes the medieval and ancient respect for the very type of approach to reality maintained in Christian Platonism now look impossible. We need to understand this shift and bring its premises out into the open if we are to think about Christian Platonism in any other terms than fantasy. But firstly, let us seek to clarify what Christian Platonism actually is.

Christian Platonism in Its First Flowering

A great deal of the trouble for Christian Platonism today is that it understands the nature of philosophy itself in terms incompatible with the modern secular way of life. This is easily pointed out by noting that the central tenets of Christian Platonism can be best briefly outlined by reference to the Nicene Creed. That is, *Christian* Platonists in Antiquity believed, centrally, that the Christian revelation is true, and that the most central Truth—and the fount of all truths—is Christ himself. Thus a distinctive historically embedded and communally transmitted revelation, made alive to us by the Spirit of Truth that breathes the very life of God into us, was taken by Christian Platonists as *the only grounds for a valid philosophy*. Which is to say that in its first flowering Christian Platonism was not some philosophy and religion hybrid that was philosophical in some regards and dogmatic/religious in other regards. Rather, Christian Platonism, first and foremost, was a stance grounded within Christian faith and the life of the church. As mentioned in chapter 5, the early church fathers of the late classical era often saw Plato as a divinely inspired pagan forerunner of Christian faith—not unlike Moses—where the Word of God was spoken not in direct theophanies, but in the intellect. So Plato's philosophy was believed to be completed in Christianity, and Christianity was seen as the true philosophy to which Plato pointed. In Christian Platonism, then, Plato is measured and amended by Christian revelation, and Plato's highest insights and deepest longings are seen as being fulfilled by Christ, and not the other way around.

So the first thing to understand about Christian Platonism is that those who we would see as orthodox adherents to this outlook in the patristic era did not think of themselves as Christian *Platonists*, but simply as Christians. Further they did not think of philosophy and religion as separate things. *Religion and philosophy are two words for the one thing*—the way of life rightly ordered by a divinely enabled pursuit of the highest truth to which humans can aspire. That is, the love of wisdom (philosophy) as a practice of life was, in antiquity, something done with all one's heart, mind, body, and spirit, and indeed—for the Christian—this was the same enterprise as seeking to love God with all one's being and to have no god before God. That is, right worship and right thinking about truth and meaning, and right acting were all seen as inescapably integral with each other. Notions of philosophy and theology having different objects, different methodologies, and different starting points—ideas that start to emerge in the high Middle Ages—were, by and large, foreign to Christian thinkers in Late Antiquity.

Even so, today we typically do separated out theology and religion from philosophy and science, and we do tend to think of a philosophical stance as centrally identifiable by its clearly articulated and rationally defended creed.[1] So for us, it is hard to understand what a particular philosophical stance could be if it cannot be described in the terms of clear and distinct propositions. Because of how *we* understand what a philosophical stance is, we feel a need to try and identify what Christian Platonism, as a set of philosophical propositions, is. This is a project that cannot really work, though it can be made to work to *some* degree.

Defining Christian Platonism

For a number of reasons it is not easy to define Christian Platonism "philosophically." Firstly, Christian Platonism has never accepted the notion that there is a sharp distinction between nature and grace. It is only possible to specify a system of propositions as a distinctly philosophical stance, demarcated from religion, if one assumes that philosophy is discretely concerned with nature, and with "natural knowledge," and religion/theology is concerned with discretely divine and "supernatural" things, which are not accessible to "natural" reason and knowledge. As specified above, Christian Platonism is Christian before it is Platonist, but not in such a manner as to suppose that faith and reason, nature and grace, truth and belief can be treated as discrete dualities. If this excludes Christian Platonism from being seen as philosophical at all, this is because an either-or dualism is presupposed in the above list of pairs that makes it possible for us moderns to think (incredibly) that philosophy *can* be meaningfully isolated from religion. Now *perhaps* modern philosophers can think this way, but I cannot see how *Christians* can. If Jesus is the incarnate second person of the Godhead, and if the resurrected and living Son is Lord of Heaven and Earth, then the gospel is globally true (in heaven and on earth) or it is no gospel and is not true at all.

1. Interestingly, philosophy in the West seems to have followed religion in going creedal and developing rational "theologies" around belief- and life-practice stances consistent with some central belief. So to be, for example, an atheist is to believe there is no God, and to attempt to justify this creed rationally and to think through the practical implications of this belief.

Secondly, unlike modern philosophical stances, only a very superficial understanding of "Platonism" can be had along propositionally expressible lines. Indeed Plato explicitly sets out to make "Platonism" very hard to set down on paper: in all of Plato's dialogues he never once says "This is what I, Plato, think to be true." Plato refuses to put his philosophy in clear propositions before us for the very specific reason that he mistrusts written statements as being "dead" propositional substitutes for the communal and individual spiritual practices of the truly philosophical life.[2] Let us unpack this a little.

Plato only mentions himself three times in all of his dialogues: twice in Plato's account of Socrates' trial (*Apology*), and once in the dialogue depicting the death of Socrates (*Phaedo*).[3] The rareness of any self-reference in Plato's dialogues makes them of particular note, particularly if we want to define "Platonism"; for in naming himself we have our only explicit signature moments in all his written works (even though these references are carefully made in such a manner as to appear incidental). The point of the references to himself in the *Apology* seems to be Plato's determination to make it clear that his account of Socrates' defense is no mere literary vehicle for his own ideas, but is grounded in a deep and intimate knowledge of his teacher's thoughts and actions, as well as in a first-hand knowledge of the public trial in which he physically stood close at hand to his teacher. The reference in the *Phaedo* is different. The *Phaedo* opens to a moving scene where the weeping friends of Socrates are gathered around him as his appointed hour of self-execution draws nigh. In a deeply touching aside it is noted that Plato was not at the death-bed conversation that followed, because he was sick. The inference is that Plato was too viscerally disturbed by the pending death of his beloved teacher to be able to be there when he died. So the only explicit things Plato tells us about himself and his convictions in his dialogues—though still indirectly stated—are that he stood completely with his condemned teacher when Athens turned against him, and that he loved Socrates

2. See Plato, *Seventh Letter* 342a–345a. While it is very difficult to really know if any of the letters of Plato were actually written by Plato, the seventh letter is considered by many scholars the most likely to be by Plato, and certainly its content is consistent with the dialogues and with the method of "indirect communication" Plato obviously employs.

3. See Plato, *Meno and Phaedo*, edited by Sedley and Long, 44n.4. Here these commentators identify *Apology* 34a, *Apology* 38b, and *Phaedo* 59b as the only places in Plato's dialogues where he refers to himself by name.

dearly and viscerally.[4] The only decisive "Platonism" that Plato himself allows us to infer involves the preparedness to stand with justice against the will of the crowd, and to full-bodiedly love people who deeply express the unmistakable beauty of goodness, in both life and death.

Other than as an active, affective, aesthetic, and embodied existential stance, it is really too much to say what Platonism is, for, amongst other things, Plato is very careful to never speak in his own name. I do not mean to suggest that we cannot identify certain beliefs Plato adhered to—clearly we can, such as: the immortality of the soul; the Goodness beyond being of the ultimate fount of reality; the partially knowable yet eternally real existence of moral, aesthetic, and transcendent reality. Yet Plato subtly advocates a high way of life that ardently pursues wisdom, and he flatly refuses to unambiguously and overtly offer us a set of intellectual answers to abstract "philosophical" questions.[5]

It seems obvious to me that Plato abhorred the idea of Platonism. For while you can draw propositional inferences from Plato—yet even the famous "forms" are complex analogical suggestions rather than tight propositional inferences in the dialogues[6]—they are your inferences and

---

4. So much for thinking of "Platonic love" as merely intellectual and body-denying. But possibly an alternative interpretation that also makes sense is that Plato's friendship with his beloved teacher is too intimate a matter for Plato to use in his writings. For we can see why Plato should place himself in some relation to this dialogue given its topic is death and the survival of the soul. Taking the *Phaedo* as a guide, it clearly advocates that philosophy is a type of death and certainly a preparation for death—it is a means of preparing the immortal soul for its judgment. The end of life is thus the culmination of philosophy. So it seems clear that Plato has to find a dramatic excuse for not being at the death conversation of his master, for it seems that no true disciple of philosophy would miss the culmination of their teacher's philosophy. Whether the inference of "Plato was sick" is one of visceral disturbance or one of piety towards that which should not be used, in both cases an intimate and deep friendship between Plato and Socrates is implied.

5. Indeed, I think it reasonable to argue that the so called "Socratic dialogues"—the ones that end without any definite conclusion—are the pinnacle of Plato's teaching, rather than "early" dialogues promoting a skeptical ignorance that Plato "overcomes" as his thought matures. This developmental model is deeply problematic and ignores the profound unity of Plato's thought, across both the unresolved dialogues and the more "dogmatic" dialogues. On this see Jacob Howland's very important paper, "Re-reading Plato: The Problem of Platonic Chronology."

6. In Plato's dialogue *Parmenides* the manner in which we might understand how forms that are eternally real are (and are not) related to physical reality is examined in considerable depth. It seems that one of the prime objectives of this dialogue is to point out how difficult it is to understand how unchanging intelligible essences interface with material reality, which is defined by genesis, change, and dissolution.

Plato expects you to take philosophical responsibility for them. Indeed, as the above mentioned active and affective notion of Platonism implies, right action and right feeling in an actual lived life are clearly a more significant measure of philosophical validity to Plato than smart thinking.[7] Plato, in other words, encouraged the pursuit of *embodied wisdom*. Merely intellectually "believing" in the transcendent existence of the form of "The Table" (and who really knows exactly what Plato thought about this other than it was *not* a simplistic conceptual reification) does not make you either a philosopher or a Platonist.

It always amazes me that otherwise very intelligent modern thinkers often read Plato as if he is either some sort of eighteenth-century Rationalist or some sort of nineteenth-century Idealist. Apart from the obvious historical anachronism in such hermeneutic vandalism, it seems unavoidably obvious to me that Plato has far more in common with the often-indirectly spoken religious existentialism of Kierkegaard than with any other recent trajectory.[8]

David C. Schindler—in my opinion one of the best contemporary scholars of Plato—notices how Socrates in Plato's dialogues often existentially, religiously, and relationally embodies that which the dialogue is concerned with.[9] Further Schindler notices the manner in which the rich dramatic structure of Plato's dialogues makes the kind of openings possible that allows the careful reader to "see" more than can be simply said (or written).[10] Plato has a genius for contextual narrative subtlety— as does Shakespeare—so one of the striking features of his work is the manner in which his dialogues gesture beyond themselves. Further, Plato

---

Plato does not want us to have a facile or complacent idea of form. Here I read Plato as saying that material reality would not be intelligible at all if it was not for forms, and yet to try and understand forms in the categories of obvious (that is materially referenced) human knowledge can never be appropriate as this is to try and understand the primary by the light of that which is derivative. Whatever forms really are, they precede and supersede what we can reasonably say about them in the terms of normal human language.

7. It would be both pointedly true and highly ironic to say that Plato has no interest in academic philosophy. Indeed, this is precisely what the founder of what we now call Middle Platonism maintained. And perhaps the true lover of wisdom can no longer have a great deal of concern with academic philosophy today also.

8. It is significant that whilst Kierkegaard railed against Hegel, he adored Plato. See Stewart and Nun, *Kierkegaard and the Greek World*.

9. Schindler, *Plato's Critique of Impure Reason*, 167–75, 78–84.

10. Ibid., 78–84. See also another wonderfully sensitive reader of Plato, Jacob Howland, *The Republic: The Odyssey of Philosophy*, 25–55.

is always wooingly concerned to form the reader in the types of determinations for good action and right feeling that we sense Plato thinks good for our spiritual development, but such formation cannot be imposed by mere argumentative force and cannot be "obtained" with a mere proof.[11] These inherently subtle and wooing features of Plato's work are some of the things that account for their enduring power and their irreducibility to propositional formulation. Thus any "Platonism" that is merely a set of propositional intellectual formulations comprising some contained metaphysical system is no true Platonism, and indeed Platonism cannot be defined in such terms.

So it is important to recognize that when we use the phrase "Christian Platonism" it is best to do so with a certain gentle irony, a certain smiling knowingness regarding what such a term can really amount to. It is a meaningful term—as I shall point out shortly—yet its meaning is not something that can be reduced to a discretely "philosophical" set of conceptual propositions that "Christian Platonists" give mental assent to.[12] For that, indeed, would be to miss the whole point of both philosophy, as Plato sees it, and Christianity. Christian Platonism is not something that can be defined in the propositional and ostensibly objectively demonstrable terms of a modern philosophical treatise.

With the above caveats before us, let us swoop in for some sort of loose conceptual grab at what Christian Platonism is. Here, four points are particularly important.

Firstly, Christian Platonism is an entirely *integrative* outlook, yet it is not a reductive or closed (conceptually complete) outlook. That is, this stance assumes that there is one overarching ever-active Cause of reason and existence in the cosmos (God), and hence all true meanings are coherent with each other and there are no discrete zones of different types of truths/meanings that have no connection. Even so, while God knows and sustains the whole, we only ever know parts and know partially. Yet our knowledge of truth—of any sort and to any degree—is a function of the grace of divine revelation and is always "located" within an ontological and epistemic relation to God. Thus knowledge is inherently

11. Notice how Socrates ardently endeavors *not* to simply triumph argumentatively over Thrasymachus in Book One of the *Republic*.

12. Upholding the value of both detailed scholarship and, of course, of Plato's dialogues, William Desmond avoids the pitfalls of "Platonism" in this wonderful manner: "On the whole I prefer Plato as a companion inspiring thought rather than an 'object' of research production" (*Art, Origins, Otherness*, 21).

religious and we can gain a more integrative and truer perspective on reality through a deeper repose in the ever-revealing Word of God. Thus receptive prayer, quiet attention, and right worship are keys to truth and success in the active pursuit of meaningful knowledge. And here it is worth recalling that the Western university sprung out of the monastery and the cathedral school and had this contemplative religious connection to truth embedded in its original DNA. This is why we can still think that the pursuit of truth is valuable for its own sake, regardless of what use (or lack thereof) truth has, or on what topic the attention of the truth seeker (however obscure) is upon.[13]

Secondly, Christian Platonism does not think the modern idea of "pure nature" makes any sense at all. In an Augustinian fashion, all creation is understood as perpetually upheld by the Creator such that the very intelligibility and existence of any being is a manifestation of divinely gifted form made actual in embodiment.

Thirdly, Christian Platonism maintains that moral, aesthetic, and spiritual qualitative meanings are real, and are more primary than material quantitative facts. This does not make the material and the quantitative unreal, but what is apparent to the senses is not understood as intelligible or actual in anything other than a derived relationship to the spiritual realities on which all material manifestations are dependent. Further, the reality of transcendent meaning is not fully comprehensible to us, but as we ourselves (and all creation) are dependent on spiritual meanings and realities for our very being we have an innate participatory knowledge of truth to the partial extent that we are both capable of and open to such knowledge.

Fourthly, Christian Platonism adheres to the notion of ontological participation. In classical Greek, the word *on* means "being." Ontology, then, concerns the nature and meaning of be-ing, of existent reality.

Ontological participation is the idea that concrete particular beings, such as the book in your hand or Socrates, are not self-contained entities, but rather participate in qualitative powers of being that transcend their spatiotemporal specificity. Indeed the Platonist understanding of the nature of temporal beings maintains that no immediate and tangible physical appearance can be equated with that which really (that is, eternally) is. Here a clear distinction between appearance and Reality is in play, and

13. OK, in the Neoliberal university this sort of non-pragmatic commitment to the unhindered pursuit of truth *for its own sake* is now becoming increasingly incomprehensible.

this distinction operates on a couple of levels. To Plato, the intelligible essence of any being is real, and the spatiotemporal expression of that being in physical actuality is partial and derivative. Such incomplete derivation is what constitutes the very fabric of the order of reality revealed to us by our senses. Because of this derivative relationship, there is always more to any being than what meets the eye. So appearance and Reality are not independent of each other, but appearance is dependent on Reality for its intelligibility and for the mystery of its spatiotemporally expressed actuality, and that Reality cannot itself be accounted for by any appearance.

In Christian Platonist thinking, God in his hiddenness is always present as the eternal and intelligible grounds of his temporal creation. God is the ontological Source out of which all beings gain their intelligible essence (their form) and their particular existence (for beings like us, matter in space and time is the medium of our existence). Thus the Real is not immediately visible and is always more ontologically primary than the apparent. That is, Christian faith historically saw the priority of the spiritual over the material as a relation between that which is primary and that which is derivative. So an ontological perspective (and Western metaphysics used to be entirely defined by this perspective, which is why Western metaphysics itself has been so determinedly dissolved and re-defined in recent centuries) holds that what you can't simply see is more real than what you can. Christianity makes no sense at all if such an ontological perspective is denied, though in no sense does Christianity denigrate the tangible en-mattered realm that God himself took up in the incarnation.

Ontological participation is premised on the idea that there are powers of being. The most fundamental power of being is God himself. Saint Paul, quoting Epimenides, expresses the nub of this stance thus: "in God we live and move and have our being" (Acts 17:28). Here God is not "a" being, but is the Ground of all being (all that "is"), that in which all beings participate in order to be anything at all, and thus God is the primary ontological source of the concrete existence and intelligible essence of each particular being. This does not mean that the cosmos is "God on a stick"—Christian belief explicitly holds that God totally transcends his created order of beings, and also gifts beings with a degree of real autonomy from himself—but it does mean that all of reality is fundamentally dependent on God for its ongoing existence and its essential and intelligible nature. So ontological participation means that at the level of what I most fundamentally really am, I do not define and self generate the most basic reality of my being myself; I, as God's creature called into being by him, ontologically participate in God. So, as Augustine put it, God is closer to me than I am to myself.[14]

The notion of ontological participation has striking significance for how we understand the life of the church and the relation of the Christian to creation. For one thing, the notion of *communion* (as distinct from society) only makes sense if one believes that ontological participation is both possible and actual. In contrast to the notion of communion the Latin word *societas* is a business term and it refers largely to a collection of individuals who band together in such a manner that each member of the society is personally benefitted from the collective power of the group. It is, at heart, an individualistic notion. If we think of church as a society of individual Christian believers, then we are not talking about any union in a common life (the notion of communion). By contrast, the New Testament word for Christian fellowship—*koinonia*—speaks of the fellowship of believers who share a common life *in* Christ. Because each Christian is "in" Christ, there is a common life, a common being even, to the church in which each individual participates. The church is an ontological power of being in which the Christian participates. The remarkable thing about this perspective is that "being" is here a multi-layered idea rather than an atomistic unitary notion. So as a particular being I can participate in multiple orders of reality at the same time. Here who I really am (the "is"ness of my being) is not definable in terms contained simply within myself, or simply locatable at one (or any) point in space and time. So you can see that ontological participation is an idea that is at once profoundly assumed by the New Testament and crucial for just about every deep theological understanding of orthodox Christianity, and also profoundly alien to the modern life world in which we live.

That is enough of a "definition" of Christian Platonism for now. With this very scant sketch in mind, let us return to the story of the historical demise of this outlook in the West.

---

14. In *The Teacher* Augustine argues that Christ, who is the divine Truth, dwells in the inner man, and is the one who addresses the soul and calls forth every intelligible response from the soul. The soul as an intelligible inner voice is a derivative conversation partner with Truth, and thus the "I" is derivative of this primary inner relation between Christ and the knowing soul. The soul is not Christ—of course—but Augustine claims that there can be no intelligent soul without Christ. For a wonderful translation and scholarly assistance with this text, see Augustine, *Against the Academicians and The Teacher*, translated with introduction and notes by Peter King.

The Fall of Christian Platonism in the West

As previously mentioned, Christianity was born in Greco-Roman Palestine during the Hellenistic intellectual era now called Middle Platonism. Without negating areas of profound incompatibility, equally there were obvious metaphysical, moral, and theological sympathies that Christian faith shared with Plato's dialogues and the later Neoplatonist fusing of Plato and Aristotle. Because both Middle Platonism and Neoplatonism were of a distinctly religious nature anyway, the incorporation and adaptation of compatible Platonist ideas into Christian theology happened quite organically in the early centuries of the life of the church. Augustine is the great Western genius of incorporating and adapting sophisticated Platonist metaphysical ideas into Christian theology. But this fusing of horizons between Christian doctrine and a sophisticated reading of Platonist philosophy underwent a radical transition that was more or less contemporary with the death of Augustine; the demise of Classical Antiquity itself.

Just before the collapse of Classical Antiquity, the monastic movement started up and became remarkably vital. Advanced philosophical thinking did not feature (except sporadically amongst the Celts) during the great missionary age of the monastery. Even so, the monastery becomes the dominant carrier of constructive Western spiritual energy for at least the next seven centuries.

During the "Dark Ages" continuous barbarian invasion and inter-"state" anarchy, produced by the power vacuum left after the empire dissolved, coincides with the astonishing success of Celtic missionaries and monastic communities resulting in the Christianization of Europe. When wealthy cities are beginning to emerge in Europe in the tenth century, they thus emerge as cities of Christendom. This Christendom was profoundly shaped by Augustinian theology, even though it was not characterized by the same sort of interest in philosophical thinking that one finds in Augustine. Yet, when philosophical thinking revived in the West, it took a remarkable turn away from Plato and towards Aristotle.

From the eleventh century through to the time of Aquinas, a new intellectual culture was being born in Western Europe. Emerging from the cathedral schools—thus deeply located within the church—this new thinking saw itself as being in continuity with Classical Antiquity, but in fact it had very little access to the primary text of the high intellectual culture of the West's past.

Probably the greatest thinker of the early twelfth century was Peter Abelard. Abelard's sheer intellectual power and sparkling brilliance was

the promise of the coming age of the Western university. He was notable
for using this power to mock those he disagreed with; one of his fond
targets of attack was a type of Platonist metaphysical stance then called
Realism.

The advocates of "Platonism" in Abelard's day had almost no access
to Plato's texts, and were indeed lacking in philosophical sophistication.
They were also simply not in Abelard's intellectual league (though who,
according to Abelard, was?). These Platonists were known as Realists
because they maintained that *universals*—such as "human"—are *real*
transcendent "things" in which all *particular* instances of any given universal (in this case, John, Sarah, etc.) ontologically participate. Abelard
intellectually shredded the Realists. Thus at the dawn of the age of the
university, what was then thought of as ontological Realism was simply
fried by Abelard's searing polemics, devastating Aristotelian logic, and
sophisticated linguistic analysis. Indeed Abelard is amongst the earliest—
and one of the most formidable—nominalist opponents of metaphysical
realism. Yet the deep embedding of Western Christian theology in an
Augustinian metaphysical outlook meant that Abelard's burning of (unavoidably) straw effigies of Platonic realism was far from the last word on
this matter.[15]

Thomas Aquinas—born eighty-three years after Abelard died—appeared at the bright dawn of the age of the Western university and was
alive during the cosmos-transforming recovery of Aristotle's corpus in
Western Christendom. But not only was Aquinas—like Abelard—a
master of Aristotelian logic and intellectual disputation, Aquinas, with
his very expansive and subtle mind, was also deeply embedded in Augustinian metaphysics and Pseudo-Dionysian intellectual humility.[16]
Aquinas' metaphysics was thus remarkably shaped by Christian Platonist
thought. But even here, in Aquinas' lifetime, Plato's texts were still largely

15. Though, Abelard is not simply innocent due to a lack of available primary
sources. Marenbon describes one of Abelard's most typical polemic approaches to
Platonism as "dustbin Platonism because . . . Platonism [here] provides a convenient
repository for positions which Abelard wishes to throw out" (*Aristotelian Logic*, XII
109). In fact, it seems to me that "dustbin Platonism" well describes a great deal of what
has been said about Plato in the West since Abelard.

16. Pseudo-Dionysius (calling himself Dionysius the Areopagite, from Act 17:34)
is the name of an anonymous seventh-century Syrian writer who advanced the notion
of apophatic or "negative" theology. That is, with the exception of the revelation of
Scripture, what we cannot say about God is a better clue to who he is than what we
can say about God.

unavailable to the West, and the center of intellectual interest—unlike in the patristic era—was the relation of Aristotle's pagan philosophy to Christian doctrine and theology (Aquinas himself being centrally engaged in the complex synthesizing of as much Aristotelian philosophy as he was able to get into orthodox Christian theology). And this central intellectual interest in Aristotle and Christian doctrine was situated in dialogue with the most advanced (and deeply Aristotelian) classically influenced philosophical culture of the time, the Islamic world. In this context Plato's works were not merely unavailable in the West, but also somewhat uninteresting to the spirit of the times, even though the relation of Aristotle to Christian doctrine and theology was actually situated within a long tradition in which a Platonist form of Christian metaphysics was orthodox.

So the first philosophical assault on the ancient norm of Christian philosophy—a norm upholding a modified yet largely natural harmony of Platonist thought with the truths of Christian doctrine—is Abelard's nominalist attack on naïve twelfth-century realism. This assault in itself did not have any shattering impact on the background assumptions of Christian Platonism in twelfth-century Christendom, but it was an ominous warning of things to come. The relation of particular things to universals remained a hot topic for medieval philosophy, but two things became apparent in the thirteenth century: firstly, this "debate" could not be properly framed in terms of the naïve and unsophisticated realism Abelard destroyed; secondly, questions of metaphysics associated with this debate were far from matters of abstract intellectual interest.

In Aquinas' sophisticated Augustinian metaphysical outlook medieval realism receives a deft and subtle advocate. Now Plato himself did not think of transcendent forms as perfect super models of particular things that exist, as things themselves, eternally in heaven (though something like this position was Abelard's target). Further, Christian Platonism in the late classical era would not have countenanced the idea that forms had some sort of eternal self-sufficient existence. The Augustinian approach was to think of forms as *ideas in the mind of God*, which necessarily *in*form any actual, particular, existing thing with its intelligible essence. So for something to exist in the created cosmos it must be made a particular instance of something—and for beings like us, matter is the medium of our particular existence—but the intelligible essence of the particular instance of any identifiable "thing" is given to it by the Word of God, speaking form into matter, bringing an idea in the mind of God into expression in concrete material actuality. So creation is an ongoing process where everything that is is called into being by God, and for the duration of its existence as a particular instance of a certain kind of being, it is always dependent on God for its essential nature and concrete instantiation. Being tied to God ontologically and essentially, however, does not make creation a mere function of his own consciousness. This is because creation is more begotten than manufactured by the God whose nature is love. That is, although no being exists either ontologically or existentially in any measure independently of God (for God is the Ground of all created being, while fully exceeding created being), nevertheless, created beings are—to some degree—separated out, in and for the possibility of love, from God, and are thus not puppets.

Understanding the ontological relation of the Creator to creatures in these terms implies an entire life-world that structures every aspect of how we live in the world. Let us look very briefly at only four life-world notions of this outlook: knowledge, power, personal identity, and community.

Knowledge works like this. What any being finally "is" is known fully only to God, but there is an intelligible essence that is gifted to every being by God. That is, there is—from our perspective—objective truth about beings that can, in some measure, be known by us, if our minds are in tune with the mind of God as expressed in nature. Thus "science" is a form of mind-to-mind fellowship with God. What any being fully is is also far more than what its merely sensible manifestations indicate. Purpose, meaning, value, beauty, etc., are deeply a function of what a being is gifted by God to be. Thus, "is" and "ought" are equally gifted to the essential nature of any being, so the idea that you can have a merely "objective" ("is") account of anything devoid of any "subjective/moral/teleological" ("ought") account is incomprehensible to this perspective. The notion that you can have facts without values is unintelligible. Equally, the idea that knowledge is an internal attribute of the human mind, such that knowledge is a mere representation of objectively meaningless reality that we can simply use for whatever manipulative power-over-meaningless-objectivity we choose, is frankly sacrilegious to a Augustinian/Thomistic outlook.

Power is always situated within ontological communion. The king might abuse a serf, but both the king and the serf have a common ontological grounding in God such that the whole peace and unity of creation is affected by any one act, and is immediately and intimately known by God within the very immanence of each being, and is teleologically structured by the essential moral and intelligible realities God has built into nature. Here power is never a type of fiat, a type of positional sovereignty, a type of private right of self-determination.

If my own essential nature is given to me by God—even though others and I might "unfold" (or fail to rightly unfold) that essence within time as I mature and make significant life/moral/religious choices—then there is an ontological truth about who I am that is simply there. I do not just "make up" or merely "project" personas of who I would like to be or like to be seen to be. Here personal identity has an ontological grounding.

As already touched on, life together grounded in a true (metaphysically real and ontologically shared) common good looks entirely different to any form of "social" structure premised on the existence of atomic individuals.

So in knowledge, power, identity, and community, the early church and much of medieval Christendom looked very different to any configuration that is coherent with the modern social life-world, which does not "believe" in ontological participation and which does not understand an Augustinian theology of creation.

Returning to the historical sequence, we have so far briefly touched on the manner in which Abelard defies naïve medieval realism, and, perhaps unwittingly, risks throwing out the entire history of the partnership between Platonist metaphysical thinking and Christian doctrine that had largely been assumed within Western Christianity from the early centuries of the church up until the twelfth century. We have also very briefly looked at the enormous life-world consequences that are connected to the acceptance or rejection of Neoplatonist metaphysical thinking within the Christian faith. I have also briefly stated that Abelard's nominalism did not unseat Neoplatonist metaphysics in the early twelfth century, for its historical inertia remained. But things changed radically from a moment that was the decisive tipping point in medieval thinking: the condemnations of 1277.[17] To this moment we must now turn.

Between Abelard and a list of doctrinal and philosophical condemnations produced by the Bishop of Paris in 1277 (a few years after the death of St. Thomas) some very big shifts had been going on in Western Christendom. Three enormous things had happened. Firstly, Western Europe had become powerful and rich and its high intellectual life was

17. See Pieper, *Scholasticism*, 126–62.

bursting into a Springtime of vital recovery and new exploration after the long Winter started with the end of Classical Antiquity. Secondly, Western Christendom had become aware of the Islamic world via the crusades. Here was a non-Christian civilization of staggering physical size, stretching from Spain to Indonesia, with learning and technology far in advance of Western Europe. Thirdly, and most importantly, Aristotle was recovered.

In Antiquity Aristotle had been a significant figure, but he was often seen as secondary to Plato, and often interpreted in the light of Platonist metaphysics. Within late classical Christian thinking, Aristotle's belief that matter was eternal, his patronizing attitudes to religion in general, and his belief in an entirely distant and high deity utterly indifferent to us made him a fairly obvious "bad" choice as a vehicle Christian's could readily appropriate in the development of philosophy. Plato was a far easier fit with Christian revelation, and more malleable anyway, as he was not didactic in his mode of communication. Consequently, while Aristotle is important for moral thinking and for logic, he was not typically drawn on for metaphysical or theological thinking by the developing intellectual culture of the ancient church. However, at the time when the West's cultural revival was adequate to the reception of the lost intellectual treasures of the past, it was Aristotle rather than Plato who was found. The reason it was Aristotle is that this was the thinker most fully embraced by the Islamic intellectual tradition, and that was a tradition with an expansive and sophisticated heritage of commentary on Aristotle which was greatly advanced beyond anything philosophically, mathematically, and scientifically available to the West. That is, the intellectual buzz was already with Aristotle at the time the West was ready for high learning again, and this gift was given to the West via largely Arabic scholars and via translations into Latin of Arabic versions of Aristotle's corpus.

The impact of this pre-Christian and distinctly pagan philosopher, via an advanced non-Christian intellectual culture, on the West was— and remains[18]—enormous. The question of how to keep faith and reason together became of central concern to the church authorities most closely connected with the universities (such as the Bishop of Paris). The medieval rapturous love of logic (the medieval period is the unsurpassed high age of logic in the West) was delighted with the rigor and beauty of Aristotle's thought, and yet there was a fear that if logic is of universal scope

18. See Rubenstein, *Aristotle's Children*.

then this would tie God himself into a sort of strict rational determinism so that he might not be free to be the sovereign of the universe in any meaningful way. In short, the recovery of Aristotle produced a profound theological crisis in a civilization that was unified and made coherent by theology, and that had a life-world that was fully tied in with its distinctive (that is Neoplatonist) theological vision of reality.

In 1277 the Bishop of Paris condemned a range of theological and philosophical stances, many of which were associated with Thomas Aquinas. For Thomas had been a keen advocate of incorporating Aristotle into Christian theology. Thomas believed that the Christian revelation and the Neoplatonist metaphysics of the church fathers were both robust enough in their truth to have nothing to fear from Aristotle, such that there must be a means of synthesizing the new knowledge into existing Christian theology, and thus expanding and strengthening Christian philosophy's scope and power. All that was needed was suitably subtle and expansive thought situated within firm religious piety and orthodox doctrine. Clearly the Bishop of Paris did not see things the same way. He was fearful that the new learning would blow apart the synthesis of faith and reason upon which the very life form of medieval Christendom depended for its unifying rational coherence.

And here is the interesting thing. Historically, the bishop was right about the fragility of the synthesis of faith and reason in his times. Yet, the vindication of this fear by subsequent historical trends does not mean that Thomas' approach to baptizing the new learning into Christian faith was incorrect. Even so, from the late thirteenth century on, faith and reason moved in different directions in Western culture until they became entirely notionally separable (even within the life of a single individual). And this separation is what was to make a Christian Neoplatonist view of reality so historically untenable to our high intellectual culture. But the division of faith and reason does not really get a powerful head of steam up within Western intellectual culture until the fourteenth century.

As already outlined, it was Duns Scotus and William of Ockham in the fourteenth century who gave us voluntarism, univocity of being, knowledge as representation, and a revived nominalism. Further, with Ockham we get the first proto-modern advocate of a distinct demarcation between the power appropriate to the authority of the church, and the power of secular authorities. This move to demarcate fields of knowledge and action—focused specifically around a polarity between what is sacred and what is profane—blossoms in the sixteenth century into the idea that not only is the church to stick to its discretely religious sphere, but, in effect, God also—and heaven, angles, devils, and hell—is to keep out of nature, which is properly the sphere of humanity. We thus get the idea of "pure nature" that is entirely naturalistic in the modern sense as well as being entirely demarcated from the realm of the "supernatural," which is somehow outside of nature.[19] Thus the cosmos is disenchanted and nothing within nature is beyond the knowledge and sovereign will of humanity. These enormous shifts of civilizational consciousness have had a profound impact on what it means to be Western. They enable faith and reason to become functionally autonomous from each other. They removed the civilizational coherence of ontological participation from Western culture. Over time these shifts ushered in modernity with its society of atomic individuals and its government by secular liberal politics and state-sanctioned violence. These moves also gave us value-neutral instrumental scientific power, unguided by any deep and coherent substantive view of wisdom. These made the economic amorality and spiritual banality of consumer society possible. In all, modernity was born in an intellectual environment where any deep integration of faith and reason was deemed regressive and oppressive and where the very notion of ontological participation made no sense at all, not only to the thought structures but equally to the operational norms of the modern life-world. So by and large Christian Platonism has survived only as nostalgic or horrific narrative memory traces of a now lost world,[20] either romanticized into fantasy or vilified into a heavily anti-Christian take on Western history in the retelling of our cultural past.[21]

19. The emergence of modernity between Ockham and Descartes is a highly complex and often little known area of study. One of the most accessible and insightful treatments of this period is by Louis Dupré, *Passage to Modernity*.

20. Peter Berger points out that the supernatural is the pornography of the modern mind. See chapter 17, "The Devil and the Pornography of the Modern Mind" in *Facing Up to Modernity*, 253–57. Thus there is a profound fascination with "occult" stories in our popular entertainment culture, and here nothing is more "sexy" than the devil. But in this arena the romantic nostalgia of an enchanted cosmos is combined with a horrific fascination with evil in a modern context that has no real means of understanding either transcendence or debasement, which still traces—just beyond our understanding—every feature of our actual existence.

21. Plato's texts have been recovered and revived in different ways in the West from the fifteenth century on; yet this influence has been overall a secondary influence whose insights have often been re-incorporated into a secularized "Aristotelian" nominalist realism, or "Platonism" has repeated the philosophical crudities of naïve medieval realism and been hard to delineate from magic, or "Platonism" has been

So the historical "accident" that caused the fall of Christian Platonism in Western intellectual culture was—very crudely stated—the vitality of Aristotelian thinking in Islamic culture at the time of the revival of a high intellectual culture in the West. That is what *did* happen, and that "explains" in historical terms why Christian Platonism fell into abeyance and has remained there for the past 800 years (though the actual process of tearing Western intellectual culture out of its Christian Neoplatonist metaphysical womb took about 400 years to reach a decisive completion). But the strength of the modern claim to the validity and vitality of abandoning the old medieval way is one that rests on the seventeenth-century scientific revolution. *Here* is where the claim that the modern world is one that steps out of superstition, speculation, and irrational violent authority and into truth, reason, and freedom is most forthrightly asserted; and it is not a claim that can be lightly set aside. But before moving to the seventeenth century, we must stop and briefly consider the most profound nature of the civilizational change that was going on across the "lost" period of Western philosophical history—the period from the early fourteenth century to the early seventeenth century.[22]

Arguably the most important aspect of the civilizational life-world transformation that accompanied the fading of Christian Platonism and the rise of proto-modern thinking is a truly seismic shift in the assumed relationship between knowledge (*scientia*) and wisdom (*sapientia*). As this shift is central to the triumphal truth narrative of modernity, this is

made into an "analytic" set of abstract intellectual propositions, remarkably hermeneutically and existentially out-of-step with the dialogues themselves. In my opinion, it is only very recently that we have seen promising Platonist metaphysical thinking in recognized philosophical circles (even though we have always had great thinkers who were *not* well philosophically recognized—such as C. S. Lewis, etc.—within the Christian Platonist tradition). Recognition of the philosophical seriousness of theology and work produced by the likes of William Desmond, David C. Schindler, Stuart Weierter, and Jacob Howland signal new possibilities in Platonist metaphysical thinking, which has had very little oxygen over the past five centuries since the works of Plato have been available to the West.

22. Charles Schmitt notes that the least understood period of the West's intellectual history is the most vibrant period of Aristotelian philosophy in Western history, which is the period that gave rise to Modernity. "The least studied period in the history of philosophy—and for the most part, in the history of science as well—are the years separating Ockham and Oresme from Galilei and Descartes. Thus about three hundred years of the Aristotelian tradition, during which intellectual activity was more intense, the publications more numerous than at any time before or since, have been largely overlooked" (Schmitt, *Aristotle and the Renaissance*, 3).

a shift that we need to understand well if we are to seriously consider the possibility that Christian Platonism might still be viable.

Knowledge and Wisdom

What is most decisive about the break of modernity with both Antiquity and the *via antiqua* within the medieval period is the rise of modernity's very distinctive understanding of the relationship between truth and interpretation. Modernists often describe this relationship as the difference *between* speculative metaphysical interpretation and objective truth, but such claims are somewhat disingenuous, thought the matter is by no means a simple one.

The overall sweep of this issue runs like this. When Neoplatonist metaphysical thinking was respectable in Western culture (from at least as early as the third century all the way up to the early seventeenth century) wisdom was prior to knowledge in relation to truth. This stance enabled a unified intellectual vision of the world where—in a predominantly Christian cultural context—an accepted and authoritative divine revelation was interpretively prior to philosophy, which was interpretively prior to science and to the application of various forms of knowledge (moral, socio-political, and technological). This outlook was premised on the idea that meaning and purpose are given to the cosmos as a whole, and to each being within the cosmos, by God. That is, it was a theologically grounded realist outlook (where transcendently referenced meaning is taken to be *real*).

One of the great narrative moments of disdain by modernity in relation to medievalism is when Galileo wrote to Kepler in 1610 and claimed that philosophers who opposed the astronomical evidence for the defects in a geocentric model of the cosmos would not even look through a telescope to see that evidence with their own eyes. (Now this comment does reflect a genuine resistance to Galileo's evidence-based theorizing, yet the historical facts are that the most serious scientific opponents of Galileo *did* study the heavens through telescopes carefully.) Thus the genesis narrative of modernity claims that medievalism judged truth by books, by doctrine, and by authority, without even looking at the facts, but modernity firstly looks at the facts and then thinks up theories about truth that seem to fit the facts, and then it constantly tests those theories against facts. The claim is that in medievalism, pre-determined theological and metaphysical visions of truth filter what facts we can see and determine in advance what theoretical meanings facts will have, whereas in modernity facts are observed objectively and then theories about their meaning are constructed and amended depending on whether the facts can be predictably explained by the theory or not.

Now the modern outlook would not be possible had not the process separating faith from reason been underway since the thirteenth century, and had not that process culminated in the seventeenth century in the potent desire to separate what we now call scientific knowledge not only from theology, but from philosophy too. So modernity is in fact a function of the uncoupling of knowledge (*scientia*) from wisdom (*sapientia*) in such a way as to give theoretical knowledge of nature a methodology that is considered both entirely independent of religious authority and that is also philosophically neutral, such that scientific truth has an objective relation to facts with no essential relationship to theological or philosophical meanings, and paying no deference to interpretive authorities. Let truth itself speak!

As will be explored in the next chapter, this stance has some profound internal difficulties as well as resulting in the remarkable cultural assumption that reality and nature *has* no objective meaning. And on the latter point, if we are part of nature, then we ourselves—and also our language, and indeed our knowledge—have no objective meaning. Thus modernity produces postmodernism as night follows day. And modernity has effectively killed theology and philosophy leaving us only with knowledge (if, that is, it has not also killed any real meaning for knowledge). Perhaps, even, *sapientia* has now largely died at the hands of modern *scientia*. If something like this has happened, this would explain why, culturally, we can only have cosmic meaning in the discretely subjective realm of fantasy or personal religious belief now.

Yet, it is the case that the Christian version of Aristotelian cosmology that was endorsed by the authority of the church in the early seventeenth century was simply *factually wrong* about the nature of the movement of the planets and the position of the sun in the solar system. So, we might plausibly ask, was not knowledge held back by religion and philosophy, and by violent and oppressive dogmatically framed politics until the scientific revolution? Has not modernity liberated us from superstitious and factually wrong theories about the nature and meaning of nature? And, has not modernity given us rational and powerful means of advancing the human situation that medievalism with its different understanding of the relationship between wisdom and knowledge could never have given us? Let us see if these questions can be briefly addressed in such a way as to keep a doorway to Christian Platonism open.

Truth and Objectivity

The twentieth-century Hungarian theoretical chemist Michael Polanyi observed himself doing groundbreaking science and came to a range of fascinating conclusions about how the practice of science actually works. [23] Polanyi observed that objective reality is one pole of the scientific quest for truth, and the language, prior knowledge, friendships, institutional politics, and cultural commitments of the interpretive community of scientists is the other pole. According to Polanyi, you must have both poles to do science. One of the points he is making here is that "objectivity" is not a simple and obvious notion. For example, by "objectivity" we might mean three things: (1) that objective reality is not concerned with qualitative meanings but is concerned only with what is simply quantitatively "there"; (2) objective reality is directly and simply accessible to us by sensory stimulation and logical analysis such that there are no complex interpretive issues for the methodologically good scientist, and; (3) that the objective observer of reality allows no prejudged values or beliefs to color his/her accurate description of that which is simply and objectively "there" in reality. But Polanyi notes that such an Obvious and Impartial notion of Objectivity (let us call it "OI Objectivity") is actually impossible and does not reflect what really goes on when scientists make important discoveries and come to significant theoretical breakthroughs. Note here that Polanyi is in no manner throwing out the notion of objective reality simply because every meaningful scientific interpretation of reality is always humanly situated, requires astonishing imaginative leaps (and, perhaps, inspiration), and draws on a rich culturally, historically, and communally formed set of relationships to meaningful knowledge. Rather, Polanyi is drawing our attention to the fascinating *actual* relationships that exists between reality and human knowledge such that linguistic, interpersonal, cultural, and political dynamics are always integral to the scientific quest for truth. Further, there is no reason to simply presuppose that objective reality is not inherently meaningful. Stated more stridently, one could say that the prior interpretive commitment to assuming reality is "merely" objective (valid knowledge is only quantitative and all qualities and interpretations are mere human glosses) is precisely the type of interpretive commitment that such a notion of objectivity denies.

---

23. See Polanyi's classic text, *Personal Knowledge*.

That is, interpretive mediation is not optional for *any* thinker—great or small—pondering the nature of reality. Thus when great thinkers reject one frame of interpretation, with its distinctive vision of what reality both means and is, they are taking up an alternative frame of interpretation rather than simply directly comprehending the naked objective truth. And, indeed, this is exactly what Galileo did. He rejected a specific metaphysically and theologically colored late medieval Aristotelian philosophy of nature as an interpretive frame through which to understand reality, and took up another interpretive frame; one that was also latent within the intellectual milieu of the late medieval university.

Abstract mathematical thinking became the interpretive frame Galileo used in order to understand truth about reality. Galileo's preferred interpretive frame functionally assumes that reducing reality to mathematically describable relations of mass and motion in time gives one a true understanding of reality that is not only entirely adequate to the task of true knowledge, but which, as true knowledge, is interpretively prior to all metaphysical and theological meanings. Thus an abstract knowledge of quantity, duration, force, and mass becomes the best knowledge of the real (that is, it functionally becomes "first philosophy") such that a meaning-denuded and abstract *scientia* is now set up to govern *sapientia*. Scientific facts are here determinative of what counts as valid wisdom.

So modernity tries to generate science out of merely quantitative and merely apparent "data." Further, if you want to derive wisdom from science, you can do that if you want a factually true wisdom, but whether you want to derive wisdom from knowledge or not is not a concern of the scientist. The scientist deals only in facts. This seemed like quite a reasonable project when modernity was young, because it in practice still assumed that culturally tacit theological and metaphysical meanings were still prior to the cold hard objective truths of science. Galileo and Descartes were Roman Catholics, Bacon was an Anglican; people generally assumed that the new science was still something that occurred within and about creation, even if one had to re-interpret and radically re-imagine the cosmos in a way that situated this new knowledge within the religious assumptions of Western culture. That is, early and high modernity tended to assume that scientific knowledge had metaphysical and theological meanings, even though its *methodology* (thanks to the gripping explanatory power of seventeenth-century pioneers of the scientific method, such as Galileo and Descartes) was explicitly blind to such meanings. Yet, as modernity matured it became harder and harder to integrate a scientific conception of factual knowledge with any serious set of recognizably theological and philosophical stances on meaning.

The great philosophers of modernity have grappled with meaning, purpose, morality, politics, transcendence, knowledge, logic, mind, God, life, death, and the nature and meaning of physical phenomena and have all come to stances where the logic of modernity short-circuits any richly meaningful substantive outcome. For where "objective scientific truth" is the master interpretive narrative that shapes modern philosophy then "mere" knowledge shapes and limits wisdom/philosophy/theology within modernity to its distinctive value and meaning blindness. Unsurprisingly, when we start with nothing, we get nothing as our finishing point. Where the fuel we want to run our interpretive engine on is "nothing," the meaning of reality becomes, unsurprisingly, the fabulously self-defeating erasure of meaning. So the philosophical dead ends of modernity are now somewhat celebrated by "postmodern" theorists. Given a meaningless view of objective reality, the problem is now how philosophy (or human existence) can have any meaning at all; so perhaps we don't need meaning and should celebrate meaninglessness?

The Fall of Christian Platonism in Overview

To return to the questions posed just before the above subheading, the officially endorsed physical understanding of the solar system upheld by the Roman Catholic Church at the opening of the seventeenth century was indeed in error, yet the matter is much more complex that the simple struggle between OI Objective truth and dogmatically authorized factual error. Let us see if we can unpack the complexity of this situation a little.

Modern science has some things really going for it. Firstly, modern science has respect for what is observably there in concrete reality such that our theoretical models stand subservient to that which is demonstrably observable. Secondly, the preparedness to assume that the logical structures of our own mathematical thinking accurately mirrors real order in the physical universe has enabled a methodology of knowledge-construction to flourish that *is* truly remarkable. Of course, key to scientific thinking is the conviction that knowledge is always a work in process such that even something as powerful and ongoingly valid as Newton's laws of physics are now not seen as the ultimate final truth about nature. Nature is such that the more we validly know about her, the more that knowledge indicates new secrets, and the more needing of revision our previous functional certainties require. So, strictly speaking, modern science does not give us truth, but it gives us working theories about nature that must have at least some purchase on natural reality, or else they would not be working theories that show a harmony between what we expect and what actually happens. (Yet, perhaps nature is always going to exceed our reasoning about her. Perhaps this indicates that nature is grounded in mysteries that are not accessible to that which is manifest within nature.) Clearly, however, modern science tells us things about observable physical reality that, if not *finally* true, are *functionally* true and, for the time being, they are the best understanding of physical necessities that we have.

In the early seventeenth century the Roman Catholic Magisterium saw itself as the embattled keeper of the flame of truth fighting the Reformation, and it was deeply committed to the validity of an integrative view of the cosmos where the wisdom discourses of theology and philosophy were foundational to the knowledge discourses that we would now call the natural sciences. This commitment was harmonious with the established and respected Aristotelian authorities within the universities at that time. However, by this stage the role of nominalism and univocity within the established wisdom trajectories, the fragmentation of Christendom, and the rise of a functional alliance between aristocratic power and a very practically interested merchant class was radically undermining Platonist metaphysical unities within the late medieval life form. In this context intellectual norms were changing as well. *Within* those norms, a nascent modern naturalist form of Aristotelianism was making it possible for innovators to become much more open to what we would now simply call a scientific outlook on reality. In this context, when the earth-centered cosmology that the Roman Catholic Magisterium set itself to theologically and metaphysically defend was later demonstrated to be factually false, this had far greater implications that simply the displacement of the church-endorsed geo-centric cosmology. Most significantly, the rise of modern science displaced the very priority of higher wisdom over immediate knowledge that had been part and parcel of the dominant Western intellectual tradition since the rise of classical philosophy until the seventeenth century. The crash of geo-centrism, ironically, thus became the final nail in the coffin for Christian Platonism.[24]

---

24. Before Copernicus, Ficino's Renaissance Platonism did support the cosmological priority of the sun over the earth, but that is another story we will briefly touch on in the next chapter.

So the fall of Christian Platonism crashes, like an unused grand piano, through a number of rotten downward floors until it goes right out the bottom of the modern Western mind and sinks (perhaps still tunefully) into the mud of the collective subconscious underneath that mind. The first fall down is via Abelard's attack on naïve realism. The second fall down is via the trend towards the parting of faith and reason after 1277. The third fall down is via Scotus and Ockham's highly influential innovations undercutting ontological participation, replacing divine reason and love with sovereign will, and demarcating religion from nature and power. The fourth fall is the sixteenth-century development of the idea of "pure nature" and the disenchantment of the cosmos. The fifth and final fall is via the scientific revolution of the seventeenth century where knowledge comes to interpret wisdom. Thus we see how it came to be that the central intellectual energies of the Western mind lost not only the instrument, but also the music of Christian Platonism. Yet, this was not seen as a loss to modernity, but rather as a liberation. But are we *really* liberated? Was it, perhaps, in fact a real loss? Even if it was a real loss, could this instrument now be recovered and could this music be played in a new key and with new developments suitable for our times? To these questions we will now turn.

7

Is Modern Truth, without Wisdom,
Believable?

In this chapter I will critique the modern notion of truth and endeavor to show that the Christian Platonist approach to truth is by no means an unreasonable or intrinsically dated alternative.

What Is a Modern Approach to Knowledge?

The Latin word *modernus* is derived from *modo*, meaning "just now." What distinguishes a modernist from some other type of thinker is not simply that they are here in the "just now"—for everyone is contemporary with their own day—but that they do not take authorities from the past too seriously. That is, if the knowledge of some past sage is no longer "up to date," then the modernist comfortably assumes that this is because our knowledge in the present is more advanced than the knowledge of the great sage of the past.

On the one hand, there is nothing novel about modernism. There have always been modernists questioning traditional verities in every age, and some of them were great innovators of true genius. And there have always been intellectual fashions that privilege certain contemporary approaches to understanding the world over older approaches that are seen as less up to date and thus less adequate. However, while there have always been modernists, there has not always been the modern *age*, modernity.

When we speak of modernity we are speaking of a particular approach to the past and the present that began to spread across Western European culture in the seventeenth century. The key feature of this civilizational turn towards the present is what is often called the scientific revolution; a revolution in knowledge. It is important to have a quick outline of how this revolution happened in order to understand what some of the deep civilizational assumptions regarding the nature of knowledge in the modern age are. So, very briefly . . .

Historical Background to the Scientific Revolution

In the sixth century the high learning of classical Greco-Roman civilization largely disappeared from Western Europe. However, traces of this learning survived and the cultural memory of a great Greco-Roman civilization endured. In the thirteenth century, via Arabic-speaking Islamic civilization, much of Aristotle's learning was recovered in the West. Two responses to this recovery were apparent. Firstly awe: in the thirteenth century there was nothing that came close in intellectual sophistication to Aristotle's science and philosophy. Secondly, a sort of intoxication with knowledge swept through Europe and the desire to follow the ancients and forge new passageways into unlocking the knowledge secrets of reality took off. So you can see tendencies towards revering ancient authorities (sometimes called the *via antiqua*) coincided with the desire to crunch things through for ourselves, possibly even displacing ancient authorities (sometimes called the *via moderna*). Both of these tendencies were undergirded by a sustained interest in and commitment to logic. For one of the very few complete systems of ancient knowledge to be passed on to the Middle Ages from Antiquity was Aristotle's logic. From the high Middle Ages to the seventeenth century Aristotle's philosophy and theology done in an Aristotelian key were added to Aristotelian logic, and thus Aristotle came to dominated the entire learning culture of the universities of Europe. By the seventeenth century Western Europe had a confident and advanced intellectual life centered in her universities, and the tensions between reverence for the past and the desire to get on with knowledge ourselves had combined with other things going on[1] such that the forces of innovation and recreation were set to burst the damn walls of continuity with the past.

In this context it is important to recall that the seventeenth- and eighteenth-century fathers of modern science and Enlightenment saw themselves—and indeed they were—as forward-looking explorers of

---

1. Notably the religious fragmentation of Europe after the Reformation, mercantilism and the beginnings of modern credit, conquest and colonial expansion outside of Europe, large scale war, the birth of the modern nation state, the peace of Westphalia, etc.

an entirely new terrain of knowledge and social organization. The traditions, authorities, and power structures of the past held them back, and they were set to break with that past and move forward. Thus the modern age our scientific and secular pioneers ushered in thinks of itself as being inherently *progressive*, *forward* looking, innovative, and self-confident. Thus the wisdom of the past and the authority structures embedded in that past are now more or less assumed to have been regressive, dated, superstitious, and intellectually moribund. Indeed, authorities connected to the pre-modern past are often seen as inherently deferential to beliefs that were grounded in mere tradition, in notions about reality that are simply not true, and in self-interested power games.

Just about any historical documentary that you watch on the TV retelling the early modern or medieval period has an assumed self-congratulatory (for us modernists) interpretive tweak to it where we can obvious pick out the courageous innovator who was ahead of their time battling the regressive yet powerful forces of ignorance, superstition, and tradition. Curious and intelligent innovators may have looked like dangerous quacks in their own superstitious times, but we can tell the difference between an alchemist leaning towards magic and a proto-scientist leaning towards objective truth. Thus the proto-modernist is the hero and the backward looking medievalist or the conservative bastion of established authority is the superstitious villain in the struggle to advance learning, heed reason, and secure modern liberties.

At this point what I am trying to spell out is the very strong sense in which the modern age defines itself as discontinuous with the West's medieval and classical past. And this discontinuity is not simply an objective fact of history, but this discontinuity has a ready-made interpretive slant to it where "old and traditional" is naturally assumed to be regressive and ignorant (and often oppressive) and "new and modern" is naturally assumed to be progressive, grounded in truth, and moving us towards liberty. We need to unpack the nature of the cultural meaning of this discontinuity a little further as it is profoundly entwined in "modern knowledge."

The Discontinuity of Modern Knowledge with the West's Classical and Medieval Past

A significant factor in why Christian Platonism is simply not considered to be a serious stance in the modern Age is the deep-seated cultural conviction that our age's rupture with the past is both irrevocable and unquestionably good. This, of course, does not amount to an argument, yet even so, sociologists of knowledge such as Peter Berger have well pointed out that the power of cultural assumptions of this nature typically constitute nine tenths of the iceberg beneath the visible polemics of any given (and inevitably culturally situated) argument.

As touched on in chapter 3, the mythos of modernity is very powerful. In fact, our re-telling of the seventeenth century typically situates the deep cosmological narratives of the present age in nothing short of biblical terms. That is, Bacon, Galileo, Descartes, and Newton are our Moses figures leading us in an extraordinary exodus out from slavery in Egypt (our classical and medieval heritage). In this great rupture, this great exodus, the innovators of our new scientific truth-discourse define us as a new people and lead us into a new land, and it is the land of freedom. Further, after the waters of the past have closed over on the powers and life-world of our former era, there is simply no way back.

So we have come to believe a cultural meta-narrative where what we call the scientific revolution stands as a sharp historical division separating the modern world from the past and orientating us towards the future. This explains something of why we are so convinced of the tacit cultural narrative of progress. Medieval Aristotelianism got us so far, but it was simply wrong about cosmology, gravity, and purpose, so when we cut our ties with an authoritative late medieval Aristotelianism we had superseded the ancients and could learn nothing more from the past. Further, it is taken as given that we have a better criterion of truth than the ancients and the medievals, so we are able to work out what reality is really like now in ways that the ancients could not. While we appreciate that there were great thinkers in the ancient past, they were not scientific thinkers in the modern sense, and hence, they did not really understand reality. Our conception of scientific knowledge as universally and demonstrably true, and true above all metaphysical and theological claims to knowledge, means that we read even truly great past thinkers as having a rather credulous or even infantile conception of reality in comparison to us. Thus, while we think that Plato was a great sage we regard his ideas about intangible ideal forms to be weird and funny *because* such notions are not scientifically verifiable. For any modern person knows that knowledge can only be considered to be true if its object can be defined in scientific terms. So any normal modern person has a better grasp of truth than a great sage from the past such as Plato. Obviously we have a more advanced knowledge of reality than pre-scientific people. And this is obvious because we can fly planes, make nuclear bombs, eradicate polio, and explore space with our knowledge; things none of the ancients or non-Western peoples of the earth could do before us.

The modern age has no time for any knowledge claim that is not "up to date." Rather, so strong is our conception of valid knowledge within our own age's understanding of science that we view all mythologies, all religious claims, all non-Western approaches to medicine and reality through the lens of our science. Our lens is—we assume—the true lens, and other approaches to truth and meaning may have value, but their *true* value can only properly be apprehended via the vision of modern Western science.

Thus the scientific revolution of the seventeenth century is, to us, a momentous leap forward in the cultural and epistemic evolution of humanity, and this leap is also a great wall forever separating modernity from the rest of human history. We have knowledge; they only had stories. We have truth; they only had intuitive speculations—some of which were remarkably lucky (such as the speculations of the ancient atomists about the nature of matter and reality), most of which were fairytales. We have power; they only had magic. We have science; they only had religion. So a modernist is convinced—or simply assumes—that only modern scientific knowledge is valid knowledge, and any claim to knowledge that is not modern is not up to date and there is no point in even considering whether it could be a better knowledge claim than our science could make.

The assumed superiority of modern scientific knowledge over any sort of pre-modern conception of the nature of reality is not mere hubris, but is premised on the astonishing explanatory power of a very distinctive understanding of the nature of knowledge. Specifically, as already pointed out, modern thinkers maintain that scientific and objective knowledge has a truth criterion that is autonomous from the claims of religion and wisdom. Conversely, this implies that religious and wisdom claims that wish to be respected as knowledge claims about the real world must pass muster under the truth criteria of scientific knowledge, and that the claims of religion and wisdom that cannot pass muster under the bar of scientific knowledge are not knowledge claims, but are mere belief claims to which the standards of true knowledge cannot apply. To us modernists, there seems nothing terribly controversial about such an outlook, but the fact is, this is the most revolutionary feature of the scientific revolution. Here we are talking about the de-coupling of *scientia* (knowledge) from *sapientia* (wisdom) and the uncoupling of both scientific knowledge and philosophical wisdom from *revelatio* (revelation). In a genuinely unprecedented cultural move, the scientific revolution is a function of the dis-integration of human thought and the unleashing of extraordinary instrumental power that results from locating demonstrable and applicable truth only in a reductively scientific frame of reference. After the modern age we can no longer think with mind, body, and spirit as an integral unity, or with community and individual as unified in religious categories that transcend both. Our view of reality is now explicitly fragmented and structurally resistive to any attempt at an integrated vision or a transcendently referenced common good.

Modern Knowledge Is Autonomous from Wisdom and Revelation

Like so many other significant structural features of modernity, the de-coupling of knowledge from wisdom, and both from revelation, has a long backstory that starts deep within medieval theology. Controversies over the nature of the relationship between faith and reason and the relationship between ecclesial authority and temporal power greatly exercise the late medieval period and increasingly integration gave way to demarcation. This long process—strikingly accelerated by the Reformation—is the cultural back-story to the move to cut knowledge off from wisdom altogether that the pioneers of the seventeenth century set in motion.

We will focus in on the uncoupling of knowledge from wisdom in the seventeenth century, though the demarcation of sacred authority from temporal power and divine revelation from natural philosophy cannot be isolated from this uncoupling.

At least two powerful historical factors gave force to the origins story of modernity being constructed in terms of the uncoupling of knowledge from wisdom.

Firstly, the coupling of wisdom and knowledge within the theologically framed Aristotelian university was an obvious and established opposition to the new autonomous, experimental, and instrumental science that Bacon, Galileo, and Descartes were formulating. In the early seventeenth century no university had science faculties, rather what we now call science operated under the umbrella of natural philosophy. Further, even by the early seventeenth century, natural philosophy was typically situated in a subservient place to the master discourse of the medieval university, theology. To "just do science" without one's theories and experiments having to pass muster under philosophical and theological bars, one had to largely operate outside of the officially recognized avenues of professorial learning. Even so, most intellectuals attracted to promoting the new "physico-mathematical experimental learning"[2] were in the academic orbit—often physicians and parsons.

Secondly, powerful mercantile, aristocratic, and religious forces (Reformed/Puritan/Nonconformist) stood to gain much in terms of freedom and wealth from the erosion of established ecclesial authority.[3] From as early as the great mercantile city states of the fourteenth century, feudal society, with its distinctive balances of international religiously authorized power and its distinctive forms of social stratification, was relentlessly giving way to new urban and national centers of wealth and power. Moving forward to the sixteenth century, Erasmus' Greek New Testament was enormously important for the Reformation. With access to the original sources, the "plain meaning" of Scripture, facilitated by the careful scholarly exegesis of original texts, came into conflict with ecclesial power and the authority of Rome. Reformers were so bold as to interpret biblical texts in such a manner that came to grate violently with the fabulous wealth, power, and debauchery of sixteenth-century Rome. So the liberation of the interpretation of Scripture from Roman ecclesial authority, appealing to a view of truth that was above earthly religious authorities, was already deeply imprinted on Europe from the sixteenth century. This notion of a passionate commitment to evidentially construed conceptions of truth—that is truth as non-authorized, non-scholastically sophisticated, and immediately evident—carried much of the life and death idealism mingled with the rivers of blood spilt in the horrifying pogroms and religiously framed wars characteristic of Europe from the Reformation till the peace of Westphalia.[4]

2. This is the description of what the Royal Society of London was set up to do in 1660, inspired by Francis Bacon's *New Atlantis*.

3. Note: it is certainly the case that many Calvinist and Reformed polities constructed theocracies that were far more invasive and complete than anything Roman Catholicism ever tried or even thought of, yet these Protestant theocracies were all built on the doctrine of a fallible earthly church and the authority of Scripture above the authority of official institutional interpretation. So the criterion of truth was in that sense autonomous from the deliberations of any established ecclesiological institution, including their own.

4. William Cavanaugh's reading of the "wars of religion" is significant and very

Thus those who initiated the scientific revolution do not stand in isolation from powerful forces that coincided to make it not only possible, but also highly attractive, to think of knowledge as autonomous from wisdom. So when we come to Galileo, Bacon, and Descartes, we see a clear tacit commitment to the autonomy of true knowledge from the wisdom discourses of Aristotelian philosophy, and the autonomy of science from the marriage of Christian doctrine with medieval Aristotelian philosophy—though none of these three saw themselves as opponents of established religion.

Let us look more closely at how this new and autonomous knowledge of nature—what came to be called science—was conceived.

Modern Science as a Particular Understanding of Scientia

In order to understand what is genuinely unique about modern science, as a distinctive way of knowing truth, we must seek to suspend our modern naturally assumed triumphalist interpretive outlook on the history of the scientific revolution. For as long as we accept the normal modern interpretation of the positive meaning of the scientific revolution without question, we will be blind to our own very powerful interpretive bias. In order to gain a larger interpretive perspective on the scientific revolution than an uncritically modern outlook allows, I am going to draw on three very helpful sources: Thomas Kuhn's sociological analysis of the history of the Copernican revolution, Michel Henry's distinctive phenomenological understanding of Galileo's physico-mathematical reduction, and Lloyd Gerson's argument about the ongoing contemporary relevance of ancient epistemology.

---

interesting, and his central claim is that the wars that coincided with the rise of nationalistic power and the demise of Catholic Christendom have been used to justify the claims of the secular nation state to a supreme right to violence. (See Cavanaugh, *The Myth of Religious Violence*.) Cavanaugh's arguments give much-needed finesse to the all too simplistic narrative of the triumph of secular political peace and reason over barbaric religious violence in the peace of Westphalia, yet just as it is false to read "the wars of religion" as only being about religion, equally it is false to read them as not being about religion at all (not that Cavanaugh does that). Certainly the notion of a careful yet "plain meaning" interpretation of biblical authority, as standing over ecclesial authority, and the notion that truth is autonomous from all earthly powers, is a vital component of the Reformation, and this notion does indeed form a significant background to the scientific revolution.

Kuhn on the Copernican Revolution

Thomas Kuhn's landmark text *The Copernican Revolution* maps the long passage from Copernicus' initial postulate of a heliocentric solar system (where the earth goes around the sun) in 1543, to its eventual acceptance in Western Europe via Newton's mathematical exposition of the motion of heavenly bodies in 1687.[5] Kuhn points out that no scientific conception of reality is ever simply factual, as the meaning of facts is always situated in a broader cultural context and all theories are formulated within communities of scholars where an authorized conceptual paradigm gives order to phenomena such that the meaning of observations is primed and shaped by the consensus of the respected scholarly community of that day. For this reason fundamental shifts in the interpretation of facts do not happen quickly.

What was most striking about Kuhn's argument when it was put forward in 1957 is that Kuhn was claiming that there is nothing inherently different about how knowledge-construction is done now to how it was done before the Copernican revolution. Further, there are no real villains and heroes in the way in which ideas change, and reason and observation were not obviously or indisputably on the side of the Copernican innovators at the time. Further again, there are no assurances that at least some of the rock solid "truths" of the science of today will not prove to be components of a dead knowledge paradigm at some point in the future. To Kuhn, thinking progresses within an interpretive paradigm until that paradigm is no longer able to make sense of what it is explaining. With the benefit of hindsight, we can see that the geo-centric paradigm established by Ptolemy (where the sun goes around the earth) was functionally valuable and intellectually satisfying for a very long time, but that it started to be unable to interpret the world effectively for the learned class with Copernicus. Yet this was not apparent to many of the most able thinkers of Copernicus' day. So who knows which of our current theories about reality, theories that we hold to be factual, are already falling over? Perhaps it might also take 150 years or so for some current paradigm to "hit the wall" as it were, and for some contemporary outsider (who is now considered to be a crackpot) to be the great innovator ahead of their time.

There are two points I want to make here from Kuhn's work. Firstly, Kuhn gives us a very sensitive modern reading of the scientific revolution, which is atypical of modern readings precisely because it does not

5. Kuhn, *The Copernican Revolution.*

buy into the hagiographic mythos of modern truth. Secondly, Kuhn's reading is a modern reading in the most revolutionary sense precisely where Kuhn has no awareness of how strongly he is carrying the separation of wisdom and revelation from knowledge with him in his project. The first point concerns Kuhn's very real success in being far more historically aware and far more interpretively fair than the more culturally typical simplistic and biased narrative tropes about the origins of modernity. But the second point is particularly useful in spelling out exactly what the turn to knowledge (and away from wisdom and revelation) in the seventeenth century actually means.

Kuhn employs an approach to history that assumes methodological atheism. This approach sits within the phenomenological trajectory of Husserl. Here, openness to trying to understand any given perceived phenomena must "bracket out" any non-experienced and conjectured belief about what causes any given phenomena, or about what transcendent "reality" lies beneath or beyond any given phenomenological "appearance." Husserl is, in turn, influence by Kant in arriving at this approach to our attempts to make sense of the realm of experienced appearances. Kant famously distinguished between things-in-themselves (*noumena*) and things-as-we-experience-them (*phenomena*). Kant was persuaded that we only ever know our experience of things (we only ever know the world of phenomena) and we never know things as they are in themselves (i.e., everything we know we know as an experience). This means that truth is a function not of a certain and correct correlation between my ideas and the world "out there," but all knowledge occurs "in here," in our conscious awareness of experienced phenomena. So when it comes to getting valid knowledge Kant thinks there are only two sources. Firstly, there are the internal necessary structures of our mind—and these are where we get rational "a priori" formal certainties from—and secondly there is the phenomenal manifold of our experience, where we get empirical "a posteriori" substantial content from. That is, we always structure our experience of the world within the formal categories of space and time; these are prior ("a priori") givens in how we experience things. But the sensory content of *what* we experience—I see the cat sitting on the mat, for example—come after ("a posterior") the simple sensations of visual perception have been structured and meaningfully processed by my a priori perceptional framework, which enables me to make sense of the world. Structure and content are always combined in our consciousness, and certain knowledge (of the working and content *of our consciousness*) can be had only if we carefully understand what the necessary structures of our mind's ordering of experience really entails. Note, we cannot know reality in-itself, as it is "outside" of our consciousness (for knowledge is exclusively a function of our *conscious experience* of the world). So anything that claims to be valid knowledge must abandon speculation regarding noumenal reality and limit its scope to the necessary rational structures of our consciousness and to the phenomenal content of experienced appearances. In arriving at this sense of sure knowledge Kant is combining the Rationalist and the Empiricist trajectories of eighteenth-century philosophy and he is seeking to solve the foundational problem of modern philosophy, which is how to get certain knowledge of the world as we experience it. Rationalists tended towards the view that reason and thought were avenues within the thinker to a true grasp of noumenal and even transcendent reality. Empiricists tended towards the view that experience is of reality (to us, there is no reality other than that of sensory appearances), yet experience is only rational and objective by convention. Kant saw both of these approaches as fundamentally inadequate on their own. Rationalism leaned too far towards the indemonstrable speculative conjecture Kant called metaphysics. Empiricism leaned too far towards seeing phenomena as a merely subjective stream of apparent contingencies. But a careful combination of Rationalism and Empiricism would put, so Kant thought, modern knowledge on a sure footing that was both reasonable and scientific. Regardless of whether Kant actually solved the problem of modern knowledge or not, for now what I want you to notice is that what Kant is explicitly doing here is *isolating knowledge from metaphysics and religion* and trying to make knowledge stand up as self-justifying in its own terms. And indeed, this is the great (and, I think impossible) challenge of modern philosophy.

Back to Kuhn. In taking a broadly Kantian look at the Copernican revolution through the eyes of our experience of historical phenomena, the theories we can construct out of historical knowledge are not actually about the true meaning of what really happened, and historical knowledge itself is not finally about what really happened. For our knowledge is always situated within human consciousness, and is always, finally, about human consciousness. Kuhn understood better than Kant that human consciousness is as much a function of culture, history, language, politics, economics, religion, art, entertainment, and sheer contingency and accident as it is a function of the rational structures of the mind and the apparent meaning of the way the mind structurally orders our experiences.

So "science," to Kuhn, has no unique epistemic privilege as some master truth discourse that tells you how things *really* are in the way that, say, religion or magic does not. Science is a function of human consciousness that is not above, but is integral with, every other aspect of human consciousness and its extraordinarily rich socio-cultural situation. And yet . . . ! Kuhn is a modernist. Kuhn understands every knowledge input as sensory phenomena such that wisdom and divinity are functions of human consciousness and human consciousness cannot be a function of divine wisdom.

Let me underscore this. Even though to Kuhn there is no fundamental distinction between the geo-centric cosmological paradigm of pre-Copernican medieval thinking, as an intelligent and meaningful system of interpretive knowledge, and our post-Copernican heliocentric cosmological paradigm,[6] the idea that you could understand cosmology today as a function of theological truth simply does not occur to Kuhn. Metaphysics and theology have been bracketed out from knowledge. Methodological atheism has been applied. Or rather, metaphysics and theology have been subsumed within a view of knowledge that is itself not metaphysically or theologically framed. This is the real heart of the modern scientific revolution. This is the nature of knowledge within modernity.

We will return to this later, but here I want you to see that because a knowledge of the true meaning of reality is excluded from the revolutionary modern understanding of truth, which is anchored firstly to knowledge itself, we are committed to a fundamental relativism in truth discourses, and we are committed to a fundamental ignorance of reality. Now both of these commitments are profoundly self-defeating. Firstly, according to fundamental relativism a genuinely transcendently referenced understanding of reality—an outlook where divinity reveals truth

6. This is a bit complex. Kuhn claims he is not a relativist and indeed he obviously does hold that the heliocentric understanding of the solar system is true whereas the geocentric outlook was false. Objective reality itself has a significant role to play in Kuhn's understanding of science. Even so, because he correctly takes all knowledge to be interpreted by people who live in and do "science" within richly human, historically and culturally situated contexts, and because he is—without any justification that I am aware of—explicitly agnostic about any divine/transcendent source to any true meaning of reality, the human world is the entire context of interpretation such that objectivity itself is by itself no guarantee of truth. For only the existence of true meaning could make human interpretation at least partially or analogically aligned with true knowledge. Thus Kuhn the agnostic is a relativist—and, ironically, a dogmatic relativist—no matter how much he protests to the contrary.

to humanity in some form or another—should be treated as no less true than a scientific view of reality. Which is to say that they should both be seen as functions of human consciousness that cannot provide us with a true knowledge of reality as it is in itself. However, revelational approaches to truth claim to exceed the limits of human consciousness, and these claims—apparently on the basis of the merely asserted truth that the apparent world known by our consciousness is the only knowable world—we modernists simply "know" to be false. That is, Kuhn does not uphold a real relativism where the truth claims of revelation are taken just as seriously as the truth claims of phenomenal science. Kuhn's relativism is not genuine. Secondly, as this shows, Kuhn's absolutism is a profound commitment to a fundamental ignorance of reality. But fundamental ignorance is a self-defeating notion because if it is true then you could not know that it was true, and if you cannot know that it is true, then what makes you so sure that you really cannot have true knowledge?

Kuhn well illustrates the aspect of the scientific revolution that I want to bring to the fore here. Knowledge has been separated out from wisdom and revelation and made to be the master discourse of modernity. This starts to really take off, culturally, in the seventeenth century, and it is really the *instrumental power* that the new mathematico-experimental knowledge we now call science unleashed, rather than any philosophical merit, that affected this astonishing cultural revolution. We can now separate our understanding of how something "works" from questions about how we should use our knowledge and what God's intended purposes in nature are. Philosophically, making mere knowledge its own truth criteria has always been profoundly problematic, and indeed (surprise, surprise) Plato pointed out quite some time ago that this is an impossible enterprise.[7] But let us look a bit closer at the nature of modern knowledge, turning now to Michel Henry's fascination examination of modernity's physico-mathematical reduction.

Michel Henry on Truth as Physico-mathematical Reduction

Michel Henry has a profound understanding of the manner in which modern knowledge defines truth in objective, scientific, and pragmatic terms, separating truth out from wisdom and revelation. The shorthand term he

7. See Plato, *Theaetetus*. For a very helpful commentary on this astonishingly perceptive dialogue on the nature of knowledge, see Burnyeat, *The Theaetetus of Plato*.

uses for the modern abstracting of truth from meaning and sacredness is "Galilean science." He does this for good reasons even though his understanding of the effects of the modern approach to knowledge is not a critique of the value of modern scientific knowledge itself, nor is it grounded in a close historical analysis of the early modern period. In order to show why "Galilean science" is a valuable term—but also what Henry does and does not mean by it—we will start this section off by a quick historical peek at Galileo.

The early decades of the seventeenth century at the centers of learning in Padua, Venice, and Florence were times of sustained intellectual astonishment. These worlds of learning were then abuzz with Galileo's mathematics, his carefully calibrated analysis of motion, his improved observations of heavenly bodies, his insistence on the autonomy of quantitative science from qualitative philosophy, and both from theology, and his powerful down-to-earth advocacy of new theories about natural phenomena and the workings of the observable cosmos. Further, his telescopes and navigational calculations were of very direct military and economic interest to the wealthy and powerful men of action in Europe.

It is near impossible for us to grasp the excitement and apprehension, the opportunities and uncertainties, the turmoil and possibilities of the atmosphere of that time. This was a time when the Thirty Years' War wracked Europe, when the disruption of the culturo-religious unity of pre-Reformation Europe was no longer something that might pass but that unity had become an unattainable memory, and when powerful national, imperial, papal, and Islamic military forces were on the move jostling each other for supremacy. In trade and conquest this was an era when the colonization and pillage of the Americas, accompanied by a massive influx of plundered gold into Europe, shifted balances of power, propelled colonial rivalry amongst European nations, and gave impetus to the re-investment culture of early modern capitalism. Due to intense maritime activity, the world was suddenly much bigger for the restless and power-hungry Europeans who were now bent on the mastery of nature and the conquest of the peoples of the entire globe. Concerning philosophy and theology, this was a time when the very framework of familiar and assumed reality was being torn down and re-built, when the implications and final meanings of new ideas were entirely unknown, and when astonishing new discoveries were being uncovered and age-old horizons were being superseded on a regular basis.

In natural philosophy (what we now call science), momentum for change was produced by the great centers of learning that were, nevertheless, still embedded in decidedly medieval patterns of contemplation and purpose. Galileo, though he certainly was a mathematician, and not an expert in philosophy, and not a theologian, comes entirely from within the academic establishment of his day. For example, in 1588, as a promising young mathematician, Galileo had addressed the Florentine Academy on the location and size of hell, working with the cosmology Dante had incorporated into his *Divine Comedy*. During the 1580s Galileo was entirely within the Christian Aristotelian mainstream of Catholic Italy regarding the philosophically and theologically endorsed view of nature and the role of mathematics within the study of nature. Here, mathematics was formally important but substantially subordinate to philosophy and theology. But as a mature figure, and as a thinker who had a native persuasive power coupled with a genuine independence of thought, Galileo came into sharp disagreement with many of the revered Aristotelian experts of his day. His clash with philosophers—who correctly saw him as fundamentally challenging the very foundations of an Aristotelian understanding of nature—got him tangled with church authorities at a time when Pope Paul V was determined to damp down contention and innovation within the Catholic Church. This was a time when the central authorities of the Roman Catholic Church saw themselves as besieged by a sea of hostile forces seeking to dislodge them from their God-given place at the center of Western culture, power, and life. Indeed, the consolidation of the Reformation in the political and intellectual life of Europe combined with the Roman Catholic response to the fragmentation of the Christian faith in the West after Luther and Henry VIII are the most significant macro-cultural features of the early seventeenth century. In ways that we cannot here more than lightly touch, this religious context is crucial in the dynamics giving rise to and shaping the trajectory of the scientific revolution.

One of the pivotal religious dynamics directly impinging on the way in which Galileo was received by Rome concerned the Council of Trent's determination that the private interpretation of Scripture was forbidden to Roman Catholics.[8] This move was in direct counter to the Protestant approach to reading the Scripture. The Protestant claim to Christian legitimacy—and the grounds of authority appealed to in their critique

---

8. See Pope Paul III, "Decree Concerning the Edition and Use of the Sacred Books," Council of Trent, Session IV, 8 April 1546.

of what they saw as the apostasy of the Roman Catholic Church—was derived from the notion that the "plain meaning" of the Scriptures was accessible to any careful reader who, in good faith, studiously opened the Scripture and sought the direct illumination of the Holy Spirit.[9] Thus the appeal to "personal" authority, particularly against established authority, was something seen in a very touchy light. Galileo could be made to look quite "Protestant" in his approach to natural philosophy for he really was appealing to the plain meaning of the evidence of the senses as interpreted by one individual in defiance of the authorized wisdom of the day.[10] Because Galileo could not be defeated on his own terms—simple and direct appeal to the obvious meaning of the senses, as interpreted by merely quantifiable mathematical logic—his philosophical opponents sought to have him silenced by theological means. Thus the philosophers who most vociferously opposed Galileo did not find it difficult to persuade high-ranking theologians that the Copernican theory—taken as anything other than an abstract speculative device—was in contravention to the properly authorized interpretation of the teaching of Scripture about the rising and setting of the sun. Thus Galileo's observational and mathematical support of Copernicus' heliocentrism constituted a private interpretation of Scripture that was not authorized by the church. At a

---

9. Note: the Roman Catholics saw the schismatic tendency of Protestantism—well illustrated not only in their relation to Rome, but in their fractious relations with each other—as derived from a lack of an authoritative interpretive center in their reading of Scripture. That is, there is no single "plain meaning" for many important passages of Scripture, hence authoritative interpretation is required. Because the Protestants did not have the apostolic authorization that would enable them to receive the correct interpretation of the meaning of Scripture from the Holy Spirit (given to the church— i.e., the See of Peter), this is why they had departed from the truth and were full of schism and heresy. The Protestants, on the other hand, saw some obviously scandalous abuses of authority, some obvious departures from the very clear and direct teachings of the New Testament, and appeals to blind trust in authority over obvious evidence that the authority was wrong as illustrating to anyone who had eyes to see that the very human and sinful protection of institutional privilege and power was hiding behind Rome's advocacy of its divine authorization. So, without getting too tangled up here, it seems pretty fair to claim that both sides have some good points to make, and some serious internal difficulties. This probably accounts for how deeply contested Catholic and Protestant claims and counter claims were at that time.

10. Though, Protestants, starting with Luther, were decidedly more antagonistic to Copernicus than the teaching authorities at Rome were until the early seventeenth century. Indeed—again, dripping with irony—the Protestant basis of rejecting Copernicus was a "plain reading" of Scripture, the very reason Roman Catholic theologians took up against Copernicus and Galileo in the early seventeenth century.

time of great contention, including sustained violent conflict, it was not hard to get the Pope to treat Galileo as just one more threat to the stability and unity of the Roman Catholic faith. As one scholar of Galileo notes:

> [In the early seventeenth century, a] principle area of contention between Catholics and Protestants was freedom to interpret the Bible. . . . A dispute between the Dominicans and the Jesuits over certain issues of free will was still fresh in [Paul V's] mind, as he had taken action in 1607 to stop members of the two great teaching orders from hurling charges of heresy against each other. These things suggest that Paul V, if not temperamentally anti-intellectual, had formed a habit of nipping in the bud any intellectual disputes that might grow into factionalism within the Church and become a source of strength for the contentions of the Protestants.[11]

The papacy at this time had a strong desire to try and keep the status quo stable within Catholicism, and thus avoid internal contention and factions. Conveniently, then, Aristotelian philosophers who opposed Galileo's science and its cosmological and philosophical implications found this papal desire to support the traditional status quo amenable to their intention to simply quash Galileo. Thus high-ranking theologians attacked Galileo on the grounds of a breach of authorized biblical interpretation and did not even enter into debate regarding the philosophical and scientific merits or defects of Galileo's work. Thus in 1616 Copernicus' heliocentric model was deemed heresy—regardless of what telescopic evidence Galileo might put forward—and the same approach was later used against Galileo himself in his subjection to the Inquisition in 1633. Interestingly, it took the Vatican until 1992 to concede that it had taken a wrong turn in relation to Galileo on this matter, though the 1992 papal commission on Galileo still found the Italian scientist to have genuinely been in theological error.

That is enough background regarding Galileo and natural philosophy in the early seventeenth century. Here are the significant issues for this argument about the nature of modern knowledge.

After the rise of the Western university and prior to the scientific revolution, the dominant outlook of the Western intelligentsia held that practical and "this world concerned" knowledge was—while obviously useful—less inherently valuable than the wisdom of philosophy and the truth of divine revelation. Further, sensory knowledge was considered

11. Drake, *Galileo*, 63.

to be not only ontologically derivative, but also interpretively dependent on the prior truth frameworks of theology and philosophy. Scripture and the church were at the center of learning in medieval culture because the higher truth disciplines—theology and philosophy—were kept in the truth by the rule of the right interpretation of divine revelation as given to Christendom by the teaching authority of the church. That is, truth was seen as providentially embedded in an ordained hierarchy that emanated, for all human purposes, from the central teaching authorities of the head of Christ's church on earth, the Bishop of Rome. Before the Reformation, the Roman Catholic Church was pretty convincing as The Universal Church as far as Western Europe was concerned, so the maintenance of a relative unity within a dynamic plurality of bishops, priests, orders, intellectuals, saints, laity, social classes, secular authorities, cities, and racial groupings was, if not an accomplished fact, at least a relatively stable governing ideal. The Reformation changed all that most profoundly. The civilizational connection between the right order of a providential hierarchy and the authority structures of established visible human institutions was breaking down. In a sense truth was being liberated from a complex mediating structure of human institutions and truth was being uncoupled from the coherence of an integrated civilizational life form. The vision of the cosmos in medieval Christendom was deeply integrative. Here meaning, knowledge, value, belief, immanence and transcendence, work and holiday, community and the individual could all be conceived of within a coherent yet dynamic unity. This unity started to give way to a life form that became (after the rise of modern political liberalism) premised on a deep commitment to fragmentation, pluralism, and individualism in the realm of value and meaning. Here the deep common meaning ties to qualitative and human truth were being undone and replaced with common meaning ties to truth that were to become, in the end, almost entirely quantitative and objective. We see here a radical shift from a *qualitative* civilizational unity where truth is tied to wisdom and revelation and embedded in the concrete human realities of lived existence, to a *quantitative* civilizational unity, where truth is tied to science and is embedded in abstract mathematical and objective categories. This shift is what Michel Henry identifies with the scientific revolution, which is to say, with "Galilean science."

There was an order of interpretive and integrative authority structuring the medieval life form. At the top of this order the church is the guardian of revealed and orthodox doctrine and presides over the correct interpretation of Scripture. At the next level of authority under the church there is valid theology, which stands over valid philosophy, which stands over a useful knowledge of the natural harmonies and purposes of creation. This structure has feedback processes in it and had regions of relative autonomy within it, but it remained structurally hierarchical, seeing these human hierarchies as reflecting divine order. Galileo defied this chain of hierarchy and this qualitative and hierarchical vision of reality. Galileo insisted that a valid knowledge of nature should not be determined by anything other than quantitative objective observation and a sound grasp of purpose-blind and value-neutral mathematical natural laws.

Once quantitative mathematical natural knowledge is granted autonomy from revelation, theology, and philosophy, then one of two things can happen. The priority of revelation and wisdom over natural knowledge can be upheld, whilst upholding the freedom of science. Or, science can become the sole criteria of truth, and revelation and wisdom can effectively sit under the authority of science. When Michel Henry talks of Galilean science, he is talking about this later shift. That is, in "Galilean science" *truth* becomes reduced to quantitative mathematical knowledge. Such "truth" has no understanding of quality, no understanding of meaning, and is constructed in terms of objects (not subjects), quantities (not qualities), extrinsic relations (not intrinsic relations), and purely mechanistic and formulaic notions of universality (not free and ontological notions of universality). Further, this abstract knowledge is manipulatively useful, but the use of merely manipulative knowledge is also an abstract type of use, for it filters moral and sacred considerations out of the categories of use, as if people can act without moral or religious implication.

Henry maintains that primary forms of truth are philosophical and theological because these are non-abstract forms of truth that are intrinsically integral to the real life situations of existing people. But when an abstract and instrumental conception of knowledge comes to define truth, this is the Galilean reduction that Henry so carefully calls barbarism. Henry has seen how modern scientific knowledge has hoisted its notion of extrinsic certainty and instrumental validity onto the very idea of truth, and has displaced the non-abstract human realm of meaning from the notion of truth. The Galilean reduction has thus constructed an abstract, value-free, and "objective" notion of truth, and this modern truth works powerfully towards the destruction—ultimately—of not only our humanity but of knowledge and of the very idea of truth as well.

To clarify, Henry finds modern science, and the technological use of this knowledge to be—when properly understood—valid and highly powerful, but this type of knowledge is only properly understood when we bear in mind that it is an abstract and secondary form of knowledge that is not self-justifying. Yet if we use the abstract, merely instrumental, and existentially derivative conception of scientific truth as the standard of truth itself, and then judge the knowledge of wisdom and revelation by the criteria of modern science, then we are destroying culture, real life, and real meaning, and this is the essence of what Henry describes as the great barbarism of our day.

According to Henry, the process of barbarism becomes possible with the seventeenth-century scientific revolution, but does not really get into the air culturally until this outlook causes the industrial revolution. Barbarism becomes civilizational via modern production and modern economics:

> When production *became economic* and acted for the sake of making money—that is to say, when an economic reality took the place of goods useful for life and designated for it—the entire face of the world was changed. . . . Production changes altogether once it is the production of money and no longer of use value. . . . [This replacing of human realities with an inhuman and mechanical logic can only occur where] a natural process has been reduced by science to its abstract and ideal parameters, to the physico-mathematical determinations of the world of Galilean science.[12]

Human Resource Management, the demise of universities as places where truth is contemplated for inherently human reasons, the replacement of political ideas with economic management, the triumph of entertainment over actually living, the subservience of people to technology, the subservience of nature to economic realism, the inherent exploitation of the global economy, the degradation of all living spiritual cultures by Western consumerism, all these normal dehumanizing, desacralizing, degrading features of modern reality are a function of what Henry calls barbarism. And this barbarism starts because a reductively

12. Henry, *Barbarism*, 48–49. Italics in original.

abstract scientific view of objective truth has come to define *truth itself* in the modern world.

So what are we to make of all this?

Galileo advocated a view of merely objective, merely quantitative, directly perceived, and mathematically interpreted truth. This is the invention of modern science as a way of seeing reality. This was, indeed, a profound civilizational revolution, one that makes the French revolution look rather insubstantial in comparison. Further, this way of seeing truth is very powerful and has an astonishing revelatory capacity concerning how material objects actually work. Our view of objective reality is greatly enhanced because of modern science. However, this way of seeing truth operates within a very restricted bandwidth within the spectrum of human experience. For this way of seeing truth is blind to value, to meaning, to transcendence, to the sacred, to God, to human dignity, to love, to mystery, to beauty, to all those things that makes us concretely human. Rather, when the modern scientific vision of truth is applied to understanding how we can measure and mechanistically manipulate value, meaning, love, the sacred, etc., these inherently human realities are reduced to the categories of objective quantification and mathematical mechanisms. Thus, what the reductive gaze of science sees and labels as "value," "meaning," etc., in exactly *not* value and meaning as any real human being experiences value and meaning. Scientific truth applied to all of life gives us reduced abstractions that can be manipulatively powerful, but which profoundly distort and violate the realities they seek to explain. Thus love is, finally, socially conditioned sexual instinct, which is a function of (finally) "mere" biology, which is itself a function (finally) of "mere"—that is objectively and inherently meaningless—chemistry and physics, which is a function of the blind meaninglessness of material existence. So life itself disappears into an abstract yet quantified and mechanistically understood object of no meaning.

Christian Platonism is a way of seeing truth and reality that is grounded in the full bandwidth of human existence. Genuinely qualitative and transcendently derived realities are taken as primary truths by Christian Platonism, but such a conception of truth is outside of the bandwidth of modern quantitative and materially manipulable scientific truth. Thus Christian Platonism's deepest insights are incomprehensible or impossible when viewed through the lens of modern scientific truth and so they are explained away. But here is the big question: is what Henry calls the barbarism of the universally objectifying and quantifying gaze of Galilean science actually how things really are, or is this view of truth an impossible and horrifying reduction that violates the very grounds of human experience out of which it (ironically) arises? Which is to ask, is it possible that the reductive gaze of Galilean science *could* be true? To this question we now turn.

Ancient Truth verses Modern Truth—Lloyd P. Gerson

The Canadian classics scholar Lloyd P. Gerson has written a careful and insightful text titled *Ancient Epistemology*.[13] (Epistemology is a branch of philosophy concerned with the nature of knowledge.)[14] This is a detailed and, in places, technical text that looks at the kind of difficulties some of our most able contemporary modern epistemologists (notably the Oxford scholar Timothy Williamson) are grappling with, and seeks to interface ancient epistemology with those concerns. That is, Gerson is arguing that ancient epistemology may well have answers to some of the deep conundrums that modern epistemology has been, to date, unable to solve.

In the brief treatment of Gerson that I will give here, I will not delve into the philosophical details of the arguments for I am writing a book I hope is accessible to all thoughtful readers. But if you already are a reader of involved philosophical texts, I would highly recommend getting this book and reading it carefully.

Let us situate Gerson's text with a few broad observations about modernity and epistemology.

Unsurprisingly, philosophical questions about the nature of knowledge have been at the center of modern philosophy since its beginning with the meditations of the great French mathematician René Descartes. (Descartes was a younger contemporary of Galileo, and also a Catholic.) As modernity is intimately tied up with the scientific revolution, and as the scientific approach to truth is an approach grounded in quantified

---

13. Gerson, *Ancient Epistemology*.

14. Note also, a distinctive kind of knowledge and a distinctive approach to truth is at the very core of the modern life-world. So if modernity is having unsolvable problems in relation to truth, morality, high ideals, and meaning—as many a "postmodern" critic is keen to point out—then no genuinely new approach to our entire life-world perspective will arise until we have a new positive understanding of knowledge and truth. "Postmodernism" simply as a negative stance, simply as a rejection of the truth of modern knowledge, cannot really take us anywhere. Thus epistemology is not only at the heart of modernity, it is the area that needs real attention if we are trying to find a genuinely new approach out of the conundrums that modernity has given to us.

and mathematized sensory knowledge, if modernity cannot justify the truth of its primary vision *of* truth, then it is in serious philosophical trouble. And the reality is, philosophical debate concerning the nature of modern scientific knowledge has always been, and remains, a philosophical minefield.

Let me outline the nature of the philosophical terrain here in broad terms. The seventeenth century saw the new mathematico-experimental learning take off. Isaac Newton was the mega-star of this new learning with his laws of motion, his optics, his astonishingly accurate understanding of celestial motion, and the development of differential calculus. Newton gives us a calculative knowledge-based power over the movement of material objects unrivalled in human history. After Newton, this new approach to knowledge became deeply embedded in the mainstream of Western academia. Yet even before Newton this new mathematico-experimental knowledge was, of course, immediately technically useful and was taken up for military and trade applications very rapidly. This knowledge was indeed power. Francis Bacon had already put forward the idea that the new knowledge—liberated from Aristotelian philosophy—was the key to fulfilling the human mandate to rule the earth. Bacon saw it as the destiny of a new age of scientific knowledge to give us the power to bend creation's natural inclinations towards the advancement of humanity. Bacon's vision of a New Atlantis was a specifically theological and practical vision predicated on the voluntarism of his Calvinist-influenced background and a total disinterest in Aristotelian metaphysics. To Bacon the essential feature of God's nature is *total power*, and we humans, as creatures made in the image of God, express the essence of what humanity is when we exercise power over the rightful arena of our domain, nature. Through the new experimental scientific method we can literally take nature captive and interrogate her, whether she wills it or not, and extract her secrets (usually by torture) thus giving us power over her. Exercising power over nature frees us from her destructive caprice and enables us to exercise our God-given right to total sovereignty over the world God has given to us.[15] So the new learning got rapidly into the air in the seventeenth century because it had decisively won a scientific victory over Aristotelian physical cosmology and because it was so obviously useful for the rising wealth-motivated and power-concerned middle and upper classes of the day. Thus the philosophers of the new

---

15. Bacon, *New Atlantis*. See also Merchant, *The Death of Nature*. See also Matthews, *Theology and Science in the Thought of Francis Bacon*.

scientific age showed no sustained interest in carefully assessing the merits and defects of a quantitative approach over the merits and defects of a qualitative approach to natural philosophy. The rising modern philosophers simply assumed that the old Aristotelian approach was obsolete in relation to physical science and hence that Aristotelian notions of the observable qualitative and purposive dimensions of nature were also obsolete. (Catholic moral thinking, however, never abandoned Aristotle and performed all sorts of remarkable intellectual gymnastics to try and have Aristotelian natural purposes and modern scientific credibility at the same time.) Thus the great age of Aristotle simply passed into the night. That which was considered obsolete was not closely examined and a new set of justifications for modern scientific truth was really the only philosophical game in town. Yet big philosophical problems were evident from the outset.

From the beginning Descartes postulated a fundamental difference in kind between mind and matter such that merely material matter—objective, quantitative, mechanically determined, mathematically mappable—is what is known, and mind is what knows. A number of serious philosophical problem arise from here. If we accept Descartes' mind/matter dualism, then it becomes hard to see how the non-material mind could interface with the material reality of the brain if the mind is indeed non-material. But if mind is material, if the mind simply *is* the brain (that is, if we can indeed understand mind in the quantifiable, deterministic, and objective terms of modern science) then is subjective consciousness just a fancy illusion? If that is so, it seems there is some fundamental irony, some basic procedural incoherence, in arriving at the idea that mind is an illusion via the process of careful thinking. Further, if subjective consciousness is all we actually know, then there is no way we can check up on the correspondence of our subjectively known perceptions with the real world of material objects, without reference to our perceptions. So how are we going to know that the immediate world of objects our perceptions make known to us really exists?

In other words, the problem of how to adequately understand the mysteriously qualitative experience of mental subjects knowing quantitative, non-mental objects—the basic operational premise of the modern scientific notion of truth—has proved to be an astonishingly difficult problem from the very outset of modern philosophy. This difficulty is particularly challenging since modern philosophy is now deemed fully rationally independent of theology. This new secular philosophy is also opposed to anything that seems in any way reminiscent of medieval metaphysics. So epistemology had to bear the full burden of justifying the nature of truth for modernity, and this type of epistemology had to be fully autonomous from theology and speculative (non-scientific) metaphysics.

Roughly speaking, during the seventeenth and eighteenth centuries, trajectories in Rationalism (where "reason" was situated within the knowing consciousness of the individual mind) and trajectories in Empiricism (where "perception" was situated within the knowing consciousness of the individual observer) put forward different attempts at establishing modern scientific truth without reference to theology, and, increasingly, without reference to anything like Aristotelian or Platonist metaphysics. Kant synthesizes these two approaches towards the turn of the nineteenth century in such a vigorously modern manner as to seek to do away with the metaphysics of transcendence once and for all, and to establish entirely non-theological and epistemologically solid grounds for valid belief in reason, morality, and science. But, as impressive as Kant's achievements were they proved inadequate: they were immediately contested by the linguistic critique of Hamann, then Kant's stance was fundamentally reworked by Hegelian idealism, and that in turn was immediately contested by the religious existentialism of Kierkegaard, by the inversion of Hegel by Marx (such that philosophy was replaced with political action), and by new forms of entirely pragmatic, materialist, utilitarian, and analytical philosophy in England and America. The heyday of vigorously materialist and scientific philosophy was in twentieth-century Britain in the era of Bertrand Russell and A. J. Ayer, and this philosophy is characterized by being profoundly deflationary, such that all the important substantive questions of philosophy are reduced to meaninglessness via linguistic analytical means. But of course, this deflates British materialist reductionism too such that Ayer- and Russell-styled English-language philosophy became an arcane branch of rarefied symbolic mathematics that seemed to have little interest or application in the lived human world of ordinary people. And then came postmodernism questioning of the validity of the entire project of modern epistemology, and we are now in the position that any grand picture of truth itself seems philosophically impossible, and no one quite knows what will become of modernity.

From the above brief sketch, the point I want to make is that modern philosophy has never even come close to solving some of its most basic justificatory problems in relation to a powerfully coherent and persuasive account of why we should really believe modern scientific knowledge is true. Even so, this has not stopped modernity—as a cultural life form—from acting on the assumption that *only* modern scientific notions of truth are valid notions of truth. The justification is simply power—it *works*. An entirely quantitative and instrumental understanding of knowledge gives us power over material objects, and that power is true enough, whatever its philosophical problems.

Now to Gerson. Modern philosophy starts from the perspective of the individual knower. Galileo observes the world, and the representations of the material world that occur in his mind can be mathematically discerned such that he is able to predict what the motion of external objects will be as he comes to understand the physical regularities governing their motion. Reason is a faculty within his mind, and the world of objects can be reduced to the categories of quantification and necessary mechanical causation, and, presto, scientific truth arrives. All matters of metaphysics and theology are irrelevant to this truth, and the warrants of this truth can be had by any individual who makes the same carful observations and notices the same causal mathematical laws governing mechanical objective necessity. However, the philosophical difficulties regarding how mind interfaces with matter, regarding whether mind is matter or not, and regarding how subjective consciousness can be genuinely certain of its representational grasp of the real world of material objects, has plagued this perspective from the time of Descartes to the present. Perhaps, suggests Gerson, the ancients had a better approach to knowledge.

If you start with the mind of an individual knower, and the assumption of the reality of a purely objective quantitative world, you get into insolvable problems very quickly. Plato in particular, saw this sort of trap, a long time ago, and refused to start off down that track. Plato's dialogue on knowledge—the *Theaetetus*—spells out a number of intractable problems that show that seeking to establish a discretely epistemological foundation for truth was never going to be philosophically viable. Knowledge cannot be its own justification. So, following Plato's lead, the ancients simply didn't start thinking about truth as if an immediate sensible knowledge of material objects provided it with a philosophically adequate approach to true knowledge.[16] Rather, their starting point was outside of human subjective consciousness altogether.

16. Of course, Aristotle, and Aquinas following him, maintain that sensation is the only avenue by which knowledge comes to the human mind; but this does not

In general terms—and Gerson well justifies his characterization of what the identifiable mainstream of ancient epistemology entailed—the ancients start with the fact of thought and meaning in the cosmos, rather than starting with the reductively objectified sensory perspective of the individual knower. So—a la Galileo—you can see how the ancient "big picture" metaphysics of intrinsic intelligence and inherent purposive intention in the cosmos might tweak your interpretive outlook on the world such that a strongly mathematico-experimental methodology premised on the mere objectivity of material reality might never get off the ground. (And indeed, because of the limitations of ancient natural philosophy, the ancients did not work out how to build airplanes, nuclear bombs, pace makers, etc.) Yet this different starting point in thinking about truth and the intellectual realm that our minds live within changes everything.

If one treats divine Reason as intrinsic to reality, and the human knower as a subset of that reality, then what is known through sensory experience is never simply objective and quantitative, but is irreducibly a function of divine grace such that all of sensible material reality is as fundamentally qualitative and as inherently intelligible as it is objective and quantitative.

The ancients distinguished between wisdom and what we call science along these lines. Wisdom concerns fundamental truths that are ontologically prior to sensory knowledge. Wisdom is essentially a contemplative (spiritual/prayerful) insight that cannot be a matter of opinion and approximation, but is true knowledge if one has it at all. All scientific knowledge is more a matter of opinion and revisable theory, and can never attain truth in its own terms. Thus valid epistemology must be grounded in valid metaphysics, which is in turn grounded in some sort of divine revelatory gift to the genuine seeker after truth. So the ancients were simply not that interested in science as we understand science, even though Aristotle certainly was a most insightful and brilliant observer and theorizer of the natural world.

---

imply, to the ancients or the high medievals, that the knowledge-faculties of the human mind, working with the material of sensation alone, can define truth. Aristotle and Aquinas are simply fascinated with the knowledge of nature revealed through the senses, and yet they still see this knowledge as premised on the inherent intelligibility of the cosmos, which is a function of divine Logos operating within the cosmos. Thus theology—which is what Aristotle meant by "first philosophy" or "metaphysics"—is the grounds of natural knowledge, but natural knowledge cannot provide its own grounds as if it is self-generating.

What should be apparent here to the Christian reader is that the ancients saw knowledge itself in the kind of terms that are natural to Christian faith. Augustine saw loving communion with the Creator as the vital grounds of any deeply true knowledge of creation. An openness to the Source of created meaning and reality alone can enable the derived human knower to attain a true knowledge of inherently meaningful reality. Thus the ancient Christian knower is not the locus of truth, but by being rightly related to the Truth, the knower can also know truth (to some degree). To the ancients, the "knowing I" is not, and cannot be, the self-standing center of valid knowledge. But to modernity, the "knowing I" is the center and origin of a valid knowledge of objective quantitative truth.

There are some obvious reasons to think that the ancients might well be right, and that the unsolvable problems of distinctly modern epistemological foundationalism are a function of simply not recognizing the ongoing power of the ancient stance, and of not being honest about the unsolvable conundrums that a modern understanding of truth cannot get around.

Firstly, for the ancients the very notion of truth is framed in categories that presuppose the intelligibility of reality external to my consciousness. Meanings about true reality are not something that can be known if "what I know" is entirely situated within the categories of human subjectivity, as is the case in modernity. The idea that we can meaningfully contemplate even the very idea of truth if we refuse any gifting of meaning and reality to things beyond the internal ken of our subjective epistemic landscape simply collapses into incoherence. Not all philosophers find this situation worrying. Thinkers such as Richard Rorty say, fine, we will simply drop the notion of truth. But if you drop the notion of truth then "knowledge" is merely a word for use value in what we conventionally take to be the manipulation of external quantitative matter and "meaning" is merely a sort of artistic construction of culturally communicable feelings about things. But if that is the case then one hardly seems able to take the sophisticated arguments Rorty engages in seriously (for no sort of true knowledge and no sort of meaning connected to reality beyond culturally situated feelings about meaningless facts is deemed, by Rorty, either possible or useful.) So on the one hand science is deemed to have replaced medieval Aristotelian cosmology because it is true; yet, on the other hand, we find the very notion of truth itself has become obsolete within significant forms of modern and postmodern philosophy.

Kant—in arguably the pinnacle achievement of distinctly modern philosophy—makes rational and sensory knowledge, as accessible to the individual knower, the center of philosophically valid truth. Here knowable reality revolves around the individual human knower. This is the nub of the modern understanding of valid truth, but is it in any way reasonable? Can knowledge justify the notion of truth when knowledge itself is a profoundly complex and mysterious thing that knowledge itself cannot really sound out? Does it not make more sense to think of knowledge as a derivative function of meaning and intelligence that is prior to the individual knower? For how can one finally escape the problem of solipsism if my own consciousness is the only site of final truth?

Gerson points out very ably that the ancients had a very different outlook on truth such that they could not confuse a quantitative mathematized understanding of material objects with truth. Probably the easiest way to point this out is to think a little about the relationship between the modern notions of information and knowledge.

No quantity of information ever simply adds up to knowledge, even though knowledge requires information to be knowledge. Knowledge (for the purpose of this discussion) is the intelligent interpretation of information such that information has communicable meaning that reflects—it is hoped—the reality of how the objective world really is. So knowledge is a higher order of thought than information accumulation, not because knowledge is more basic than information, but rather because knowledge rests on information yet is itself not reducible to information. Likewise—to shift sideways a bit from a simply modern perspective—no quantity of knowledge ever simply adds up to wisdom. No amount of intelligent knowledge of how the world of objects really *is* will tell you how the world *ought* to be, or what qualitative *value* any state, reality, person, or accomplishment really has. Again, wisdom is a higher order of thought than knowledge not because it is more basic than knowledge, but exactly because it is dependent on knowledge but is not reducible to knowledge. So in this hierarchy of different forms of thought, the higher is always dependent on the lower in material and chronological terms, but the higher cannot be accounted for by the lower, and indeed, the lower is only essentially meaningful in terms of its relation to the higher. That is, the higher has ontological priority over the lower, even though the lower has in a sense, mechanical priority over the higher in terms of functionality.

Here we come to see how the very power of the quantitative-math-ematical-experimental conception of scientific truth deeply differs from the ancient conception of truth. For to us moderns—particularly since Darwin—the lower always explains the higher, and the simple laws of mechanistic necessity ultimately define everything from the bottom to the top. (And the functional replacement of *Genesis* with the *Origin of Species* in our intellectual culture profoundly re-organizes our civilizational view of the origin of reality such that a broad cultural belief in the higher causing the lower is replaced by a broad cultural belief in the lower caus-ing the higher.) So for modernity, information must produce knowledge, and wisdom does not exist—matters of "ought" and value have no objec-tive reality. Yet to the ancients, wisdom is more ontologically primary than knowledge, which is more ontologically primary than information. Indeed, what we call knowledge can never be true to the ancients, for it is always a function of incomplete and contingent information, and our theoretical constructions about the realm of change and appearance are always revisable and never finally certain. Only in the realm of wisdom can we find truth (or more accurately, be found *by* truth), and the realm of wisdom cannot be reduced to the terms of propositionally expressible knowledge about information concerning the state of physical reality. And yet, thought itself is needed for any perception, any knowledge-interpretation of perception, and any encounter with value, meaning, purpose, quality, etc., and thought is exactly *not reducible to matter*. So the high is in fact basically presupposed in any sort of mental operation, and it does not make sense to hold that the high can be produced by the low, but it does make sense to hold that the low is, ultimately, a function of the high; of the essentially intelligent and intelligible nature of being itself. And here the ancients are very hard to nay say.

Assuming that intelligence and intelligibility are primary, observ-ing the world, ordering those observations into intelligible meanings, and discerning values and purposes that qualify the world—that is, the normal process of thought, life, and moral action—makes perfect sense. Assuming that intelligence and intelligibility are somehow secondary by-products of merely quantitative, meaningless, material facticity, seems self-defeating regarding the value of thought and knowledge in the first place. This is because it implies that every aspect of our ordinary experi-ence as living, thinking beings within an intelligible cosmos is some sort of delusion that (ironically) intelligent people cannot take seriously.

To the ancients, true knowledge is not within the ambit of scientific theory about the material world. True knowledge is not even within the ambit of directly correlated propositions such as science might have about the physical properties of any given object of its observation and theorizing. Rather, true knowledge resides in the highest order of intellect, the order of wisdom. This is a luminous type of intelligence that is gained not by the cumulative acquisition of knowledge, but by contemplation, by an ontological openness to the intelligible Ground of Being itself. Wisdom cannot be framed in terms of the kind of beliefs about the state of the material cosmos that modern science and modern philosophy is concerned with.

The modern outlook basically holds that if something cannot be demonstrated in mathematically necessary and empirically observable terms, then it does not exist. Wisdom does not exist as truth. Rather, people's beliefs about the value things have, etc., exist as definable psycho-propositional assertions, and these we can meaningfully talk about. However, one has to think in order to come up with this modern outlook, and thinking itself is still not scientifically quantifiable. Is modern truth, then, a bit mad?

The nature of modern knowledge is objective, quantitative, mathematical, averse to metaphysics, and rejecting of any revelatory grounds for any warrant of truth. Further, the barbarism of modernity is a function of this distinctly modern approach to truth being applied across all spheres of human reality. But then modern epistemological foundationalism has some deep-seated internal problems. The ancients did not think such an approach was in any way workable and we certainly haven't been able to make it work philosophically. Yet it is precisely because we are culturally committed to a modern vision of truth itself that Plato's approach to truth seems impossible to us. For we want divinity held discretely away from knowledge, we want metaphysical presuppositions (first-order meaning commitments that are *prior* to knowledge claims) to be separated out from epistemology and to have no bearing on "pure reason," and neither of these stances will Plato accept, arguably for good reason. So perhaps we cannot take Plato or Christian Platonism seriously today because we are blindly committed to modernism and refuse to consider the possibility that our modern take on true knowledge is profoundly problematic, leading quite naturally to the postmodern rejection of the very idea of truth.

Can Christian Platonism Be Revived within Modernity?

If the above is the case, then Christian Platonism may simply be waiting there for us to pick up and rework as a potentially fruitful and viable philosophical alternative to both modernism and postmodernism. And indeed, given the philosophical difficulties of modern truth, and given the ongoing vitality of a broadly ancient approach to epistemology—as Gerson has argued—I can see no reason why this option should not be considered very seriously today.

But . . . even if Christian Platonism is theoretically viable today, is it in any way *practically viable* to be a Christian Platonist within the modern life-world? The answer to this question is that it is not. The modern life-world only allows the people who live within it to function normally under the operational assumptions of modern ontological nihilism (that reality itself has no meaning). If Christian Platonism is to come alive, this will require some form of life-world rebellion, some great pioneers of a new form of collective life that is a radical alternative way of living to that which is normal to modernity. As we have seen in this book, such astonishing changes in civilizational life-world have happened before, so why should they not be able to happen now?

The last chapter of this book will seek to address how we might start addressing the task of returning to a Christian Platonist understanding of reality as a viable life-world alternative to the metaphysical and practical parameters that define the governing principles of the modern age. I believe this task must be attempted for two reasons. Firstly, a Christian metaphysical outlook is not optional to the Christian. Secondly, if we stay within the reality framework of the modern age we are powerless to do anything to re-direct the unstoppable destructive tendency of modernity to burn itself out (along with the entire globe) due to its profound functional blindness to the primary realities of meaning, purpose, moral truth, sanctity, and God.

PART III

APPLIED CHRISTIAN METAPHYSICS

8

Returning to Reality

Over the past three days two of my daughters have been at a music camp. We live on the eastern coast of Australia in the beautiful sub-tropical city of Brisbane, and at this music camp Aurora and Claire have been playing their violins with four hundred other primary-school aged music students from state schools in the northern suburbs. This evening we had a two-hour concert where the children displayed their achievements to over a thousand admiring parents and relatives. They played music in two string orchestras and three stage bands, but the highlight was the massed choir at the end. They sang some fun songs and they also sang the Jewish blessing "shalom chaverim." It was most beautiful: the luminous faces of the children, the sweetly sung words of blessing, the adoring eyes of the parents, the undisguised joy of the conductor. I found myself marveling at the richness and simplicity, yet astonishing spiritual abundance, of this lived enactment of shared beauty. We all touched, and were touched by, something remarkable. In Michel Henry's terms, we were inside a primary truth of human life. And deeply, beyond words, we knew this was primary. And yet, this contact with primary truth was not simply beyond words, it was also outside of the very language and beliefs of our social reality. Because we are all modern Western secular consumerists, we *have* no words, no ideas, no logic, no common religion, no understanding of metaphysical reality in which to place this primary and most sacred truth, so its meaning touches us but also amazingly escapes us. We cannot reason about objective meaning, we cannot speak of meaning in terms of truth, we can only feel it, and articulate our delight in terms of how we each individually feel. Meaning is a subjective and personal feeling state to us moderns, not any real thing about which the "real world" of objective, demonstrable, useful "truth" might be concerned.

185

Alas, it is all too obvious that even though we are deeply and fundamentally embedded in primary truth, in most significant public contexts, reasoning and acting on the grounds of this reality *does* escape us. Our dominant discourses of reality, of public life, of financial reality, of power, of learning, and of action operate within parameters that make no reference to primary truth.

Just a week before this wondrous music camp the manner in which modern reality is disconnected from primary truth was all too forcefully displayed in a federal election in Australia. For though we live in a peaceful, safe, and rich land, though all our children have all their material needs met and nothing to be afraid of, we as parents had just voted in an election where the platforms of both of our dominant parties were almost entirely sub-human. The "real" objective issues of the election were merely quantitative economic issues, and the "real" subjective issues of the election were defined in terms of base—and apparently amoral—notions of fear and greed. Further, in this election both our major political parties, through a highly technically and psychologically competent use of the mass media, politically manipulated the public. Thus the public was conditioned to vote in conformity with an astonishingly mean-spirited, calculative "logic" of both atomized and collective competitive advantage. Our election was fought over which political side could be more inhumane to asylum seekers, which side would put more money in our pockets, which side would be more attractive to foreign mining companies and big business, and which side would slash public spending most (including more cuts to education and universities) in order to bring the nation's public spending budget out of its modest deficit. In Henry's terms, only abstract, secondary, quantitative, pragmatic, and "value neutral" concerns were considered "real" to our public political discourse. So we voted like narrowly self-interested, amoral pragmatists, and we seem to have thought that that was the only realistic type of political option we had. And yet, we touch truth of an entirely different sort—which is real truth, not abstract—when we listen to our children sing. But that truth is simply outside of the discourse of "realism" that dominates the actual public decisions we make.

Imagine another world. In this other world we could have a collective understanding of the priority of the qualitative over the quantitative, the priority of the essentially human over the instrumentally pragmatic, the priority of wisdom over science, and an understanding of wisdom as a divine gift. Imagine, that is, if we were all Christian Platonists. Or, imagine if at least Christians were Christian Platonists marching to a different drum to the metaphysical nihilism of the reality vision of the modern world's dominant public truth discourse. Imagine if the church was a witness to an entirely different way of *seeing* and *living* primary truth in our times. Imagine if Christians were working to bring wisdom back to a place of priority over merely quantitative objective knowledge and power.

What would such a church look like, and how would it move in the larger "barbaric" world of modern truth and power in order to transform that world so that our actions and reasoning could line up with the metaphysical truths in which we are primarily embedded? How would our science and technology, our business and education, our collective care capacities look if they were consciously run to cut with the grain of divinely-given truth rather than without any comprehension of that grain? What transcendently referenced common beauty, what true common richness, and what reflection of divine goodness would we be a part of then? What meaning would each one of us knowingly and actively participate in then?

Interestingly—but not surprisingly—what sociologists call anomie is one of the defining features of our "advanced" modern Western life. Anomie is a self-destructive sense of cosmic disorientation in the individual. This results from the breakdown of shared social values, the erosion of common frameworks of sanctity and intrinsic meaning, the fragmentation of familial and locational ties, the disintegration of coherent personal identity due to the multiplicity and separation of the different functional contexts of our lives, and the destruction of the very language of qualitative reality. Depression, suicide, and mental illnesses that are related to such a sense of intrinsic pointlessness are strongly on the rise in Westernized city living.

The 1999 movie *Fight Club*—based on the novel of the same title by Chuck Palahnick—is an insightful artistic exploration of the underlying topography of urban anomie in the contemporary West. The story opens by depicting the central character as an IKEA catalogue junkie with no substantial human ties to anyone, whose only access to meaning and satisfaction is the depthless fantasy world of shimmering advertisements, pointless work, and compulsive consumption. This is a very interesting movie for not only is anomie starkly depicted here, but as the plot develops the movie explores the idea that we need a radical metaphysical re-framing of normality, integrated with a radical praxis of revolution, once we can clearly see that the very fabric of our society is existentially weightless and inherently exploitative.

The theology and metaphysics of this movie are situated within a post-consumerist nihilism where the absence of transcendence is taken as true. So its unremitting darkness never escapes the 1DM transcendental ceiling that we have critiqued from a Christian Platonist stance in this book. *Fight Club*'s depiction of reality is not actually true to real life, which always retains traces of transcendent meaning, and the idea that you can find revolutionary empowerment through the rage of anomie is highly idealistic. Yet, as an artful expression of the myths and power structures undergirding the rising anomie in our culture, this movie is very significant. Most frighteningly, it well discerns that a neo-fascist Nietzschean will-to-power is all that is left to the metaphysically and theologically sensitive if real transcendence is fundamentally denied by the practices of meaning, normality, and power in which people live.[1]

In Australia the deforestation, overgrazing, and over-farming of our semi-arid lands has resulted in the degradation of the fragile topsoil, a rising of the water table, and the lifeless salinization of vast tracts of land. Our modern Western ways have rendered much of this vast and beautiful country a wasteland. Culturally, we are seeing something similar. We are seeing the continuous expansion of a qualitative wasteland that results from the clear felling of "old" meanings, beliefs, and patterns of community organization. This clearing away of the "old" must happen in order to facilitate the smooth running of the cultural industries that generate the ever-new personal-identity constructs that have replaced human and spiritual meaning in our "free" and hedonistically self-determined social landscapes. We now live in an endless artificial maze of wires and pipes

---

1. As an interesting aside, the manner in which *Fight Club*'s nihilistic outlook must draw on Christian motifs of radical sacrifice and of death and re-birth—though they are without transcendent reference, and hence are radically inverted—is very significant. You cannot even make nothing up as a life-directing vision of constructed purpose and liberating action without borrowing and inverting motifs and practices from the substantive metaphysical convictions of living religious traditions. Thinking of the great modern mis-adventures in collective meaning—imperialism, nationalism, Nazism, Marxism, consumerism—mythico-religious motifs are unavoidable in any collective life form which endeavours to create meaning out of merely contingent immanence and power. Richard A. Koenigsberg's explorations into the socio-psychology of modern nationalism and its relation to ritual acts of blood sacrifice in war are very insightful on these matters. See his *Nations Have the Right to Kill*. James K. A. Smith's exploration of the rituals and liturgies of consumer culture is also very interesting. See his *Desiring the Kingdom*.

and roads connecting atomic personal identities with mass-produced goods, services, and information. For not only does modernity produce a spiritual and relational wasteland, it also treats it.

The dominant cultural response to the passing of old meanings, in keeping with the technocratic objectivity of modernity, is consumerism. We buy things, experiences, and entertainments that sedate, titillate, and distract us, and we engage in a relentless life of self-promoting work and self-actualizing activity. We do this to distract ourselves so that we do not need to hear the horrifying silence of meaning that forms the backdrop to both our personal lives and the collective human cultural context in which we live. And the fact is, the Christian church is deeply embedded in the relentless "sound and fury" of the meaningless idiocy of consumer culture.

Unsurprisingly, most contemporary Western Christians understand what it means to be a Christian in modern and Western categories. That is:

- nominalist and voluntarist thinking shapes our theology very deeply;
- acceptance of secular and scientific conceptions of objectivity and subjective and personal conceptions of religious faith are simply assumed to be both valid and good;
- the scientific revolution, its technology, and its social manifestations in the mass media, etc., are the unnoticed practical and intellectual realities that define our very view of the world;
- modern notions of "society" and personal freedom of conscience govern our understanding of what the church is;
- "amoral" consumerism is the unnoticed wallpaper to our way of life, and;
- metaphysical reasoning is incomprehensible to us.

None of this is surprising for the striking reason that late medieval nominalist and voluntarist theology and post-Reformation individualist notions of truth and authority have largely generated the modern world in which we live. But what if defining truth in the terms of modern objectivity is actually theologically impossible for orthodox Christian faith? What if much of the late medieval and early modern theology that has produced the modern World, and modern Western Christianity, is seriously off key in its understanding of truth and reality? What if the very conceptual lens through which we see reality as modern Western Christians is giving us a distorted view both of who we are as Christians and of what the world is as God's creation?

But the picture is complex. To a Christian Platonist, transcendently referenced reality is real, whether it is recognized by pragmatic modernity as real or not. And indeed, quantitative know-how in the service of qualitative truth is a great human good. Thus modern science can indeed be a wonderful tool in the service of goodness . . . or a cold and degrading tool in the service of mere instrumental organizational efficiency, or a horrifying tool of sacrilege and violence in the service of greed and mere force, and, indeed, of evil. It is not modern science in itself that is bad, it is assuming that truth is constructed only within modern scientific parameters that is the problem. Recalling the first chapter's discussion of one-dimensional and three-dimensional metaphysical visions of reality, we find that people are actually embedded in a three-dimensional reality and actually exist within the truths of qualitative meaning. And yet, a one-dimensionally quantitative outlook has grasped control of the public discourses of power, possibility, commerce, and usefulness, and now shapes the very assumptions of the modern Western mind in the realm of what we (wrongly) believe is collective and objective reality. Our collective mind is powerfully enchanted with an entirely unreal view of reality.

But this *is* complex. For as strongly emphasized in John's Gospel, what we believe about the nature of reality has a fundamental impact on how we live.[2] So the first hurdle we modern Christian's face is to really believe in unseen reality. For, for all practical purposes, we can happily do our religion in entirely tangible and practical terms. We make the church run by fund raising, careful management, programs, outreach strategies, charismatic speakers, beautiful and musically gifted worship leaders, and so on. But what about prayer? What about contemplation? What about the attentive mental disciplines of inner stillness, inner openness to God?

---

2. John uses different forms of the Greek word for "believe" ninety-eight times. Those who change their outlook on reality (*metanoia*) and actively *believe in* the liberating reign of Christ in the kingdom of God are saved and are transformed into the children of light, but those who do not believe are judged by the Word that was spoken to them. Believing, "seeing," and acting—both in salvation and in judgment—are integral in John. Thus, not believing entails not seeing and entails acting within the logic and perceived necessities of a false vision of reality; the vision projected by the enemy of our souls, "the ruler of this world" (John 14:30). The New Testament gives no scope for metaphysical neutrality; all metaphysical visions are tied up with orders of power: the powers and authorities of the kingdom of God, or the powers and authorities of "the present evil age" (Gal 1:4).

We still do some of that stuff sometimes, and in liturgical churches we still have the sacramental consciousness of earthly things participating in spiritual realities that are "bigger" than the tangible expression of those truths; but really, all of this runs counter to the tangible, activist, mastery-of-knowledge trajectories of modern truth and modern power. Given the very "here and now" framework of assumed public truth in our societies—even as Christians, even as worshipers—do we really believe that God, who is unseen and conceptually uncontainable, is more real than objects that we can see and manipulate? Do we really believe that prayer is primary and that our Christian action is a function and extension of prayer and dependent on divine enabling for its kingdom-of-God validity? Do we believe that it is God who gives wisdom and knowledge to whomsoever he chooses (Dan 2:20–21), so that when we think, research, and study, the truth validity (in both wisdom *and* knowledge) of that action is entirely dependent on the grace of God? Is it possible, then, to be a true thinker without being a person of prayer, without being a person who is a disciple of Christ, without being a person on the pathway of sainthood?[3]

To clarify, I am not in any way advocating a disconnection between spiritual life and practical action here; rather I am warning that we can so easily *replace* spiritual life with practical action, or with mere propositional knowledge, within the knowledge and action norms of the modern way of life. We need to recover the priority of the unseen, the intangible, the essentially qualitative, the ontologically dependent, and the inherently relational over the tangible, the quantitative, and the pragmatically activist if we are to resist the cultural power of the modern world to define our faith to us in terms that are entirely foreign to the reality-perspective of the New Testament.

3. Consider the ninth-century Celtic sage John Scotus Eriugena's perspective: "Observe the forms and beauties of sensible things, and comprehend the Word of God in them. If you do so, the truth will reveal to you in all such things only he who made them, outside of whom you have nothing to contemplate, for he himself is all things. For whatever truly is, in all things that are, is he. Indeed, just as no substantial good exists outside of him, so no essence or substance exists that is not he." From Eriugena's homily on the prologue to the Gospel of St John, XI, as translated in Christopher Bamford, *The Voice of the Eagle*, 89. Eriugena is commenting on the prologue to John's Gospel here, so he is not advocating pantheism, rather he is noting the radical ontological and existential dependence of creation (which, of itself, is called "out of nothing") on Christ. For this reason all learning is worship, all knowledge is knowledge of the meaning of God (the Logos) expressed in creation, and there is no profane truth, but truth is divine, for all created reality is given and sustained by God.

And here is where belief, imagination, and reality re-connect. When it comes to believing in the reality of the invisible, we must build imaginative pathways towards such primary truths that we know are not those truths themselves, but which nevertheless give us a realer connection to reality than any abstracted and mere objectivist "realism" allows. Here John Milbank has very helpfully discussed the manner in which poets, wise people, saints from various religious traditions, and our own medieval Western heritage—in a very non-modern way—has often understood imagination to be deeply connected to truth.[4] This, of course, links in with the ancient Platonist tradition too. To that tradition the qualitative cannot be derived from the quantitative. If this is the case then it is inherently pointless to expect to bottle primary truth within the categories of modern realism. Analogy, narrative, poetry, art, music, prayer, religion, conversation, and life lived in the contemplation and enactment of the Good, the Beautiful, and the True—*this* is what philosophy as the love of wisdom is really all about. This is why Plato's dialogues are so richly imaginatively constructed; this is why Plato simply makes up myths to try and communicate some of his most central insights; this is why Plato's dialogues always gesture beyond what can be propositionally expressed about truth in the faltering and incomplete categories of human words and thought, to truth itself; this is why Socrates *embodies* the truths Plato is seeking to communicate, rather than simply didactically expounding on truth in the terms of (falsely) sure human knowledge. And this is why the works of Lewis and Tolkien speak so powerfully to us about human truths that no positivistic psychology manual can touch.

Here, also, the individual and the community must re-engage. Faith—as a practical confidence in any distinctive reality outlook—has both a personal and a corporate dynamic. It is neither simply personal (as modern individualism would have us assume) nor simply corporate (as "realist" executive corporate "leadership" would have us accept, and as "market confidence" would have us believe). In our day, "normality" is situated within a grating dissonance that is a running feature of the dynamic between corporate belonging and individual autonomy. We believe fiercely in our rights and freedoms of individual autonomy and yet, because our secular corporate and financial world has no conception of a transcendent reality that stands above all human constructs of power, we live in culture fixated with both arbitrary personal freedom and an

4. See John Milbank's Stanton Lectures of 2011. Online: http://theologyphilosophycenter.co.uk/online-papers/.

amoral "realist" political conformity to mere institutional force. Thus the corollary of the ideology of liberalism at an atomized personal level is a remarkably amoral conception of executive power.[5] If we take either of these attitudes to personal freedom and corporate realism with us into the church, we have abandoned the Christian vision of church. Without that vision we cannot proclaim an alternative *reality* to the fallen "realism" of "the world," and our attempt to witness to a vision of creation as visited by the redemptive in-breaking of the kingdom of heaven has no credibility.

What we believe about reality constructs the boundaries of the possible within the cultural world in which we live. For this reason there is no power more fundamental than the power to define and control our basic imaginative boundaries concerning the nature of reality and the possible.[6] Thus, the implementation of a Christian understanding of the priority of divinely given wisdom over practical knowledge, the priority of the spiritual over the material, the priority of quality and meaning over quantity and merely manipulative power must be done in a community. Can Christians imagine a reality together that is different to the intrinsically meaningless modern notion of reality and the life-world of consumeristic individualism that goes with it? Can we build a different practice of life to the modern realism of our times? If we cannot, then I suspect that Christianity will entirely fail in the post/modern West. If the West becomes bereft of its own indigenous spiritual heritage, then it will simply run out of spiritual fuel and implode, destroyed by its hubris, its unrestrained will-to-dominate, its lack of language appropriate to existential reality, its metaphysical emptiness, its loss of any high vision of human dignity and divine reality.

Jesus himself noted that salt that loses its savor is good for nothing and that as the salt of the world his followers have a preserving and flavoring role to play in the world. I doubt that Western civilization will long endure after it is bereft of any vibrant understanding of inherently qualitative and spiritual reality. Another spiritually vital civilization will arise after the ruins of the West have settled into the dust of the past, but if it is really true that Christ is Lord of heaven and earth, this would be a grave loss to the world. Then again, so globally powerful is the West now,

5. See Hamilton and Maddison, *Silencing Dissent.*

6. This is the central message of Plato's famous analogy of the cave in *The Republic*, as well as the central message that C. S. Lewis conveys in his own Christian version of Plato's cave analogy in *The Sliver Chair.*

so acidic to all spiritual vitality, that its swan song could intone cataclys-
mic disaster for human civilization itself. The West needs the church; but
it needs a Christian witness that is not conformed to the metaphysical
blindness of our times, and it needs a Christian witness that takes the
radical claims of the Lordship of Christ seriously in both the church *and*
the world.

Kurios Iesous

On one decisive point, Christianity was born with a radically different
reality vision to the larger Greco-Roman world that was its civilizational
mother. The center of that difference was not the conviction that reality is
inherently meaningful, not that wisdom is a divine gift, not that the unseen
is more primary than the seen; the central difference was the firm conviction that God had become human in Jesus of Nazareth, and that this Jesus
had triumphed over the grave and was not only the eternal *Logos* of God,
but was Lord of all reality.

The central ancient creedal affirmation of the early church was *Kurios Iesous* ("Jesus is Lord," Rom 10:9). These two words signal the fundamental non-conformism of the followers of Jesus with the realism of their
time. For, of course, realistically speaking, everyone knew that Caesar
was lord. And Caesar had the armies, the wealth, the tangible institutions dispensing power and justice, and the civic divinity and collective
mythology to back up his claim. So this creedal statement of the early
church was nothing other than a rejection of the very concrete political
and religious realism of its day. Christianity could have happily existed
within the Greco-Roman world as a private cult, along with a vast pano-
ply of personal salvation religions each equipped with their own inner
mysteries, their ecstatic altered states of mind, their special teachings,
and their moving rituals. But by claiming that Jesus is *Lord* the privileges
and protections of a private cult were denied to Christianity. For this was
a statement in direct defiance of the public cult of the emperor. Believe
whatever you like in private, but in public you must give appropriate
(and surely harmless) ritual gestures of obeisance to the emperor whose
very concrete power and glory provides for your needs and keeps order
and unity in the vast empire of Greco-Roman civilization. To do less is
to display seditious ingratitude to the power that sustains your life and
the vitality and glory of the Greco-Roman civilization. For very good

political reasons, such sedition was not tolerated.[7] And for that sedition many of the apostles and many an early saint were martyred. All for refusing to sprinkle a bit of incense on an alter to Caesar. (Note what high significance the church gave to small ritual acts.)

In our day the lordship of Caesar is expressed in the unassailable realisms of meaning-less economic, technological, military, surveillance, information, and mass media power. These are the "real" functional overlords under which we live our lives. And, as in ancient times, our earthly lords have made provision for private religious cults. Of course, those cults are only allowed because they do nothing to challenge the lordship of the powers under which we live, and they even complement those powers nicely by giving those people who seem to require it some sense of ultimate (yet private) purpose and meaning. The supernatural comfort private cults provide is situated safely beyond the cold, hard realism of the meaningless powers to whose beat all must, in reality, march.[8] Let them have their personal ecstatic meanings, their good-time sing-along cult meetings, and their life-after-death salvation, just so long as they quietly give their bodies, time, work, spending, belief, practices of life, and small ritual loyalties to this cold, hard realism now.

So the confronting question about Christianity as a faith that expresses uncompromising fealty to the Lordship of Christ and is tied fundamentally to a view of reality that will always be "unrealistic" to what Saint Paul calls "the natural man" (1 Cor 2:14) is simply this: have we conformed too readily? Does our Christian faith fit within the atomized, subjectified, constructed, commodified, privatized, discretely supernaturalized, enterainmentized, personal salvation arena that the modern secular West has set aside for religion? If it does, well, the sooner our religion

7. All human power structures rely on collective belief in order to operate. Provided the undergirding myths of valid authority, the legitimate use of force, and of the cosmic appropriateness of established institutions and procedures are simply assumed by a populace, there need be no show of force in upholding right belief in relation to the undergirding myths on which collective power rests. But should any basic challenge to the validity of the primary mythos on which the powers and authorities of any given society appear, the establishment's days in power are numbered—no matter how big their armies—if that challenge gains momentum. This the ancient Romans understood very clearly.

8. See Budde, *The (Magic) Kingdom of God* and Budde and Brimlow, *Christianity Incorporated* for some penetrating, theologically sensitive sociological thinking about the manner in which the contemporary Western church all too easily finds itself playing the role of a supportive chaplain to the secular state and commercial powers that run the world we currently live in.

fades to black the better. But there are alternatives. And then, there is the Holy Spirit to enable the impossible. But if there is to be hope we must shake off the metaphysical enchantment and the many shadow plays of dependency and seduction projected onto the cave wall of modern realism, to which we have now grown so deeply accustomed. Waking up and returning to reality will not be easy. Even so, Christian, if it is really true that Jesus *is* Lord, then this reality requires us to choose our most basic allegiances against the realism of our times, just as it required it of the apostles and martyrs of the early church.

Applying Christian Metaphysics Against Modern Realism But For the (Really) Real World

So far this chapter has sketched a big-picture outline of how incompatible the prevailing 1DM realism of modernity is with the 3DM understanding of Christian faith. If the Christian Platonist view of reality is taken seriously by Christians then there is scarcely any normal feature of modern life that the church should not be fundamentally challenging. But, given the global nature of the incompatibility, how could a 3DM Christian understanding of reality actually be brought to bear on the modern world?

The New Testament provides us with three very powerful words that show us a way forward. These words all concern Christian metaphysics of a 3DM nature. They are *metanoia*, *pisteuo*, and *koinonia*. *Metanoia* refers to a change of mind, a change of metaphysical outlook, which apprehends the higher realities that the Christian revelation proclaims. *Pisteuo* is a verb, it is the practical actions of believing in the reality that the Christian revelation proclaims as true. *Koinonia* is the context of Christian fellowship in which the shared vision of the Christian revelation is practically put into action.

Metanoia—Transformed Metaphysical Vision

The Greek word *metanoia* is composed of *meta*, meaning "after," and *noia*, meaning "mind" or "consciousness." In the New Testament *metanoia* signifies a fundamental change of mind, a shift of consciousness, a move from a spiritually dark mind—the unregenerate *protonoia* ("before-mind") of the "natural man"—to a mind that is illuminated and transformed by divine truth (the *metanoia*, the "after-mind") of the new creature in Christ.

In today's English New Testament the word *metanoia* is often translated as the word "repent." This is a controversial linguistic choice, the controversy of which goes right back to the earliest translations of the Greek New Testament into Latin. Back then Tertullian argued against translating the Greek *metanoia* into the Latin phrase *paenitentiam agite* ("do penance") from where the English sense of repentance, as used in translating *metanoia*, ultimately springs.[9] Repentance has strong connotations of being firstly retrospectively sorrowful, then prospectively reformed in action, and the roots of the English word are tied up both with pain and penance. Feeling and action are emphasized in this word choice; the vision of the *mind* is not central. *Metanoia*, however, is centrally focused on the mind. It is firstly concerned with what you are changing your mind *to*, more so than what you are changing your mind *from*; thus it is *a forward looking* word tied up with the liberation of revelation and the actions that flow out of the transformed vision—and, indeed, the transformed being—which one receives from God. So the phrase "repent and believe" (Mark 1:15) can be more literally (and more accurately) translated as "change your mind and believe."

9. For a helpful potted history of the manner in which *metanoia* has been translated into Latin and English—including this reference to Tertullian (p. 33)—see Anton, *Repentance*, 27–43. Perhaps one of the reasons why Latin translators shied away from rendering *metanoia* as "change of mind" is nervousness about Christian conversion being seen as simply a gnosis (a form of knowledge) rather than an entire change of being (body, soul, mind, action and spirit). Gnosticism was a powerful force in the early centuries of the church; various gnostic sects maintained that special revealed knowledge was the pathway to salvation, and these sects were largely intellectualized, esoteric, and "spiritualized" to the point where the body and the world were things to be left behind. These sects also often enjoyed safety within the larger Greco-Roman world as private cults that had no interest in the powers of Caesar, or in the Lordship of Christ over those material and temporal powers. By emphasizing personal feeling and public acting in the translation of *metanoia* the Western church differentiated Christian conversion from the initiation processes of gnostic mystery religions. However, it seems fair to note that while the Christian meaning of *metanoia* does indeed incorporate personal feelings and public acting, and Christian conversion is not gnostic salvation, yet the New Testament clearly implies that the change of *mind* is the locus of the work of the Holy Spirit in affecting the transformation of the full mind-body-soul being of the Christian, along with ontological incorporation via the sacrament of baptism into the church. Christian conversion understood just as a feeling-state and as the performance of penance for past wrongs badly misses the centrality of the mind in the New Testament dynamic of conversion. A lack of interest in metaphysics—which entails a lack of interest in the deep reality assumptions of the mind—in modern Western Christianity may well be an unintended legacy of a necessary defense against Gnosticism in the early centuries of the church.

Expressed in English "change your mind" doesn't seem like all that big a deal, but *metanoia* is a primary and global change word in the New Testament, for *noia* in Greek means the highest powers of the mind, those powers connected with (or failing to connect with) eternal realities. A "change of mind" at this most primary level of insight thus implies a total change of life, such that conversion—the transformation of our mind, heart, and actions—is what *metanoia* results in. Thus, the nub of *metanoia* is not the emotive experience of remorse, it is not the determination to make amends in our actions for past wrongs, it is the change of consciousness that is produced by the Holy Spirit in harmony with the active trust of the believer. *Metanoia* is the change of our very understanding of reality, accompanied by a divinely enabled change of our being. *Metanoia* is the center of a dynamic process of non-conformism to the most basic reality assumptions of the non-Christian cultural world in which we live. Non-conformism to the very structures of the assumed reality vision of "this world" is possible, Paul explains, when *our* understanding of reality is transformed (literally, metamorphized—moving into an "after form," like a butterfly after the "before form" of a caterpillar) by the renewing of our minds (Rom 12:2).

Pisteuo—The Action of Belief

As Mark 1:15 depicts it, Jesus explodes into public life with this radical claim: "The kingdom of God is near. Repent [*metanoeite*] and believe in the good news [*pisteuete en to euangelio*]." As noted, this "repentance" is a call to a radical change of consciousness. To perceive the spiritual reality of the kingdom of God as manifest in the person of Jesus, in the flesh, is to receive a new mindset, a new lens through which to see reality, a new consciousness. But this vision is to be an active and committed vision, a believing *in* the good news.

The Greek stem *pist-* is the root of both the Greek noun "faith" (*pistis*) and the Greek verb "belief" (*pisteuo*), and this root's primary meaning is confidence (indeed, the Latin origins of the word "confidence" are *con* meaning "with," and *fide* meaning "faith"). The pre-philosophical, pre-theological meaning of the *pist-* root is a relational term of public trust, of reliable reputation, of business confidence. And this old meaning denotes both relational reliability and active, publically enacted confidence. In harmony with this "market place" meaning of faith/belief, the Christian "believing in" Jesus is not simply a passive and personal conviction, for John makes it clear that to believe in Jesus is the *work* that God requires of us (John 6:29), and that the good news is to be publically lived and proclaimed. Relational trust is expressed in an active and public reliance on the one in whom one has confidence. So to believe in Jesus is not simply to "see" the revelation that Jesus is the Son of God (Mark 1:1), the divine Logos (John 1:1), and the cosmic Lord (Col 2:9–10), as if this "knowledge" was a private and subjective religious belief; rather, to believe in Jesus is to put into practice an active and public confidence in this vision of who Christ is, and what created reality is as a function of the creating power of Christ.

I am seeking to here connect *metanoia* with *pisteuo* in the manner in which the New Testament connects them. That is, the change of consciousness that the revelation of the divinity and Lordship of Christ produces is to be worked out in a relational loyalty to the divine King of heaven and earth, and that loyalty is to be worked out publically and in defiance of all authorities and pretended higher powers and supposed realities that bind and deceive those who do not believe. To the modern liberal and scientific ear, this is nothing short of radical religious nuttery, of intolerant and arrogant fundamentalism, of superstitious mania. And yet, if the Christian gospel has no spiritual power and little cultural, moral, and public-affairs-shaping impact on our world, one has to wonder if it is actually the Christian gospel that we believe (in).

Accepting at least some degree of offense to the realism, values, and sensibilities of liberal scientific secular modernity, it looks as if the Christian "repent and believe" will either turn our world upside down if we actually do change our mind and act on our stated confidence in the Lordship of Jesus Christ over heaven and earth, or it will demonstrate that Christians are indeed great fools and the reality outlook of Christianity is simply delusional. Let us proceed on the possibility that it is the former rather than the latter that is the case. Here the vision of truth and reality revealed by God in Jesus is to be applied in the world in direct defiance of the false outlook on reality that structures "the world" that does not heed the authority claims of Christ. As a function of true humility and obedience to the revelation of God, this will not entail ignorant and barbaric intolerance or dogmatic arrogance or a head-in-the-sand blanket rejection of the validity and value of modern learning and social life forms. But the inherently three-dimensional metaphysical vision of reality, and a willingness to actively believe the revelation of God in the Scriptures and the life of the church must clash with those aspects of modernity that simply reject the very possibility of the Living God being actively engaged in human history. Where modernity has a false vision of reality—a reality that is functionally governed by the sovereignty of humanity as exercised via our instrumental power over physical nature—the governing socio-cultural principalities and powers that shape the norms and operational regularities of this present age must be actively opposed by the church if Christians are to be true to the meaning of their faith.

Koinonia—The Shared Life of Faith: Christian Fellowship

Koinonia is the word used by the New Testament that means "fellowship." We might have a revelation of divine truth and change our mind about the nature of ultimate reality, and we might seek to actively believe in that vision; but the fact is, we always see reality—including the reality seen by faith—in the context of a shared lived world. Thus re-working an established culturally situated vision of reality—such as announcing that the time has come, the kingdom of God is at hand!—cannot be done by one person. The walk of faith is not a private and discretely personal walk. To be in Christ is to be in his body; it is to be incorporated into the church. Jesus gathered his disciples together and by the power of the Holy Spirit this gathering was transformed into a public assembly (*ekklesia*)—this is the New Testament meaning of the word "church"—that both saw and enacted reality differently. After Pentecost, the established visible realities and powers governing the commonly accepted norms and the metaphysical assumptions of the "common mind" of the larger Greco-Roman culture were countered by a different vision, a different mind, and a different power in the church. So the infant church was a fellowship of divinely mind-transformed, active believers who together enacted a different understanding of reality to the stories, the powers, the class structures, the political and economic necessities, the gender relations, the religion, and the operational norms of the pagan Greco-Roman world in which they lived.[10]

If we are Christians merely *within* the discretely personal, non-political, autonomously-value-determining enclosure that the ruling powers

---

10. Certainly the process was two-way. The cultural world of Greco-Roman times did indeed shape the manner in which Christian communities understood themselves, yet the manner in which the church of the martyrs often recklessly defied key power and meaning structures of the Greco-Roman world is testimony to their being governed by a different understanding of reality and final loyalty to the world in which they lived.

of liberal modernity have set aside for us, then it is hard to see that we have the first inkling of what *koinonia* is, or what the radical claims of the reality vision that proclaims that Jesus is Lord are. For under the conditions set aside for religion in secular liberal consumer society, we cannot meaningfully proclaim the Lordship of Christ, but rather we bow to the realism of a functionally materialist, amorally pragmatic, and profoundly disintegrative and atomistic consumer society that is in dark bondage to the godless and idolatrous spirit of our times.

Against the Atomism and Imperialism of Modern Realism, for the World

Probably the first challenge faced by any Christian who wants to repent metaphysically and who lives in the modern world is the problem of atomization. That is, the world of "liquid modernity"—as the sociologist Zygmunt Bauman describes it—is one where all collective ties, all locational ties, all ties to the past and the future, all common, transcendently referenced values are dissolving. The individual increasingly finds herself freely floating in the powerful cultural and political currents generated by the global economy, consumer society, the nation state, and the mass media. What is striking about this—as another thinker Jürgen Habermas points out—is that when you have no middle-order social institutions that resist this atomization of the individual and this free flow of powerful collective currents, then the role of speech and meaning becomes entirely lost in modern liberal society. That is, if we only have, on the one hand, the individual and, on the other hand, massive, "efficient" and impersonal corporate and bureaucratic powers, then the distinctly public sphere between the individual and the impersonal necessities of power dies off. The absence of humanly concerned and locally scaled civic life results in the death of the public sphere even if the democratic ritual of public voting still occurs. In other words, without a living public sphere the very idea of government for and by the people towards human and meaningful ends becomes redundant. Thus atomized "society" containing individuals with scant humanly rooted middle-order communities who thus have very limited power to shape the larger environment in which they live, end up being astonishingly easy for large instrumental powers to handle. We are seeing the death of political ideas, civic consciousness, and participatory community engagement as our politicians are increasingly governed by the economic necessities set up by large corporate players, and as citizens retreat from public life into the realm of their own non-public spaces.[11] This is very bad for any attempt at moral governance in the interest of the common good of the people. All manner of exploitation of the vulnerable, the poor, and the non-human, and all manner of freedoms for the rich and the powerful increasingly overshadow the human spaces in which we live. To the Christian the exclusion of moral reality from public life is a travesty that the prophets of old constantly railed against, and that the people of God can in no manner simply accept.

Saint Augustine and Stanley Hauerwas are right in recognizing that the church is a polity, and that the City of God must resist the atomization of the associational and locational dissolving that modernity accomplishes. We must recover the polity of the church if we are to resist that dehumanization of the process of power in our broader society, and indeed in our global context. For it is one thing to perform various acts of micro-resistance to the entrenched exploitation and immorality of consumer society on a personal level. Micro-resistance to the moral failings of our times—such as ethical shopping, renouncing private transport, writing to politicians, growing your own food, renouncing TV, volunteering in local community concerns, etc.—are all good to do, but their reach is essentially into the arena of personal morality. What is needed to counter the powers is *collective* acts of micro-resistance at a humanly scaled and locationally rooted level of fellowship. If Christian responses to the moral blindness, the instrumental indifference to value and meaning, or the subordination of real people to abstract financial necessity, etc., remains a personal response that has to do only with our personal sense of religious and ethical authenticity in the exercise of our private freedoms, then the powers that govern the mainstream remain entirely indifferent to our futile micro assertions of private displeasure.

So here is where repent and believe (*metanoeite kai pisteuete*) kicks in for us regarding atomization. Do we grasp the revealed truth that the church is an ontological reality in which we participate as believers, which is a publically assembled polity with its distinctive center and life in Christ, which is the very body of Christ on earth? Or do we see church as a club, a collection of autonomous free individuals who each have their

11. The internet and mobile phones do not often re-animate the middle-order political sphere as the rootless, individualized virtuality of cyberspace tends to re-enforce contextless personal freedom as interfaced with higher level power (be it political or market power). While it is certainly possible to influence higher-level power by "viral" facebook means, this type of power is inherently tied in with image and public opinion, which is the natural currency of higher power, and thus remains within its ambit and under its control.

own personal religious convictions? Do we see the mission of the church as one that expresses the life of Christ in the world, confronting all principalities and powers that raise their head in defiance of the Lordship of Christ? Or do we see the mission of the church as propagating a merely personal and "spiritual" response to the work of Christ aimed only at saving people's souls, while leaving the larger world just as it is? Do we see the work of the church as something that is done, in fellowship, by all Christians living faithfully to the Lordship of Christ in conflict with the lordship of the powers that structure the normal dynamics of power, value, and purpose under which our world largely lives? Or do we see the mission of the church as something we put money in the plate for religious professionals to worry about? Do we *believe in* the metaphysical vision of the church in an active manner that expresses a real confidence in the truth of this vision, in defiance of the accepted atomistic vision of reality upon which the norms of personal consumer satisfaction and corporate and bureaucratic power depend?

Can we "see" that the church is not just what it appears to be to the modern outlook on social reality? To the modern vision churches are—let's face it—tribally discrete, lose religious associations of private individuals and institutions that propagate themselves over time. But can we see that the church is actually *the ontic reality of the body of Christ* where this unseen reality transcends the individual personal identities of the Christians who participate in her? Can we then actively believe in that reality in such a manner that it shapes how we live? If we can, then we must get serious about practices of collective micro-resistance to the atomizing and de-personalizing features of liquid modernity.

Church that re-builds humanly meaningful localized communities under the Lordship of Christ is going to clash with the powers of our times. For such a church will be outside of the undergirding mythos that sustains power in the modern world. In modern liberal consumer societies, the sacrosanct freedoms are of personal value, personal belief, and private association, with a corresponding conformism to the laws and "objectivity" of public spaces that are explicitly deemed neutral with regard to (private) value and meaning. These "value free" operational forums for public power and objective facticity then become amazingly free of moral constraint. In the world of high finance and global corporations, this translates into creating ingenious ways of speculatively and exploitatively inventing huge quantities of money and paying hardly any tax on astronomical "stateless" corporate profits, all legally. And because these powers are *so* powerful—because money is the currency of power—our politicians largely facilitate the protection of enormous private wealth out of the public purse and the processes of civic politics. This was seen, sickeningly, in the donation of inconceivably large amounts of public money to "too big to fail" private financial institutions in the US in the 2008 financial crisis. The money-accumulative interests of the corporate world, its public exploiting and degrading power, and its functional alliance with government, gives an interesting gloss on James' ancient rhetorical question "is it not the rich who are exploiting you?" (Jas 2:6).

If our modern world is basically OK and modern Western Christians within it can make positive adjustments to how things already are, then everything this book has said about the metaphysical vision of Christian Platonism and about *metanoia* is moonshine. Modern reality is just fine and we need no fundamental change of mind. If, however, modern notions of truth, meaning, personal identity, markets, money, and power are not only going to destroy us, but are fundamentally at odds with a Christian metaphysical vision, then no amount of positive adjustment to the modern world is going to help us (or it). Fighting pornography, defending Christian notions of the family unit, running Christian schools and universities, doing "Christian" marketing/business/entertainment, strategizing and achieving successful ministry targets, etc., is just re-arranging the deck chairs on the Titanic if that is all we can do. For the very hope of a basic shift in our civilizational direction there needs to be an alternative vision of the very nature of reality. And there needs to be a community, a fellowship of believers, who can imagine and enact an alternative way of life via acts of intelligent collective micro-resistance premised on the ontological reality of the Lordship of Christ and the participation of Christians in the body of Christ on earth. If this later scenario is the case then metaphysics *really matters* and Christians who do not understand the metaphysical implications of their faith—let alone take them seriously—are part of the problem of our times rather than salt and light to preserve the good and illuminate the true in our times.

Positively stated, only what modern realism must see as an unrealistic vision of value and meaning can provide us with the spiritual fuel that can change our civilizational direction. The logic of instrumental power in the service of the amoral self-interests of the already rich will not take any reasonable action to divert longterm disaster or unsettle established patterns of exploitation—no matter how reasonable and how morally necessary such actions might be. One cannot but have a certain pity for our politicians. They—like the public they serve—are small pawns in an entrenched game of big power that they seem essentially powerless to affect. The media controls them just as they control the public through the media, and big business operating globally sets the bottom line of what can and cannot be done by public policy and national laws in a political environment where the only bottom line is the bottom line.

How, then, might we change?

A Church under the Lordship of Christ, Redeeming the Public World

The kingdom of God is a "place" where the reign of God is willingly honored by people. That is, the gospel is about power and authority, and it is about the total transformation of people and communities such that God's will might be done on earth as it is in heaven. To think that the gospel is just about saving people's souls after they die must be the most astonishing heresy of our times.[12]

As pointed out, the conditions of modernity erode the public sphere where the middle order of humanly significant and locally rooted concerns (*ekklesia* concerns) mediates between individuals and large powers. Within liquid modernity individuals readily become lost in narcissistic fantasy realms of self-construction, large powers tend towards functioning without any wisdom-based or sanctity-aware restraint, and mere instrumentality in the service of the accumulation of financial power tends to become the governing norm under which we live. The metaphysical dynamic that underpins this set up is the relegation of meaning and value to the realm of private and personal freedom. The church's metaphysical vision of *real* meaning and *real* value, of the ontological participation of the Christian in the collective life of Christ, and of the Lordship of Christ over heaven and earth must challenge the very structures and underlying

---

12. Of course, the atonement between God and humanity won by Christ via the cross does indeed save our soul and does indeed give us access to the resurrection of the dead in the life of Christ. But this atonement is cosmic not merely personal and "other-worldly." The victory of Christ over sin, death, and the devil via the cross is a display of the love and power of God, yet the atonement is a means of entry to the kingdom of God and the reign of Christ over all powers and authorities, and not the end point of salvation. It is just as heretical to hold that Christ does not save our soul and preserve our life in him beyond the grave, as it is to hold that the powers and affairs of this world—which Christ came to save (John 3:17)—are of no concern to the gospel.

mythos of what the modern world has become. To do this, it must animate the middle order of social reality with the life of Christ expressed
in the church.

In what follows I am going to think through a hypothetical scenario
of kingdom-of-heaven community transformation, as specifically located
in the public realm. The particular hypothetical example I have picked is
not of central interest here; it is the recovery of the public nature of the
advancement of the kingdom of God under the reality vision given to the
church that is of central concern.

Take the issue of domestic energy supply in Australia as a hypothetical scenario for change.

In Australia we have soaring household energy bills and we use coal-
burning electricity generators—which used to be state-owned assets—to
supply the vast majority of our nation's power needs. The coal industry
and privatized owners of energy companies make very tidy profits from
how things now work. And yet, we have every natural resource and the
technical know-how to solve our nation's energy needs by entirely renewable means (though this would by no means be a simple challenge). Em-
barking on this challenge could also create a large pool of useful technical
jobs in an era when large manufacturing firms are going off shore leaving
most skilled manufacturers redundant in Australia. However, supplying
anything more than a token fraction of Australia's energy needs with
state-initiated renewable energy plants will never happen. No matter
what the science on climate change says, no matter how good it might
be for the ordinary Australian consumer and worker, the established
processes and players of high financial power, of public opinion manipulation, and of party politics could simply not see such an aim as in any
way realistic. For power is its own thing, it does not exist for the common
person, or the common good, or common sense even; it exists for its own
preservation within the existing structures of power, wherever it is found.
Thus, because of how we see political power, we cannot change. We have
no vision of meaningful reality that *subjugates power to truth*, that puts
wisdom ahead of short-term self-interest, that upholds the dignity of the
common person and the integrity of local communities over the impersonal powers of human resource management, bureaucratic efficiency,
and financial necessity. And, as the Scriptures put it, without a vision the
people will perish. Folly and destruction is what you get when wisdom is
silenced. But—pity them—our governing powers *cannot see* any meaningful truth; they can only see instrumental necessity, the amoral realism

of power, the existing matrix of limits within which they must operate. Due to a near-complete lack of spiritual vision, no hope for a better world will come to us from our governing powers now.

In no sense am I advocating that Christians give up on the public sphere but I am arguing that we must now work to redeem the shared reality of our public world by means other than those embedded in the official structures of political power.

So here is an idea. Australia—like Canada—saw a profound demographic collapse in active church affiliation in the 1960s and 1970s. Even so, about one in five Australians still find themselves in church at least once a month. So the "remnant" of the Christian population in Australia is by no means insignificant. Imagine if Australian Christians came to see land-care as a significant issue of faithfulness to the Scriptures. Let us suppose that Ellen Davis' compellingly argued book *Scripture, Culture and Agriculture* went viral in Australian Christian circles and Australian Christians came to see locally produced renewable energy as a significant issue within that context. For indeed, Davis' book makes it unavoidably clear that locally concerned land-care is a profoundly significant biblical issue and that all manner of moral and natural exploitations tied up with imperial power undergird the entrenched powers that oppose the will of God on these matters. Imagine that Christians in regionally concentrated areas (Australia's population is almost entirely composed of less than twenty large cities) decided that some pooling of resources could be justified to buy a property on which they could build a wind farm. So the property is bought and funds are made available to buy a few wind turbines. Then a strictly not for profit renewable energy company is formed in each region which has the financial aim of raising revenue that will enable it to employ more people, buy more turbines, and expand its renewable energy scope with the aim of eventually powering its entire local area—for the good of that area, not for private profit. But that too is only a starting aim. For the bigger vision is to get large enough to manufacture our own renewable energy equipment and fund research into cracking the holy grail of renewable energy, which is storing energy in a form suitable to meet fluctuating demand. Imagine the Christian churches decided this entire process must be done separately from government funding and from "for profit" businesses in order to keep the logic of the enterprise carefully focused on human and transcendently referenced ends (doing something that is good *because it is good* and *because God requires it*). Imagine that through intelligence and hard work, and through the blessing of God, this Christian-based initiative to transform Australia into a 100 percent renewable energy country gained a head of steam and really took off. Over time enough people will be working in locally based renewable energy that these concerns will start to penetrate the electorate in a serious manner. Political parties will have to get on board and renewable energy will become an unavoidable political necessity. Legal and commercial structures will have to be adjusted to bring the governing norms in line with the will of the people. The powers will have to adapt to the vision of the people.

In this hypothetical scenario *metanoia, pistueo,* and *koinonia* would all play decisive roles in transforming the church in Australia from a loose collective of factionally divided private religious associations into public assemblies that are actively engaged in transforming the very principalities and powers under which we live. By this pathway the church would become salt and light in the world, and would affirm the Lordship of Christ in the real and public world. Correspondingly, the reason why such an enterprise has not happened—and is not even thought of—is because of failures in *metanoia, pistuo,* and *koinonia.*

Metanoia comes first. If our consciousness of both the ultimate and the operational realities in which we live sets Christ *among* the powers, but primarily as a personal religious deity, then we may enter our Christ into the arenas of politics, commerce, education, foreign policy, land use, or whatever, but as subject to the existing powers that govern those secular spheres. With such a mind not only do we not challenge every power and authority that raises itself against the Lordship of Christ, we actually bolster the existing powers by giving their authority our tacit religious endorsement. Given that the powers of modernity do not recognize any publically real notion of meaning and value, but situate all meanings and values in the humanly constructed and naturalistic arena, collectively acceptable meanings, values, and regulations become simply one power that amoral and meaningless pragmatic power itself has to shape or contend with as it pursues its own advantage by whatever means simply come to hand. If the church is not committed to real meaning and value, and if it is not prepared to actively *believe in* that real meaning and value by refusing to live subservient to the amoral pragmatism of our times, then it does not have the mind of Christ (1 Cor 2:16) and it cannot function as the body of Christ in the world, advancing the kingdom of God as a sacrament of the eschaton. If this is the case, there is not much real difference between the church and any other non-professional social club that simply accepts the reality it is situated in and tries to further its own interests within that reality.

Another crucial area of *metanoia* concerns which vision of the church we accept as real. If our professional religionists are primarily concerned with the political realities internal to their local congregations and institutional structures, and if they see "running" church life in terms of management, marketing, quantifiable "vision," programs, and the protection of the morals and cultural identity of their flock, then they will operate within the pragmatic realities of their operational environments in a manner that is entirely situated within modern realism. Further, if Christians in congregations and parishes see their faith in terms of discretely personal or ritual faith, and if they treat church like a society in which they are free associates as autonomous modern individuals (not bond-slaves of Christ, not family, not members of an ontological reality that is more primary than their individual identity), then again, there is no biblical vision of church as an ontological reality in which they participate, and that is enlivened not by the flesh and will of man, but by the very Spirit of God. And then there is ecclesial parochialism. In John 17 Jesus specifically prays for unity amongst his followers, and tells us that unity will powerfully witness to the world of the truth that God has sent Jesus into the world as its redeeming Lord. But we are divided into Catholics, Baptists, Orthodox, Pentecostals, Anglicans, etc., and we have very little interest in acting as the one body of Christ in the location where we live. We do not see Christ's vision of Christian unity and we do not believe in that vision in practice but keep largely to our own kind as scattered across the city. I do not intend to diminish the very significant matters of doctrinal distinctives and historical events that cannot be glossed over when Christians from different "churches" (not a notion that is compatible with the New Testament or the Nicene creed) seek to act together under the common Lordship of Christ; but I do not see that the effort for collective action can be ignored if one takes John 17 seriously. In reality our "churches" run as worlds unto themselves and this fits in with the atomistic trends of our times where localized collective action hardly ever succeeds against the powerful cultural forces of individualization, bureaucratization, mass communications, and corporatization. But perhaps only the congregations of believers in a localized area can revive the human vitality of local communities, because they have a vision of reality that is inherently meaningful, that is morally realist, and that has access to the ontological life of Christ expressed in the church. If the church is not challenging the anti-human and exploitative powers of our times, what hope is there for the world?

So *metanoia* is crucial, but then *pisteuo* and *koinonia* must be integral with *metanoia* if the church is to actually live out the advancement of the kingdom of God on earth; if we are to *be* the key mode of answering the Lord's prayer—Thy will be done on earth as it is in heaven—in the age of the church before the eschaton. We are to resist the reality vision and operational ways of "the world" in order to live effectively for the best interests of the world in our times. We can only do this if we have our minds fixed on realities the world cannot see.

C. S. Lewis famously noted:

> If you read history you will find that the Christians who did most for the present world were just those who thought most of the next. The Apostles themselves, who set on foot the conversion of the Roman Empire, the great men who built up the Middle Ages, the English Evangelicals who abolished the Slave Trade, all left their mark on Earth, precisely because their minds were occupied with Heaven. It is since Christians have largely ceased to think of the other world that they have become so ineffective in this. Aim at Heaven and you will get earth "thrown in": aim at earth and you will get neither.[13]

We must return to a vision of reality that is grounded in revealed truth of a genuinely spiritual and transcendently sourced nature. Without such vision, we will only have amoral power, instrumental exploitation, and a deepening blindness to the actual human truths that give meaning and purpose to our existence. Christians have a deep heritage of such a divinely given vision of reality, but it has been sorely degraded in recent centuries by the advance of a form of realism that knows no intrinsic human or natural meanings, and that recognizes no divine reality above human power.

And yet . . . can modern realism really be believed? Is meaning and value just subjective? Is transcendence as traced in every tangible expression of beauty, goodness, and truth mere illusion? Is God himself no more than an idol made in our own image; merely a product of human cultural, economic, psychological, and biological need? If Christians accept these corollaries of 1DM modern realism, then this can signify only one thing—our faith is dead. If we look for life in our faith, then

13. Lewis, *Mere Christianity*, 116–17.

we must reject the metaphysical perspective of modern realism and we must return to the rich reality vision of the gospel and actively believe in that vision in the fellowship of other believers. This active believing will again proclaim that the kingdom of God is at hand. This proclamation is valid not as mere words, but as community transformation, pushing back the darkness and futility of the powers of violence and exploitation that are deeply embedded in the modern world and which quietly undergird every aspect of our normal lives. But this confrontation of the modern reality-vision is, as C. S. Lewis well described above, a confrontation that is profoundly *for* the real good of the world. We must aim at heaven, and with the vision of heaven in mind, to genuinely change the earth for the better. Only such vision *can* change the very structures of power and authority under which we live. Metaphysical truth is the only way to morally effective politics.

Bibliography

Anton, Edward J. *Repentance: A Cosmic Shift of Mind and Heart*. Spring Hill, TN: DPI, 2005.

Aristotle. *The Complete Works of Aristotle*. Edited by Jonathan Barnes. Princeton, NJ: Princeton University Press, 1984.

Augustine. *Against the Academicians and The Teacher*. Translated with introduction and notes by Peter King. Indianapolis: Hackett, 1995.

———. *City of God*. Translated by Henry Bettenson. New York: Penguin Classics, 1984.

Bacon, Francis. *New Atlantis and the Great Instauration*. Wheeling, IL: Davidson, 1991.

Banks, Robert. *Paul's Idea of Community*. Peabody, MA: Hendrickson, 1994.

Bercot, David W., editor. *We Don't Speak Great Things—We Live Them*. Amberson, PA: Scroll, 1989.

Berger, Peter L. *Facing Up To Modernity: Excursion in Society, Politics, and Religion*. New York: Penguin, 1979.

Betz, John R. *After Enlightenment: Hamann as Post-secular Visionary*. Oxford: Wiley-Blackwell, 2009.

Boersma, Hans. *Heavenly Participation: The Weaving of a Sacramental Tapestry*. Grand Rapids: Eerdmans, 2011.

Brueggemann, Walter. *The Prophetic Imagination*. Minneapolis: Fortress, 2001.

Brunschwig, J., and Geoffrey E. R. Lloyd, editors. *Greek Thought: A Guide to Classical Knowledge*. Cambridge, MA: Harvard University Press, 2000.

Budde, Michael. *The (Magic) Kingdom of God: Christianity and Global Culture Industries*. Boulder, CO: Westview, 1997.

Budde, Michael, and Robert Brimlow. *Christianity Incorporated: How Big Business is Buying the Church*. Grand Rapids: Eerdmans, 2002.

Burkert, Walter. *Babylon, Memphis, Persepolis: Eastern Contexts of Greek Culture*. Cambridge, MA: Harvard University Press, 2007.

———. *Greek Religion*. Oxford: Blackwell, 1987.

Burnyeat, Myles. *The Theaetetus of Plato*. Indianapolis: Hackett, 1990.

Cavanaugh, William T. *The Myth of Religious Violence*. Oxford: Oxford University Press, 2009.

Chesterton, G. K. *Heretics*. London: Baronius, 2006.

———. *The Man Who Was Thursday*. Fairford, UK: The Echo Library, 2006.

Copleston, Frederick. *A History of Philosophy*. Volume 1. London: Continuum, 2003.

Cornford, Francis M. *From Religion to Philosophy*. Princeton, NJ: Princeton University Press, 1991.

Davis, Ellen F. *Scripture, Culture and Agriculture*. Cambridge, MA: Cambridge University Press, 2009.

De Lubac, Henri. *Paradoxes of Faith.* San Francisco: Ignatius, 1987.

Desmond, William. *Art, Origins, Otherness.* New York: SUNY, 2003.

Dodds, Eric R. *The Greeks and the Irrational.* Berkley, CA: University of California Press, 1951.

———. *Pagan and Christian in an Age of Anxiety.* Cambridge, MA: Cambridge University Press, 1965.

Drake, Stilman. *Galileo.* Oxford: Oxford University Press, 1980.

Dupré, Louise. *Passage to Modernity.* New Haven, CT: Yale University Press, 1993.

Eriugena, John Scotus. *The Voice of the Eagle: The Heart of Celtic Christianity.* Translated by Christopher Bamford. Great Barrington, MA: Lindisfarne, 2000.

Ferguson, Everett. *Backgrounds of Early Christianity.* Grand Rapids: Eerdmans, 2003.

Gadamer, Hans-Georg. *Truth and Method.* New York: Continuum, 2004.

Gerson, Lloyd P. *Ancient Epistemology.* Cambridge, MA: Cambridge University Press, 2009.

———. *Aristotle and Other Platonists.* New York: Cornell University Press, 2005.

Gilson, Etienne. *History of Christian Philosophy in the Middle Ages.* London: Sheed and Ward, 1953.

Hadot, Pierre. *Philosophy as a Way of Life.* Oxford: Blackwell, 1995.

———. *What is Ancient Philosophy?* Cambridge, MA: Harvard University Press, 2004.

Hamilton, Clive, and Sarah Maddison. *Silencing Dissent: How the Australian Government Is Controlling Public Opinion and Stifling Debate.* Sydney: Allen & Unwin, 2007.

Harnack, Adolph von. *History of Dogma.* Volume 1. Translated by Neil Buchanan. Reprint. Charleston, SC: BiblioBazaar, no date given.

Hauerwas, Stanley. *The Peaceable Kingdom.* South Bend, IN: University of Notre Dame Press, 1991.

Henry, Michel. *Barbarism.* New York: Continuum, 2012.

Heschel, Abraham. *The Sabbath.* New York: Farrar, Straus and Giroux, 1951.

Hopkins, Gerard Manley. *Poems and Prose.* London: Penguin Classics, 1963.

Howland, Jacob. *The Republic: The Odyssey of Philosophy.* Philadelphia: Dry, 2004.

———. "Re-reading Plato: The Problem of Platonic Chronology." *Phoenix* 45.3 (1991) 189–214.

Jaegar, Werner. *The Theology of the Early Greek Philosophers.* Eugene, OR: Wipf and Stock, 2003.

Kierkegaard, Søren. *Concluding Unscientific Postscript to the Philosophical Fragments.* Princeton, NJ: Princeton University Press, 1992.

Klein, Jacob. *Greek Mathematical Thought and the Origin of Algebra.* New York: Dover, 1992.

Koenigsberg, Richard A. *Nations Have the Right to Kill.* New York: Library of Social Science, 2009.

Kuhn, Thomas S. *The Copernican Revolution.* Cambridge: Harvard University Press, 1957.

Lewis, C. S. *The Abolition of Man.* Reprint. London: Fount, 1999.

———. *The Last Battle.* Reprint. London: Penguin, 1964.

———. *Mere Christianity.* Reprint. Glasgow: Collins, 1977.

———. *Perelandra.* Reprint. New York: Scribner, 1996.

———. *The Silver Chair.* Reprint. London: HarperCollins, 1980.

Lindbeck, George. *The Nature of Doctrine.* London: Westminster John Knox, 1984.

MacDonald, George. *The Princess and the Goblins.* London: Puffin Classics, 1997.

Marenbon, John. *Aristotelian Logic, Platonism, and the Context of Early Medieval Philosophy in the West*. Farnham, UK: Ashgate, 2000.

Matthews, Steven. *Theology and Science in the Thought of Francis Bacon*. Farnham, UK: Ashgate, 2008.

Merchant, Carolyn. *The Death of Nature: Women, Ecology, and the Scientific Revolution*. New York: HarperOne, 1989.

Milbank, John. The Stanton Lectures of 2011. Online: http://theologyphilosophycentre. co.uk/online-papers/.

———. *Theology and Social Theory*. 2nd ed. Oxford: Blackwell, 2006.

Moltmann, Jürgen. *Theology of Hope*. Minneapolis: Fortress, 1993.

Nietzsche, Friedrich. *Beyond Good and Evil*. New York: Dover, 1997.

Osborn, Eric. *The Beginning of Christian Philosophy*. Cambridge, MA: Cambridge University Press, 1981.

———. *Tertullian, First Theologian of the West*. Cambridge, MA: Cambridge University Press, 1997.

Osborne, Catherine. *Eros Unveiled: Plato and the God of Love*. Oxford: Clarendon, 1994.

———. *Presocratic Philosophy: A Very Short Introduction*. Oxford: Oxford University Press, 2004.

Pieper, Josef. *Scholasticism: Personalities and Problems of Medieval Philosophy*. South Bend, IN: St. Augustine's, 2009.

———. *The Silence of St. Thomas*. South Bend, IN: St. Augustine's, 1957.

Plato. *Complete Works*. Edited by John M. Cooper. Indianapolis: Hackett, 1997.

———. *The Dialogues of Plato*. 5 vols. 3rd ed. Translated by Benjamin Jowett. Oxford: Oxford University Press, 1892.

———. *Meno and Phaedo*. Edited by David Sedley and translated by Alex Long. Cambridge: Cambridge University Press, 2010.

———. *Plato*. 12 volumes. Loeb Classical Library. Cambridge, MA: Harvard University Press, 1930–89.

Polanyi, Michael. *Personal Knowledge*. Chicago: University of Chicago Press, 1958.

Ricoeur, Paul. *The Symbolism of Evil*. New York: Harper & Row, 1967.

Rubenstein, Richard. *Aristotle's Children: How Christians, Muslims, and Jews Rediscovered Ancient Wisdom and Illuminated the Middle Ages*. New York: Harcourt, 2003.

Schindler, D. C. *Plato's Critique of Impure Reason*. Washington, DC: The Catholic University of America Press, 2008.

Schmidt, Charles. *Aristotle and the Renaissance*. Cambridge, MA: Harvard University Press, 1983.

Shakespeare, William. *The Oxford Shakespeare: Complete Works*. Oxford: Clarendon, 2005.

Siegle, Lucy. *To Die For: Is Fashion Wearing Out the World?* London: HarperCollins, 2011.

Simpson, Christopher B. *The Truth is the Way: Kierkegaard's Theological Viatorum*. Veritas. Eugene, OR: Cascade, 2011.

Smith, James K. A. *Desiring the Kingdom: Worship, Worldview, and Cultural Formation*. Cultural Liturgies. Grand Rapids: Baker Academic, 2009.

Smith, Ronald G. *J. G. Hamann 1730–1788: A Study in Christian Existence*. New York: Harper, 1960.

Stewart, Jon, and Katalin Nun, editors. *Kierkegaard and the Greek World, Tome I: Socrates and Plato*. Farnham, UK: Ashgate, 2010.

Tertullian. *Tertullian: Treatises on Penance: On Penitence and On Purity*. Ancient Christian Writers Series vol. 28. Mahwah, NJ: Paulist, 1958.

Twain, Mark. *Following the Equator*. Hartford, CT: American, 1898.

Weierter, Stuart. *Understanding Life and Death through Plato and Socrates*. Lewiston, NY: Mellon, 2012.

Weil, Simone. *Waiting for God*. New York: Harper & Row, 1973.

Wink, Walter. *Engaging the Powers: Discernment and Resistance in a World of Domination*. Minneapolis: Fortress, 1992.

Wright, N. T. *Paul*. Minneapolis: Fortress, 2009.

Yoder, J. H. *The Politics of Jesus*. Grand Rapids: Eerdmans, 1994.

Name Index